ADVANCE PRAISE

"This is a great book on the topic of Customer Experience. It is thorough and detailed. I love the structured, easy to follow layout. And the case studies are very helpful for readers to put the suggested framework into action."

Annette Franz, Founder and COO, CX Journey Inc.

"The authors ask: "But with all the resources out there on the subject, why is a great customer experience so rare?" – My answer to this obvious question: Knowing is one thing, doing is another. When you describe service as 'taking action to provide value for someone else,' it becomes clear that it's about DOING and not just KNOWING. In their new book, Alan and Dave describe how DOING can actually be lived and how CX exists as a value-based culture rather than a buzzword in the company. For leaders aiming to stay ahead in a rapidly evolving digital and behaviour-driven marketplace, this book is not just informative but transformative, a key to unlocking unparalleled customer satisfaction."

Prof. Dr. Christian Coenen, Professor for Marketing and Services Management, ZHAW – Zurich University of Applied Sciences

"As a customer service consultant with two decades of experience in industry dealing with internal and external customers, I love the way this book is fused with frameworks, tools and industry case studies. This holistic book is a must-read, if you are an organization or an individual seeking to be a transformative service experience leader in an ever-changing world where the only differentiator is service excellence. The book is a practical masterpiece, and I am particularly enthused with the chapters on alignment and employee engagement, as I strongly believe it takes inclusion and collaboration to make any service agenda happen effectively. It is a valuable resource for industry leaders, CX practitioners, frontliners, entrepreneurs, human capital managers, operations supervisors and students of customer service who are passionate about making the 'wow' factor of customer service happen."

Dr. Genevieve Pearl Duncan Obuobi, CX, SME Consultant, Banker, Author

"This easy to read, understand and use book makes CX come alive. The importance of the customer is highlighted over and over, using wonderful quotes. I am happy to see the authors focus on consistency and enabling which are often overlooked areas. Great case studies and new insights on action to improve CX make this a must-read book."

Gautam Mahajan, President, Customer Value Foundation, Founder Editor, *Journal of Creating Value*

"A thoroughly enjoyable book for its insightful focus on making Customer Experience (CX) a valuable contributor to an organization's success. I resonate with the emphasis on alignment of all functions in delivering value to customers, a concept I refer to as 'business harmony.' What sets this book apart is its exploration of the connection between CX delivery and the brand, a topic not commonly addressed by many customer experience professionals. The many practical examples are also exceptionally helpful."

Olga Potaptseva, CCXP, Founding Director CXPanda

"As customer experience becomes THE strategic differentiator, this well-researched book crafts a distinct holistic approach to excelling in CX. If you are serious about creating a competitive advantage through CX, this book should be your top priority."

Lior Arussy, Author of *Customer Experience Strategy* and *Next is Now*, Chairman of Imprint CX

"*Supercharging the Customer Experience* is a must-read for leaders seeking to design and implement an effective Customer Experience (CX) strategy. With its actionable insights and powerful examples, this book will inspire you to look at CX as a company culture versus a function, how to measure and report outcomes, and enable your organization to perform more effectively, more efficiently and more profitably. I enjoyed every moment unpacking this wonderful book and I wish it had been written years ago because I would have been successful a lot sooner."

Dr. Tabatha Erck, President & CEO, Zipari

"This book does a great job of helping the reader navigate and understand its main arguments by providing an in-depth analysis of the background factors and the context. It is written for practitioners using their language and provides excellent examples of all the concepts covered. The comprehensive approach touches all three corners of a service triad: organization – brand identity, employees – employee engagement, and customers – customer experience. This is quite different from many others that adopt a narrower lens. *Supercharging the Customer Experience* is a must-read book for marketing professionals, practitioners, and should be included in reading lists for MBA and Executive MBA-level courses worldwide.

The 'Top Tips' should be framed and hung on the walls of every service organization and included in their organizational handbooks."

Sertan Kabadayi, PhD, Joseph Keating SJ Distinguished Professor in Business, Professor of Marketing, Director of Professional MBA Program, Gabelli School of Business, Fordham University

"This book is a fabulous reminder for organization's leaders to keep our customers' requirements 'front of mind' and to use the tools it shares to be a truly customer-centric business. But more important than this is how the authors identify the crucial fact that, at the centre of everything, customers are people with very basic characteristics, and these come with emotional needs. If we don't recognize and fulfil these simple human drivers, everything else can become irrelevant and superfluous."

Karen Leftley, President, British Quality Foundation

"Not just another CX book but rather a powerful, practical guide, packed full of great content and tools to support any leader who is charged with driving improving customer experience."

Vinay Parmar, Founder & CEO, Dhruva Star

"*Supercharging the Customer Experience* is *the* field guide to the contemporary landscape of customer experience. A work of great depth, this book is rigorously researched, chock-full of relevant case examples, and perceptive in its presentation of practical approaches to aligning organizations around the values that earn customer loyalty. Bravo to Alan Williams and David Stubberfield for expanding our minds and hearts to the new reality of the customer experience."

Jim Kouzes, Coauthor of *The Leadership Challenge*, Fellow of the Doerr Institute for New Leadership, Rice University

"The world of customer service and customer experience has changed drastically in my 40 years in the field. This book provides a powerful framework that will help give any organization a laser-like focus on the customer experience."

Shep Hyken, Customer service/CX expert and *New York Times* bestselling author

Published by
LID Publishing
An imprint of LID Business Media Ltd.
LABS House, 15–19 Bloomsbury Way,
London, WC1A 2TH, UK

info@lidpublishing.com
www.lidpublishing.com

A member of:

businesspublishersroundtable.com

ISBN: 978-1-915951-28-1
ISBN: 978-1-915951-29-8 (ebook)

Cover and page design: Caroline Li

ALAN WILLIAMS & DAVE STUBBERFIELD

SUPERCHARGING
THE CUSTOMER EXPERIENCE

HOW ORGANIZATIONAL ALIGNMENT
DRIVES PERFORMANCE

MADRID | MEXICO CITY | LONDON
BUENOS AIRES | BOGOTA | SHANGHAI

CONTENTS

This book is dedicated to every single person
who plays a part in designing and delivering
memorable experiences for customers,
whether they are front-line service people,
supporting behind the scenes or senior executives.

ACKNOWLEDGEMENTS

A big thank-you and appreciation to all the wonderful people we have encountered in our formal education, working lives, ongoing growth and personal development – past and present clients, work colleagues, service partners, collaborators, connections, friends, competitors, teachers and tutors. These people, their knowledge and shared experiences have made this book possible, and without them, there would be no book at all.

Special mentions go to Martin Liu and colleagues at LID Publishing, who have been partners for three previous coauthored books and now this latest project.

Invaluable feedback and positive appreciation for this book have been received from a wide range of people around the globe. Some of these people have been connections for more than 40 years and others are recent acquaintances. Among them, they hold a rich variety of roles and interests, ranging from senior executives in the private and public sectors to leading academics and experts in marketing, brand identity, customer experience, employee engagement, psychology, organizational development and leadership. They are based in an equally diverse range of locations: Australia, Canada, China, France, Ghana, Hong Kong, India, Japan, the Middle East, New Zealand, Singapore, South Africa, the UK and the US. It is a privilege to be associated with these people and their interest, time and giving spirit are much appreciated. We would like to extend our thanks to:

- Lior Arussy, Author of *Customer Experience Strategy* and *Next is Now*, Chairman of Imprint CX
- Bruce Barclay, Head of Property and Facilities, Rehab Group

- Moira Clark, Professor of Strategic Marketing, Founder and Director of the Henley Centre for Customer Management, Henley Business School
- Grant Cochrane, SVP/President Global Healthcare and Trade Services, FedEx
- Prof. Dr. Christian Coenen, Professor for Marketing and Services Management, ZHAW – Zurich University of Applied Sciences
- Dr. Tabatha Erck, President & CEO, Zipari
- Annette Franz, Founder and COO, CX Journey Inc.
- Shep Hyken, customer service/CX expert and New York Times bestselling author
- Sertan Kabadayi, PhD, Joseph Keating SJ Distinguished Professor in Business, Professor of Marketing, Director of Professional MBA Program, Gabelli School of Business, Fordham University
- Jim Kouzes, coauthor of *The Leadership Challenge*, and a Fellow of the Doerr Institute for New Leaders, Rice University
- Karen Leftley, President, British Quality Foundation
- Gautam Mahajan, President, Customer Value Foundation, Founder Editor, *Journal of Creating Value*
- Shawn Nason, Founder & CEO, MOFI
- Dr. Genevieve Pearl Duncan Obuobi, CX, SME Consultant, Banker, Author
- Vinay Parmar, Founder & CEO, Dhruva Star
- Olga Potaptseva, CCXP, Founding Director CXPanda
- Neil Skehel, CEO & Founder, Awards International
- Robert Spector, Speaker, Author
- Adrian Swinscoe, Customer experience advisor, Author
- Bruce Temkin, Head of Qualtrics XM Institute, Cofounder CXPA

We would also like to acknowledge ChatGPT. From the outset, we made a conscious choice not to use ChatGPT in the writing of this book, partly because we had so much content between us already and partly because we didn't think it was right to put our names to a book we had not written ourselves. However, where we did find ChatGPT helpful was in the review and editing stage and in identifying additional research and articles we might otherwise have missed.

FOREWORD

In the ever-evolving landscape of contemporary business, the domains of customer management and customer experience stand prominently at the top of many boardroom agendas. How to attract, retain and create advocates from customers is a top priority for executives all over the world.

Supercharging the Customer Experience emerges as a commendable contribution in this arena, demonstrating a profound understanding of the shifting dynamics that organizations navigate today. Drawing from a wealth of personal experiences in research, teaching, consultancy, and as a discerning customer, I know that things are different now from how they have been before. The authors illuminate the transformative differences defining the present era. Contemporary customers are more demanding, diverse and have high expectations. They seek affiliations with organizations that align with their values in a 'want it now' world.

When I set up the Henley Centre for Customer Management in 2002, the ambition was to create a unique collaboration between business and academia, to develop and encourage excellence in customer management practice across industries, to build transferable knowledge focused on the issues that mattered most, and to equip our members with the tools and models needed to turn these actionable insights into best practice within their organizations. This book strikes a delicate balance between 'theory heavy' academic texts and 'theory-light' airport business management texts and 'theory-free' but entertaining 'concept' materials. The authors present conceptual thinking grounded in practical reality, supported by sound research, all conveyed in an organized, accessible and comprehensible manner.

At the heart of the book lies a compelling concept—the power of values-driven organizational alignment. Leaders, particularly, would benefit from considering this carefully because, in my experience, it is all too rare. I work extensively in the area of culture and climate and the critical linkages between employee behaviour and business performance. You've really got to get the right kind of organizational climate if you want a good customer centric organization. What gives the book an edge is that it explains how this precious alignment can be achieved in practice. In many ways, the methodology that is put forward is very simple and that is what makes it so widely applicable. Yet it has a richness and depth, drawing on years of research and operational wisdom, which renders it supremely sophisticated. The book offers a plethora of practical tips, enriched by mini case studies, reinforcing a consistent message throughout—to implement strategies tailored to you and your organization's particular situation.

Anyone involved in the delivery or leadership of customer service and customer experience will be able to apply the knowledge gained from this book in their own organizations. I encourage you to read the book and, more importantly, to implement whichever actionable insights you choose in your organization to supercharge the customer experience.

Moira Clark
Professor of Strategic Marketing,
Founder and Director of the Henley Centre
for Customer Management,
Henley Business School

CHAPTER 1
INTRODUCTION

"The pace of change has never been this fast,
yet it will never be this slow again."
Justin Trudeau[1]

We are living in extraordinary times. Whichever your preference of acronym – VUCA, BANI, RUPT or TUNA,[2] we have never experienced such a sense of uncertainty about the present and the future. When Prime Minister Trudeau spoke at the 2018 World Economic Forum in Davos, Switzerland, he used the above quote about the pace of change. Nobody could have foreseen the extent to which his words would ring true some two years later with the seismic impact of the COVID-19 pandemic. Even though the global public emergency has officially been declared 'over,' the ongoing repercussions seem likely to continue for some time yet. It is clear (to us at least) that there will be no return to the way things were and, instead, a next way is already forming. In the area of customer experience (CX), many traditional approaches are no longer relevant because the landscape of brand identity, employee engagement and customer experience itself is changing ... all at the same time, all the time and at an accelerated rate again in the 2020s.

Customers' expectations are increasing, and they vote with their wallet or contactless card. Consider the growth of the Fairtrade brand, which started in 1994. According to the Fairtrade International Annual Report for 2020,[3] global retail sales of Fairtrade-certified products reached nearly $14 billion. Similarly, there has been a rise in green consumerism, where people (particularly younger generations) are willing to pay extra for eco-friendly or sustainable products.[4]

Some brands are now connecting with their customers at a deeper, more emotional level, e.g., The North Face, Apple and Tesla. Notwithstanding all that is being said and written about AI and the digital world, people are still a critical factor because the behaviour of the people representing the brand strongly influences customers' perception. We know that customers' brand perception is significantly influenced by their experience with the organization's employees[5] and 96% of customers say customer service is important in their choice of loyalty to a brand.[6] This is a contributory factor to improved customer experience being the fastest-growing priority area for customer-care leaders.[7] And yet, at the same time, customer experience quality and ratings are falling for many brands.[8]

The area of customer experience has exploded in recent years[9] to become a powerhouse driving growth and revenue at companies around the world. As the discipline has grown, so too has the number of people working in the field and its importance and credibility. CX is still put forward as leading-edge thinking in many areas of business. It might, therefore, be a surprise to you that the term 'the experience economy' was coined in 1998.[10] This was more than 20 years ago ... in the previous century. Have we not moved forward from this? We believe that we have: that an 'experience' is no longer enough for a customer; that customers want to know more deeply about the organization providing the service, what it stands for and what it believes in before they decide if they want to be 'associated.'[11] This customer interest extends beyond the organization to its supply chain, as demonstrated in the film about the clothing industry, *The True Cost*.[12] Companies must begin thinking in terms of transparency-by-design to bridge the gap and safeguard brand resilience through trust-building. Companies can't simply say "trust us" when customers are demanding "show us."[13]

We predict that the successful organizations of tomorrow will be those that establish a sense of shared values with customers and other stakeholders (employees, service partners, owners or investors, and local communities).

> "I've learned that people will forget what you said,
> people will forget what you did, but people will never forget
> how you made them feel."
> **widely attributed to Maya Angelou, among others[14]**

ALIGNMENT IS THE KEY

These developments have created a time like never before when the customer experience bar needs to be raised. And yet, with all the resources out there on the topic, why is great customer experience so rare? (see **Chapter 4:** *Beginning*). This is the acid test of traditional approaches in the area and why we believe our fresh perspective can create so much value. For any organization wishing to excel in this area, we suggest that our tried-and-tested approach can provide a means to sustained performance against the backdrop of the emerging landscape. First and foremost, it is a pragmatic operating tool that provides a framework for the day-to-day leadership of the organization (as opposed to some sort of purely conceptual or theoretical model). The essence of the methodology is organizational alignment and coordinated execution. The framework consists of what we refer to as the five Elements: the Elements of Brand Identity, Employee Engagement and Customer Experience, are supported by the Elements of Systems & Processes, and Measurement & Insight (this is why you will see these terms capitalized throughout the book when we are referring specifically to the framework). The approach facilitates synergy and helps to minimize duplication and waste, creating significant value. A structured framework enables any organization to assess its performance, explore opportunities to do things differently and assist business planning, using the framework on an ongoing basis to maximize organizational alignment in 'business as usual.' It can help to mobilize everybody representing the organization in an aligned way, rather than relying on the CEO or leaders from other functions, and it helps prevent organizational structures and in-company power dynamics from adversely affecting the organization's direction and performance. It is, in effect, a business excellence model, which aligns activities to deliver measurable impact and creates a culture of customer-focused, high-performance, continuous improvement.

We introduce the concept in **Chapter 5:** *SERVICEBRAND* and provide an in-depth examination of the five Elements in **Part Three:** *Delivering* and **Part Four:** *Enabling*.

"Authentic brands don't emerge from marketing cubicles or advertising agencies. They emanate from everything the company does."
Howard Schultz[15]

HOW TO USE THIS BOOK

We have written this book to show how leaders of any service-focused organization – irrespective of size, geography and industry sector – can use a tried-and-tested approach to supercharge their customer experience. We share insights into how and why the methodology works in the emerging business landscape, as well as practical examples and stories. The approach has been successfully adopted by large and small companies, across sectors, all over the world.

The purpose of the book is to:

- Provide a practical and theoretical context by sharing information about the evolution of the customer experience concept alongside the approach we use to help leaders of service sector organizations design and implement a customer experience strategy (**Part One:** *Backstory*).
- Explore the importance of context over content and an overview of how our suggested approach enables this (**Part Two:** *Context*).
- Offer a detailed exploration of the practical design and implementation of an effective CX strategy. We share our thinking on how customer experience is best viewed as a whole organizational culture rather than a function, a process or set of tools, how it is inextricably connected to the rest of the organization, and explore some of the tools and techniques that can be drawn upon (**Part Three:** *Delivering*).
- Explain how the organizational infrastructure (systems and processes) and a focus on measurement and insight can support delivery of the customer experience strategy (**Part Four:** *Enabling*).
- Provide a practical perspective with a variety of mini case studies featuring organizations in different sectors, geographies and stages of maturity (**Part Five:** *Practice*).
- Highlight some key topics to consider when planning the future development and implementation of a customer experience strategy in your own organization (**Part Six:** *Future*).
- Encourage you to implement what you have learned about our approach in some way, large or small, to create value.

We have used a simple structure of 'bite-sized' chapters so you can explore in the way that appeals to you. You can read from the first page to the last page or dip into the book in a more random way. The content is divided into clearly labelled parts and chapters to help your navigation. How you make use of the book is entirely up to you. We have made a conscious effort to keep the style accessible and practical, supported by academic and business references where appropriate. We have also signposted carefully chosen additional resources (books, articles, posts and videos) to help you explore a range of topics more deeply if you want to. Finally, we offer two 'top tips' at the end of each chapter for you to consider. These are our personal suggestions deliberately focused on implementation and provide just two key takeaways to apply in practice in your organization. For ease of reference, there is a compilation of the top tips featured throughout the book after the final chapter, **Chapter 19:** *Summary*.

One way to think of the book is as a practical reference guide to understanding a fresh perspective of customer experience and why and how our approach to the topic can create so much value. It is not another regurgitation of all the customer experience content available in various formats. However, it is important to realize that our suggested approach in itself is not what will make the difference. The essence of our framework is that 'content' is vastly overrated and what is far more important is 'context.' It is the way the customer experience strategy is implemented by the people in an organization for its own unique situation that will determine the level of value creation.

We have been delighted to receive feedback that the book achieves a rare sweet spot of presenting a deeply thought-through concept in an accessible way supported by robust academic theory and offering tips for practical application.

WHO IS IT FOR?

We have written *Supercharging the Customer Experience* for a global audience. It is for progressive leaders all over the world who consider the area of customer experience to be important and who want to optimize performance. The book will be as valuable to senior executives and team leaders in small- or medium-sized enterprises as it will be for those in large multinationals in any sector or in the public sector. It is relevant to business-to-business and business-to-consumer environments, as well as to the public and third sectors, and even to internal service/ support functions within an organization. Clearly, it will be of interest to you if you have an academic interest or role in the functional area of customer experience. However, because of the focus on systems thinking and organizational alignment, it might also be helpful for people in the areas of marketing, branding, HR, culture, employee engagement, employee experience and organizational design.

Throughout the book, we bring together thinking and practice from great academic minds and well-known achievers in business, and we also introduce real day-to-day stories from our personal experience of working with leaders, being leaders ourselves and observing others. Our personal perspective is multifaceted, combining 40 years of work experience and organizational leadership (coauthor Alan) with a point of view enhanced by the knowledge and 15 years of experience in continuous improvement and customer engagement (coauthor Dave).

PART ONE: BACKSTORY

The first part of the book provides an introduction and background information to help you navigate and understand the content that follows. Through an introduction to the concept of customer experience and our unique perspective of the topic, you will gain an immediate level of familiarization and understanding at both a conceptual level and a practical level. You will also become familiar with the terminology used throughout the rest of the book.

Chapter 2: *CX Evolution* shares some of the thinking, research and philosophy that make this topic the cornerstone of the book. **Chapter 3:** *Alignment* describes how a more positive impact can be created when customer experience is a culture across the whole organization rather than a function operating in isolation. **Chapter 4:** *Beginning* describes how we came to coauthor this book and create the British Quality Foundation (BQF)-accredited customer experience development programme, CX in ConteXt. The general background provides a practical and theoretical context for the detailed explanation that follows.

PART TWO: CONTEXT

This second part of the book explores the importance of context over content. **Chapter 5:** *SERVICEBRAND* provides an overview of the approach we use and how this is helpful in designing and implementing a customer experience strategy that is tailored to the specific needs and situation of your organization. This is a crucial point. A customer experience strategy cannot be copied from another organization and 'dropped in' to be effective. Instead, it must be carefully designed and executed to take into account the organization's circumstances and environment. Please consider the relationship between the five Elements of our approach in your own organization. Many organizations operate in functional silos, devising their own unilateral strategies and missing many opportunities to improve the performance of the whole organization. We have seen this situation play out in large corporate organizations and smaller businesses. **Chapter 6:** *Landscape* then explores the wider context of the landscape in which organizations exist and operate, referencing the fundamental role of values and the emerging paradigm referred to as the Values Economy.

PART THREE: DELIVERING

The third part of the book explains in detail the three core Elements of our approach: **Chapter 7:** *Brand Identity*, **Chapter 8:** *Employee Engagement* and **Chapter 9:** *Customer Experience*. We describe what each Element is, identify the component parts and explore how the Elements can be aligned to create the most positive impact.

PART FOUR: ENABLING

The fourth part of the book explains in detail how the three core Elements covered in **Part Three:** *Delivering* are supported by the other two Elements of the framework with **Chapter 10:** *Systems & Processes* and **Chapter 11:** *Measurement & Insight*. We describe what these two Elements are and identify the component parts. This part of the book encourages you to consider how these two Elements support the areas of Brand Identity, Employee Engagement and Customer Experience in your organization.

PART FIVE: PRACTICE

This part of the book features four carefully selected mini case studies. We share real experiences with you, using the lens of our suggested approach to identify areas of best practice, benefits and challenges that have been faced. This practical, operational perspective brings to life the thinking we share throughout the book. The principles and methodology remain the same whether you are in a single business unit in any country or for a global organization. It is industry-sector agnostic. The framework accommodates varied contexts, and we explore the implications using examples from quite different industry sectors, geographies and stages of maturity. In some of these, we have worked directly with the organization and in others we have used the framework as a lens to look at the organization's performance. We summarize key CX in ConteXt takeaways for each situation. Our deep gratitude goes to our connections in these organizations for making this part of the book possible.

PART SIX: FUTURE

In the final part of the book, we highlight key topics to consider when you are planning the development and implementation of your customer experience strategy: **Chapter 16:** *Behaviour*, **Chapter 17:** *Digital* and **Chapter 18:** *Disruption*.

Our intention is that, by sharing our thoughts on these subjects, you will develop your insight into why and how you could design or develop and implement the customer experience approach for your organization from an informed and practical, operational perspective. To finish, we offer a recap and summary in **Chapter 19:** *Summary* followed by a compilation of the two top tips from the relevant chapters.

As you make your way through the book, you will notice the illustrations introducing each chapter, featuring Cai the CX SuperHero (who you can learn more about on page 274). The purpose of these illustrations is to provide a 'customer experience' thread as you read and a continuous reminder of the fundamental principle of our approach: everything in the organization is geared toward creating, delivering and improving the customer experience for sustained performance. We hope that you enjoy them as much as we enjoyed cocreating them with illustrator John Montgomery.

TO CONCLUDE

We are all too aware that there are many books on the topic of customer experience. Despite the best attempts of business professionals, researchers, scientists, philosophers and thinkers, there is no agreed, fixed formula that will deliver best-in-class customer experience over a sustained period. Each individual, group and organization's evolution is a process of constant interaction with and adaptation to the environment and context they find themselves in – which is why this won't be the last book on the subject. However, our framework helps organizations align and coordinate a range of activities in a sustained way. There is freedom within the framework to allow each organization to design and implement its own unique, fit-for-purpose customer experience solution that can evolve over time. It facilitates agility and scaling. It also enables synergies to be realized and duplication and waste to be minimized, and we have seen, first-hand, how it can deliver remarkable results across a balanced scorecard of measures. Of course, it is not a 'fix-all' solution – nothing is – and successful application depends on effort, collaboration, discipline and resilience.

We trust you will enjoy *Supercharging the Customer Experience* and find much within our suggested approach that resonates with you. We hope it will deepen your knowledge and awareness of how and why you would want to create a customer experience-focused organization or be associated with one. Our book will prompt you to ask and explore some of the questions that might be helpful and stimulate ideas about how to design and deliver great customer experience for sustained performance. If, by reading our book, you are inspired to take at least one action, small or big, then we will have succeeded in what we set out to achieve. We look forward to hearing your stories of how your CX thinking and practice has enabled you to create an even more effective organization. Naturally, we would be delighted to assist you on this journey!

TWO TOP TIPS

- No matter how volatile or uncertain the world may be, there will always be customers ... so treat them well.
- From the beginning, avoid treating customer experience in isolation, because it is inextricably connected to the rest of the organization.

PART ONE
BACKSTORY

The first part of the book provides an introduction and background information to help you navigate and understand the content that follows. Through an introduction to the concept of customer experience and our unique perspective on the topic, you will gain an immediate level of familiarization and understanding at both a conceptual level and a practical level. You will also become familiar with the terminology used throughout the rest of the book.

Chapter 2: *CX Evolution* shares some of the thinking, research and philosophy that make this topic the cornerstone of the book. **Chapter 3:** *Alignment* describes how the customer experience function can deliver the most positive impact when it is aligned with the rest of the organization and there is interdependency (rather than exist in isolation and be siloed in an organization). **Chapter 4:** *Beginning* outlines the development of our approach and how it creates value.

Our intention is that this general grounding will stand you in good stead for the rest of the book, making it an accessible, smooth-flowing experience.

CHAPTER 2
CX EVOLUTION

"It is not the strongest of the species that survives,
nor the most intelligent that survives.
It is the one that is most adaptable to change."
Charles Darwin

The earliest examples of the existence of customers through trading or purchasing can be traced back to ancient civilizations thousands of years ago. Specialized markets where customers could purchase various goods such as grains, textiles, pottery and livestock were located in densely populated city centres, or near temples that served as important economic and social hubs. Customers visited these markets to exchange goods or obtain items they needed by bartering or using early forms of currency such as barley, silver or gold. So, we've had customers for millennia, but the term 'customer experience' is brand new in comparison.

Lewis 'Lou' Carbone is credited for the term 'customer experience' and is widely regarded as the father of the experience movement. His 1994 article, "Engineering Customer Experiences"[1] in *Marketing Management* magazine is regarded as the beginning of the customer experience discipline. However, the origins of having a focus toward the customer can be traced back to the words of renowned business magnate Henry Ford,[2] who once famously said, "A business absolutely devoted to service will have only one worry about profits. They will be embarrassingly large." Although there is debate about the exact wording of this quote and when it was said, the sentiment is clear. You could argue that this laid the foundation for a shift in business strategy, emphasizing the importance of prioritizing the needs and satisfaction of customers, even though Bruce Temkin[3] coined the term 'CX' several decades after Ford's death.

> "The goal as a company is to have customer service
> that is not just the best, but legendary."
> **Sam Walton[4]**

Early pioneers in customer-centric business practices have left an indelible mark on the way organizations approach customer experience. The founder of Walmart, Sam Walton's emphasis on delivering exceptional service has helped to lay the foundations for customer-centricity in the retail industry. Harry Gordon Selfridge[5] was an American retail businessman who revolutionized the retail industry with his department store, Selfridges, in London in 1909. He introduced several customer-centric practices, including attractive window displays, product demonstrations, a 'one-stop shop' experience, and a focus on customer service. He famously coined the phrase "The customer is always right" to emphasize the importance of prioritizing customer satisfaction. Marshall Field,[6] an American entrepreneur and founder of Marshall Field and Company (now Macy's), was a pioneer in the concept of customer satisfaction. He implemented a revolutionary approach in the late 19th century by offering a wide variety of quality merchandise, unconditional return policies, and exceptional customer service. Field focused on creating a positive shopping experience. These early pioneers in the retail sector have paved the way for businesses to embrace customer-centricity as a core principle, demonstrating that a strong focus on customers is essential for long-term success and differentiation in a competitive marketplace.

The area of customer experience has exploded in the last decade or so, evidenced by the emergence of The Customer Experience Professionals Association (CXPA),[7] the premier global nonprofit organization dedicated to the advancement and cultivation of the customer experience profession, founded in 2011. The founder, Bruce Temkin, saw that the profession needed a single voice that would advocate for its growth.

To sustain the customer experience movement, the starting point was a common language and a philosophy of sharing best practices.

At the first major event, Bruce told the attendees that they needed to start using the acronym 'CX' to describe customer experience. The growth of the CX profession over the subsequent decade and beyond has been remarkable – there are now more than 4,000 CXPA members. The most telling impact is that companies are now hiring CX people – that didn't happen before. Secondly, individuals view themselves as CX professionals, and they're proud of it. This was a critical step for sustaining the profession, because once people self-identified as CX professionals, they became much more interested in helping other CX professionals – even those who worked in other companies.

> "The purpose of a business is to create
> and keep a customer."
> **widely associated with Peter Drucker[8]**

The concept of prioritizing customer experience has evolved over time, guided by the understanding that happy customers are the lifeblood of any successful enterprise. In our opinion, customer experience is not a department or a process or a set of tools. It is a philosophy to be embraced by every single employee, all the way from the CEO to the most recently hired. We believe this mindset is key to cultivating a customer-focused culture throughout an organization.

The shifting business landscape we describe in **Chapter 6: Landscape** has seen the emergence of customer-centricity as a powerful competitive advantage. We're in an era of rapid digital transformation and organizations have recognized that prioritizing customer experience is a key driver of innovation and success. According to a report by PwC,[9] 73% of all people point to customer experience as an important factor in their purchasing decisions. Delivering exceptional experiences to gain a competitive edge is growing more important by the day.

> "We see our customers as invited guests to a party,
> and we are the hosts. It's our job every day to make every
> important aspect of the customer experience a little bit better."
> **Jeff Bezos[10]**

The relentless pursuit of improvement and customer satisfaction is a crucial aspect of staying ahead in a dynamic business environment. As organizations embrace customer-centricity, they not only build loyal customer bases but also cultivate brand advocates who can help drive organic growth. In this new landscape, customer-centricity has become a necessity rather than an option, reshaping strategies and redefining success in an increasingly competitive marketplace.[11]

An example of a brand with high advocacy is Apple. Many Apple customers almost attach more importance to the brand and sense of connection than the quality of the product and own a range of products: iPhone, iPad, Apple Watch, Mac or MacBook – or even both – AirPods, AirTags or even Apple TV. Apple has cultivated one of the most fervent and dedicated communities of brand advocates in the tech industry, which has profoundly influenced the evolution of customer experience in comparison to Android devices and manufacturers. Their commitment to a seamless and integrated ecosystem, marked by the legendary ease of use, design aesthetics and a robust support system, has fostered an almost cult-like following among its customers. These brand advocates not only cherish their Apple devices but also actively promote them through word of mouth and social media. This enthusiastic advocacy translates into higher customer loyalty, premium pricing and a virtuous cycle of innovation. In contrast, the Android ecosystem, with its fragmentation and diversity of manufacturers, struggles to replicate a similar level of uniform customer experience. While Android offers versatility and choice, Apple's brand advocacy has consistently set the bar high for user satisfaction, pushing competitors to refine their products and services to stay competitive in the ever-evolving tech landscape.

> "Customer service shouldn't just be a department;
> it should be the entire company."
> **Tony Hsieh[12]**

Having a great experience as a customer is different to designing and implementing CX. Implementing effective customer experience strategies has its challenges and barriers. Our approach is totally aligned with Tony Hsieh's quote above, and we wonder whether the creation of the CX movement has, in some ways, hampered this whole organization approach by creating a single function that might be seen as 'responsible' for the area. Additionally, a report found that leaders of organizations rely mostly on customer satisfaction scores and other survey-based feedback to assess their CX strategy.[13] The lack of organizations having dedicated CX strategies emphasizes the challenges in developing a cohesive roadmap and approach for implementing customer-focused initiatives. You simply can't tell your service or support teams to 'do' customer experience, nor is it something you can claim to focus on unless everybody in the organization is aware of what the CX strategy is.

Overcoming resistance to change is arguably the biggest barrier for organizations globally in this area. Traditional ways of working and operating need to be challenged to foster a culture that embraces customer-centricity. Addressing all the challenges and barriers that relate to change is crucial for organizations to successfully navigate the path toward delivering great customer experiences.

THE AGE OF ...

We have entered an era where customers have more choice, information and power than ever before, known as the 'age of the customer.' We're going to explore the previous ages and how they have led to where we are now.

The '**age of manufacturing**' started around 1900 and lasted until around 1960. This period marked a transformative era in the age of manufacturing, shaping industries and economies around the world. This era witnessed the rise of assembly line production, with Henry Ford famously stating, "I will build a motor car for the great multitude." This mass-production approach revolutionized various sectors, including cars, consumer goods and electronics. If customers wanted to discover a new company or product, they would likely find it in their local town or hear about it from a neighbour. They also had to go to the store to purchase it or order it from the company's mail-delivered catalogue. Companies dictated the entire buying process, and any information published about the brand was promoted by the company. Manufacturing output in the United States increased from

$357 million in 1900 to $6.3 billion in 1960.[14] The Second World War propelled manufacturing to new heights, as Winston Churchill noted: "Give us the tools, and we will finish the job." The manufacturing sector became crucial for wartime production efforts, driving technological advancements and leading to sustained economic growth. The age of manufacturing stands as a testament to human ingenuity, fostering progress, and transforming societies through industrialization.

> "Any customer can have a car painted any colour
> that he wants so long as it is black."
> **Henry Ford[15]**

The '**age of distribution**,' from 1960 to 1990, saw a reshaping of the way goods and services were delivered to consumers. During this era, advancements in transportation and logistics played a pivotal role. The rise of computerized inventory systems and the arrival of containerization revolutionized global supply chains, enhancing efficiency and reducing costs. Modern transportation made it possible to deliver products all over the world. Businesses were no longer limited to their local geographical markets and could start to think globally in terms of distribution. Distribution statistics from this period demonstrate its impact. Containerized cargo traffic at ports worldwide grew from around 11 million TEUs (20-foot equivalent units) in 1968 to over 72 million TEUs by 1990.[16] This era witnessed the growth of retail giants like Walmart and the expansion of global trade. The age of distribution epitomized the power of effective logistics, enabling businesses to reach wider markets and providing consumers with greater convenience and accessibility.

> "The information about the package
> is as important as the package itself."
> **Fred Smith[17]**

The 'age of information,' from 1990 to 2010, ushered in a digital revolution, transforming the way knowledge is accessed, processed and shared. The emergence of the internet and advancements in computing technology propelled the information age forward. During this period, the volume of digital data exploded exponentially. In 1993, it was estimated that the total amount of digital information stored worldwide was approximately 15.8 exabytes. By 2014, that number had surged to 5,000 exabytes,[18] reflecting the vast expansion of digital content. One exabyte is made up of 1,000 petabytes, and this is the amount of data that the world generates per day. Given that 1,000 terabytes make up one petabyte, that means the world generates one million terabytes of data every single day! The internet not only revolutionized access to information but also transformed industries such as media, entertainment and commerce. Social media platforms like Facebook and Twitter allowed individuals to share stories, ideas and experiences on a global scale, fostering a culture of connectivity. The age of information propelled humanity into an interconnected era, empowering individuals, businesses and societies with unprecedented access to knowledge and communication.

"Information technology and business
are becoming inextricably interwoven.
I don't think anybody can talk meaningfully
about one without talking about the other."
Bill Gates[19]

The 'age of the customer,' since around 2010, has seen organizations increasingly prioritize customer-centric strategies and experiences. Forrester marks the age of the customer as starting in 2013, but we really entered this era in 2008 with the rise in popularity of social media platforms like Facebook and Twitter. This customer-centric mindset has reshaped industries and taken the importance of customer satisfaction to new heights. Eighty per cent of customers now consider their experience with a company to be as crucial as its products or services.[20] Moreover, the rise of social media and online reviews has empowered customers like never before. Customers have become active participants, sharing their experiences and shaping brand perceptions.

The age of the customer has driven companies to prioritize personalized experiences, with 72% of customers expecting businesses to understand their needs and tailor interactions accordingly.[21]

Customization and personalization have become essential strategies across various industries to enhance the customer experience, highlighting the importance of tailoring experiences to individual preferences. In the retail sector, research shows that, in some categories, more than 50% of consumers expressed interest in purchasing personalized products or services, and half said they were willing to wait longer for these features.[22] This statistic highlights the growing demand for customized offerings that cater to specific customer needs. Moreover, in the hospitality industry, a study revealed that 83% of travellers are willing to share their data to receive personalized experiences,[23] highlighting the value customers place on this feature. These examples illustrate how customization and personalization have become integral strategies for businesses across industries, enabling them to create memorable and highly tailored experiences that meet the unique preferences and demands of their customers.

Personalization and relationships have become more important too[24] in a world where customers have more choice than ever before and can demand bespoke products or services to meet their needs. In today's competitive landscape, personalization is a key differentiator, enabling organizations to forge meaningful connections and create memorable experiences that resonate with their customers' unique values, preferences and expectations. This personal data can now be collected and analysed to create tailored experiences and has become a crucial strategy in seeking to meet and exceed customer expectations. In some ways, data is the new oil, as there is a growing recognition of data's immense value and potential. In line with this, research reveals that 52% of consumers are likely to switch brands if they don't receive personalized communications.[25] This statistic highlights the importance of leveraging customer data to deliver relevant messages that resonate with individuals. Furthermore, organizations that effectively use customer analytics are more likely to outperform their peers in terms of revenue growth and customer loyalty, demonstrating the impact of data-driven personalization on business success.[26]

"We are not in the coffee business serving people,
but in the people business serving coffee."
Howard Schultz[27]

Customers have so much power today that they take into consideration company values even before considering a purchase.[28] This has led to the values-based customer, and you can read more on this in **Chapter 6:** *Landscape*. In the age of the customer, companies will live and die by their customer experience. While it's hard to predict the future and age we are heading for next, it is likely that elements of the age of the customer will continue to influence businesses over time. After all, we still use manufacturing to create products, modern transportation to distribute globally, and the internet to research and discover new brands.

THE OMNI-CHANNEL EXPERIENCE

Throughout the ages of manufacturing, distribution, information and the customer, there has been a dramatic shift in communication and its importance. In the manufacturing and distribution ages, the supplier organizations were in control but the introduction and development of technology in the age of information gave consumers a louder voice to promote or complain about a business or product. Customers and organizations' control of brands has shifted from ownership by the organization to co-ownership by customers and other stakeholder groups with multiple different channels at their disposal (see **Chapter 6:** *Landscape*).

The evolution of customer experience across multiple channels has transformed the way organizations interact with their customers and 75% of customers expect a consistent experience across multiple channels.[29] There is an increasing demand for seamless interactions and personalized experiences regardless of the 'channel' used. Channels are the different mediums of communication, with telephone, email and in-store being the more traditional methods, to which social media was added. The latter has evolved from being a single channel to being multiple and segregated because Facebook, Twitter (or X), Instagram,

LinkedIn, Snapchat, TikTok and Threads attract different demographics and users. The popularity of social messaging options like WhatsApp and Facebook Messenger has exploded in the last few years.[30]

Alongside the communication channels, the different devices that people use need to be considered. People change frequently between their phones, tablets and desktop devices throughout the day, which underlines the importance of providing a consistent and integrated, seamless experience across various touchpoints. Organizations need to be visible, promoting their brand and products while providing easy two-way communication with their customers, making it easy to engage, interact and buy products.

In response to this evolution, organizations have had to embrace omni-channel strategies, aiming to deliver cohesive experiences across different online and offline channels. Customers are looking for a consistent experience, irrespective of time, geography or channel.

"A brand is no longer what we tell the consumer it is
– it is what consumers tell each other it is."
Scott Cook, cofounder of Intuit

Creating a consistent omni-channel experience presents both challenges and opportunities for organizations. Maintaining a consistent brand image across multiple channels is a challenge, because customers' perceptions are shaped by their interactions and conversations with an organization. Seventy-three per cent of customers use multiple channels during their shopping journey, highlighting the need for businesses to provide a seamless and integrated experience.[31]

Significant preparation and orchestration between different functions is needed. Once again, we highlight the need for organizations to look beyond and break down internal functional silos to achieve consistency across channels. At the same time, there are significant opportunities for organizations that successfully deliver a consistent omni-channel experience. Organizations with strong omni-channel engagement strategies retain nine out of ten of their customers, demonstrating the potential for increased customer loyalty and retention.[32] Furthermore, a survey by Deloitte found that 96% of retail consumers 'expect' a seamless omni-channel experience across all channels.[33]

The word 'expect' emphasizes the shift to the age of the customer, once again highlighting the competitive advantage that businesses can gain by providing a consistent and integrated customer journey.

Several companies have set high standards in delivering exceptional omni-channel experiences. Apple is known for its seamless integration across various devices and platforms. Their omni-channel approach ensures a consistent and intuitive experience for customers, whether they interact with the brand in-store, online or through their devices. Another standout example is Disney, which has mastered the art of creating a magical omni-channel experience, seamlessly connecting its theme parks, movies, merchandise and digital platforms. From visiting a theme park and enjoying a personalized experience with Magic Bands to engaging with Disney content on multiple devices, the company ensures that customers have a cohesive and enchanting journey across channels. Nike is also renowned in this area, delivering a consistent experience through its mobile app, website, physical stores and connected fitness products. Customers can seamlessly shop online, access personalized content, and even receive product recommendations based on their activity data. Nike's omni-channel strategy enables customers to engage with the brand and enjoy a tailored experience at every touchpoint. These examples demonstrate the power of delivering exceptional omni-channel experiences by seamlessly integrating customer touchpoints, providing personalized interactions, and fostering a consistent brand experience. By focusing on customer needs and leveraging technology, these companies have established themselves as industry leaders, delighting customers and building strong brand loyalty.

In summary, the history of customer experience has evolved significantly over time, reflecting the changing dynamics between businesses and consumers. In the past, companies primarily focused on transactional interactions, where the main goal was to sell products or services. However, with the dawn of the age of the customer, which emerged in response to empowered and informed customers, organizations began to recognize the importance and need of delivering exceptional experiences. This shift in mindset placed the customer at the centre of business strategies, emphasizing the need to understand and meet their expectations and values. The meteoric rise and development of technology has shifted the balance in communication (see **Chapter 17:** *Digital*), and the rise of the omni-channel experience has played a crucial role in shaping customer experience. The combination of customer-centricity and omni-channel experience has become pivotal in fostering long-term customer loyalty and driving business success in today's competitive marketplace.

To stay ahead of the competition and meet the evolving demands of empowered, values-driven customers, it is time for organizations to embrace the age of the customer and implement omni-channel strategies. The key lies in adopting a proactive mindset, leveraging data-driven insights, and employing technology to create cohesive, consistent and exceptional experiences across all touchpoints. By doing so, organizations can not only attract new customers but also nurture existing ones, ultimately driving growth and long-term success. It's time to embrace the values-led, customer-centric revolution and seize the opportunities that the age of the customer and omni-channel experience presents.

TWO TOP TIPS

- Analyse the different ways customers interact with your organization and don't assume that what is in place today is good enough.
- Compare the experience your organization provides with experiences from other organizations, in other sectors and geographies, because that's what your customers do.

WANT TO KNOW MORE?

To explore this area further, you might enjoy the following articles and books:

Harley Manning and Kerry Bodine. *Outside In: The Power of Putting Customers at the Center of Your Business.*

Jim Blasingame. *The Age of the Customer: Prepare for the Moment of Relevance.*

Keith F. O'Brien. *Omnichannel Marketing: The Roadmap to Create and Implement Omnichannel Strategy for Your Business.*

Andreas Weigend. *The Omni-Channel Retail Revolution: How to Create Seamless Customer Experiences Online and Offline.*

Lonnie Mayne. "Evolve or Die in the Age of the Consumer." *Entrepreneur*

CHAPTER 3
ALIGNMENT

"No one can whistle a symphony.
It takes a whole orchestra to play it."
widely attributed to H. E. Luccock[1]

Being able to articulate a clear strategy is one thing, and yet an organization's ability to execute a strategy is an altogether different, usually more challenging matter. We know that many senior leaders agree.

Contrary to the central premise of many strategy studies, usually it is not the vision or aspirations of a successful company that allow it to stand out (and these goals are often remarkably similar, irrespective of organization size, geography or industry sector). What sets the top performers apart is the 'how' – the way they organize and operate to make their aspirations a reality.

"There are few original strategies in banking.
There's only execution."
Sir John Bond[2]

The answer usually lies in the organization itself and in the way that everything works. However, this is often a complex challenge to deal with because of the involvement of various internal structures, frameworks, operating practices, and functions or departments, sometimes with different perspectives, objectives and priorities.

We believe that the key to success in delivering a great customer experience is values-led organizational alignment focused on customer experience as the outcome. This is particularly important in the new paradigm of the Values Economy[3] (you can learn more in **Chapter 6:** *Landscape*), which is a double-edged sword. On the one hand, robust alignment will be recognized by all stakeholder groups and widely lauded with all the positive impact it can create. However, on the other hand, any gaps between what the organization says it is and the way its employees make decisions and behave will be exposed with potentially fatal consequences.[4]

> "Good business leaders create a vision, articulate the vision, passionately own the vision and relentlessly drive it to completion."
> **Jack Welch[5]**

But alignment is rare, and nine out of ten companies fail to execute their strategic vision.[6] On average, 95% of employees are unaware of or do not understand their company's strategy. How do you think these companies would sound if they were an orchestra?

WHAT IS ALIGNMENT?

In its simplest form, alignment means "functioning as a whole."[7] Organizational strategic alignment means lining up a business's strategy with its culture across the organizational functions, departments and operating units (horizontally) and from the boardroom to the front line (vertically). To assist vertical alignment, we encourage our clients to consider any business objective from end to end, broken down into the areas of strategy, management and delivery. In other words, what is the strategic objective, what management processes need to be put in place, and what is delivered 'on the ground'? In **Chapter 5:** *SERVICE-BRAND*, we use the practical example of a company with a strategic objective to 'develop our people' to explain this.

The alignment approach also needs to extend externally beyond the organization, to align with its customers, employees, service partners, local communities and marketplace. The approach to alignment is a process that requires careful, detailed management to align the vision for the company with that of its leadership goals, different departments, culture and individual employees at every step of the business planning process – from creation to execution.

"Clarity = speed."
Ken Perlman[8]

Most executives today know their organizations should be aligned. They know their strategies, organizational capabilities, resources and management systems should all be arranged to support the enterprise's purpose. The challenge is that executives tend to focus on one of these areas to the exclusion of the others, but what really matters for performance is how they all fit together.

Consider McDonald's. What does it take to be able to serve nearly 1% of the world's population – more than 70 million customers – every day and in virtually every country around the world? It takes fanatical attention to the design and management of scalable processes and routines, and a working culture by which simple, stand-alone and standardized products are sold globally at predictable (and, therefore, manageable) volumes, qualities and costs. Maximizing economies of scale lies at the heart of McDonald's product-centric business model. Efficiency is built into the design of its winning organization in the form of formalized hierarchies of performance accountability, a high division of labour, routinization of specialist tasks and teamwork at the point of sale. McDonald's has been the market leader in its sector for decades.

"The main thing is to keep the main thing the main thing."
Stephen R. Covey[9]

Jonathan Trevor and Barry Varcoe envisage enterprise alignment as a tightly managed enterprise value chain that connects an enterprise's purpose (what we do and why we do it) to its business strategy (what we are trying to win at to fulfil our purpose), organizational capability (what we need to be good at to win), resource architecture (what makes us good) and finally, management systems (what delivers the winning performance we need).[10] There is a strong parallel with the approach we use, which provides an additional focus on the organization's people delivering a brand-aligned customer experience.

The role of organizational culture cannot be underestimated in importance because organizational alignment is more than a process map. Values-driven organizational alignment, specifically, is the central principle of our approach and it could well be the bedrock – the foundation – upon which all genuinely successful organizational change rests.[11] Within this area sits the topic of values alignment between employees' personal values and the organizational values. Research is starting to identify the importance of this area.[12] When employees show their authentic selves at work, it allows them to focus on their strengths rather than wasting energy covering up who they are.[13, 14]

WHAT ARE THE BENEFITS?

We believe that organizational alignment can deliver a wide range of benefits and, naturally, some of these will be realized more than others or to a greater or lesser extent from one organization to another depending on their individual circumstances. Having said this, broadly speaking, we suggest that the benefits can be summarized under the three main topics: business performance, employee engagement and organizational agility.

"Alignment is that state where the key elements of a business are integrated and aligned to drive growth and profit."
George Labovitz[15]

When employees understand their individual goals and how these relate to the overall company's goals, they become more engaged with their work. Because they can see how they can make a direct contribution to the company's success, they begin to focus on finding ways to work smarter and more efficiently. This boost in employee productivity will naturally lead to increased business performance. In organizations that combine excellence in tactical project implementation with alignment to strategy, projects are successful 90% of the time; in contrast, those that neglect strategic alignment have a 34% success rate.[16] Furthermore, a study found that 44% of stronger-performing companies had almost 100% alignment in their goals at the managerial level compared to none of the weaker performers and that 67% of companies with a stronger financial performance covered all managers and some levels below with their performance management system compared to 28% of the weaker performers.[17] A study of alignment between sales and marketing functions reported 20% average growth (increase) in company annual revenue, as compared to a 4% average decrease among what it called 'Laggard' organizations.[18]

> "If everyone is moving forward together,
> then success takes care of itself."
> **widely attributed to Henry Ford[19]**

REASONS FOR LACK OF ALIGNMENT

You might be wondering: if alignment is so valuable, then why are so many organizations clearly not aligned?

We believe that the most important reason for its absence is that alignment is simply 'not on the radar' for many senior executives. You might think that the CEO (or equivalent) is where this responsibility lies but, in our experience, very few leaders take this view. Instead, they choose to focus on driving the performance of the various individual operating units and central support functions described in the organization's structure. While the structure is an important part, organizations are much more than this. Organizations are complex systems of choices dealing with strategy, work, structure, metrics and information, people and rewards, and culture and leadership practices. Key drivers of complexity are the number of employees, range of customer profiles, variety of service lines, breadth of communication channels and physical spread (by geography and time zone).

When leaders take the time to look at their organization from a systemic standpoint, they can pinpoint and diagnose misalignments and make alignment-producing adjustments. Often, they simply do not think of the component parts as connected and coherent value chains. As a result, multiple individuals and groups are responsible for different parts of the organization and no individual role or group is functionally responsible for overseeing organizational alignment.

Individual leaders are often inward-looking, seeking to drive the best performance in their own area of responsibility rather than align and improve across the entire organization. They become all-consumed with 'performance,' blinded by the demands and pressures of 'business as usual' to the possibilities of an aligned organization. They have no time or inclination to realize the potential benefits. This has resulted in the growth in power of individual operating units and central support functions, which have, in effect, developed as independent entities over a period of many years, with investment of time, expertise and finance to establish practices, processes and cultures that are often not connected to the 'mothership.' It is, therefore, not surprising that for many CEOs (and shareholders), tackling the situation is put in the 'too difficult' box.

As we have already mentioned, complexity makes sustained organizational alignment particularly challenging, especially against the backdrop of a rapidly changing business landscape. It is easy to appreciate that a small, single-service organization with a targeted local customer profile in a single location is easier to align than a large, diversified and geographically dispersed organization, whichever sectors they operate in. Many organizations are too complex for their design and management to be left to chance or to rely solely on one individual. This is why a framework like the one we recommend, which can enable organizational alignment, is so valuable, providing a structure for all decision makers to allow them to view their organization as one holistic entity, rather than as a set of individual units or functions. Looking at the organization in this way also helps to answer the question, "Where does alignment add value and where does it not?"

The final reason we suggest for a lack of organizational alignment relates to a shortcoming in communication. Many readers will have worked for a variety of organizations of different sizes and in different sectors. Consider your experience of the balance between the amount of communication (all channels – meetings, informal discussions, intranet, etc.) that occurs within individual operating units or functions versus organization-wide. In our experience, this balance is heavily weighted to the former and, where efforts are made across the organization, they often flounder through lack of support from functional leadership. The nature of alignment demands cross-functionality: communication up, down and across the organization and between teams. We discuss the importance of the communication framework in **Chapter 9:** *Systems & Processes.*

HOW TO DO IT

The short answer is to use the approach we are explaining in this book. It is not rocket science, and we were interested to discover an article published by Gallup that, in effect, summarizes the approach we use and poses some great questions:[20]

- How much, exactly, does employee alignment contribute to business outcomes beyond customer alignment?
- What would your organization gain if it could recruit people who are already poised to deliver the core elements of your brand identity and promise when they are hired?
- In what way, if any, do aligned customers or employees serve as ambassadors of the brand?
- How does brand engagement – or the marketplace's perceptions of a brand's honesty, integrity, value and irreplaceability – complement alignment?

"Consistent alignment of capabilities and
internal processes with the customer value proposition
is the core of any strategy execution."
Robert S. Kaplan[21]

Organizational alignment is simple but not easy. It's the exhausting work of getting every member of your organization focused on delivering a great customer experience, walking in the same direction and making the right contributions at the right times to reach that destination.

While it is difficult to achieve, the results can be powerful. For the organizations that get it right, the organization and the strategy are as one rather than separate entities. This can lead to dramatic (rather than incremental) improvements in performance and value creation. New growth opportunities are often realized by enabling and rewarding more entrepreneurial behaviour at multiple levels and, over time, by attracting and retaining more qualified and motivated individuals. Ultimately, adopting a new, customer-focused 'operating model' can be an effective way to align an organization's people with its strategy – which itself is the best way to drive continual improvement.

TWO TOP TIPS

- Examine how the different functions in your organization work together with the same objective and where they are working on their own in silos.
- Identify ways in which policies and procedures in your organization 'get in the way' of delivering a great customer experience and deal with them.

WANT TO KNOW MORE?

To explore this area further, you might enjoy the following articles and books:

George H. Labovitz and Victor Rosansky. *The Power of Alignment: How Great Companies Stay Centered and Accomplish Extraordinary Things.*

Reed Deshler. "The secret to organizational alignment: Becoming an alignment leader." *SHRM Executive Network HR People + Strategy Blog.*

Christopher M. Branson. "Achieving organizational change through values alignment." *Journal of Educational Administration.* 46 (2008): 376–395.

Jeffrey W. Bennett, Thomas E. Pernsteiner, Paul Kocourek and Steven B. Hedlund (2000). "The Organization vs. the strategy: Solving the alignment paradox." *Strategy+Business.*

Wouter Aghina, Karin Ahlback, Aaron De Smet, Gerald Lackey, Michael Lurie, Monica Murarka and Christopher Handscomb. "The five trademarks of agile organizations." *McKinsey.*

John Kotter. "When CEOs talk strategy, 70% of the company doesn't get it." *Forbes.*

GAP INTERNATIONAL (2023). *"The power of alignment: Fuel for high-performing teams."*

CHAPTER 4
BEGINNING

"Success is a journey, not a destination.
The doing is often more important than the outcome."
widely attributed to Arthur Ashe[1]

To complete the first part of the book in setting the scene for what follows, this chapter shares how the book that you are reading now came about. The catalyst was the coauthors' (Alan and Dave) association with BQF, the premier membership organization in the UK representing excellence and performance improvement. It was founded in 1993 by government and leading UK businesses and is an independent, nonprofit, corporate membership organization.[2] Alan has been a nonexecutive director at BQF since 2010 and Dave has been a member since 2012.

CX IN CONTEXT

In 2022, BQF President Karen Leftley was having parallel conversations with the coauthors. She was discussing with Dave the opportunity to create a body of knowledge in the area of customer experience. Dave had suggested that there was a gap in the BQF training offer because the topic of customer experience was included as a component of the Lean framework, instead of being a standalone subject. At the same time, Karen was exploring the possibility of Alan's company SERVICEBRAND GLOBAL Ltd becoming a partner to deliver

BQF-accredited training and development in the area of customer experience. Things moved quickly from this point. A couple of Zoom calls confirmed closely aligned thinking and Alan and Dave met in person near Liverpool Street station in London to scope out the design of the BQF customer experience development programme. There was a mutual desire for the programme to offer something different and fresh compared to similar products available from other providers. The challenge was provided by a simple question: "With all the content out there on the topic, why is great customer experience so rare?" The conclusion was that the main reason for the scarcity of great customer experience is that the focus tends to be on communicating knowledge, theory and content on the topic. The coauthors shared a deep operational understanding of customer experience; Alan through his initial experience in premium hospitality environments and Dave through driving operational customer satisfaction and engagement in the telecoms sector. This helped crystallize that having the customer experience knowledge is not enough because it is only the ability to apply this knowledge in practice that enables delivery of great customer experience. Furthermore, every organization is different, with its own unique situation and circumstances. Context is far more important than content.

THE BRAND

This focus on context above content led to the creation of the brand for the BQF customer experience programme: CX in ConteXt. Serendipitously, the letters C and X are in the word 'context' and a trusted graphic designer was able to interpret this thinking into a logo that has received rave reviews. It was also critical to reinforce the central importance of an attitude and mindset focused on customer experience as opposed to thinking of customer experience as a process, function or set of tools. As a result, the CX Superhero character Cai (they/them) was born. Cai is a gender-neutral name of Latin and Welsh origin meaning 'rejoice' or 'happy' and this seems perfectly aligned with the purpose of customer experience. The CX in ConteXt development programme encourages the attendees to discover their own CX Superhero within (at a personal and organizational level).

The training and certification pathway provides candidates with the necessary understanding, tools, techniques and confidence to successfully develop and execute a CX plan tailored for their organization. It covers each of the major competency areas in the framework:

1. What is CX? An introduction
2. CX in ConteXt overview
3. Brand Identity
4. Employee Engagement
5. Customer Experience – The CX in ConteXt toolbox; customer journeys, channels, personas, design thinking
6. Systems & Processes
7. Measurement & Insight
8. Action planning

The programme is suitable for ambitious individuals seeking to transform CX for their product or service, as well as individuals with a determination to learn more about CX for themselves and/or their organizations. There are different levels to accommodate everybody, from those who are at the beginning of their customer experience journey to those who are in leadership roles:

- CX Introduction – All employees (whether customer-facing or not). Also consider outsourced service partner employees.
- CX Practitioner – Employees directly involved in the design and/or delivery of CX activities (or aspiring).
- CX Advanced Practitioner – Employees with CX operational leadership responsibility (or aspiring).
- CX Master Practitioner – Senior leaders with CX strategic leadership responsibility (or aspiring).

The programme was launched at a BQF event at BT Tower, London in November 2022.

We are delighted that one of our mini case studies, **Chapter 15**: *BT Group*, became the first company to progress with the CX in ConteXt Programme.

THE BOOK

Once the CX in ConteXt development programme was designed, Alan suggested a coauthored book on the topic. It was an easy decision for Dave to say "yes" and LID Publishing, who had published Alan's previous coauthored books, was very excited to lead the project. You might be surprised to know that from the time it was decided to write the book to its publication took less than two years.

There were several principles and core themes that were agreed on for the book project. The first theme might seem obvious for a book about customer experience: focus on the customer experience. As highlighted previously, but worth repeating, this means that customer experience is a whole organizational culture rather than just an operating function, a process or a set of tools.

Another strong core theme was a combination of theory and practice: understanding the theory that helped to underpin successful practical outcomes, applying theory in practice and, finally, understanding the relationship between the two. Personal experience of working with various business models or frameworks (e.g., the EFQM Excellence model,[3] Hospitality Assured,[4] Investors in People[5] and the Service Profit Chain[6]) had also been beneficial. The key insight was the value of having an overarching organizational framework to support general management of the business instead of allowing an approach more reliant on individual functions and the organizational structure. These frameworks helped to join up the functions of a business horizontally and vertically (i.e., actively involving all members of the team and keeping them focused on the priorities of the business as a whole). Other areas that had helped to create improved business performance were putting in place various common operating systems and processes, including communication channels and methods to capture measurement and insight.

Although the various business frameworks mentioned above had all been helpful in their own way, they all seemed to have individual strengths but also areas that could be improved. One common area that seemed to be lacking was a recognition of the importance of aligning all activities with the organization's brand (where this is the personality and character rather than the logo). This proved to be the motivation for Alan to create a customer experience-focused model where all aspects were informed by the brand identity. It was designed to be comprehensive yet simple and provided a robust structure at the same time as offering flexibility to suit organizations with different circumstances. As a result, the SERVICEBRAND approach was born and is the framework used in our book to describe how leaders in any organization can design, implement and improve a customer experience strategy bespoke to their own unique circumstances and situation. The framework provides the core structure of the book with an introduction in **Chapter 5:** *SERVICEBRAND* and a deeper explanation of the five Elements in **Part Three:** *Delivering* and **Part Four:** *Enabling*.

> "That's been one of my mantras – focus and simplicity.
> Simple can be harder than complex: You have to work hard
> to get your thinking clean to make it simple. But it's worth it in
> the end because once you get there, you can move mountains."
> **Steve Jobs[7]**

AMBITION

Our best hope is that this book and the CX in ConteXt development programme can add to the existing valuable resources available on the topic to help leaders in service organizations improve the experience of their customers over time. It would be wonderful if a great customer experience could become the norm rather than the exception.

TWO TOP TIPS

- Resist the temptation to plan forever; start implementing and adjust as you go.
- Take that leap of faith to collaborate – it can keep you accountable, innovate new ideas and take you out of your comfort zone.

PART TWO
CONTEXT

This second part of the book explores the importance of context over content. **Chapter 5:** *SERVICEBRAND* provides an overview of this approach and how it is helpful in designing and implementing a customer experience strategy that is tailored to the specific needs and situation of your organization. Please consider the relationship between the five Elements of the approach. Many organizations operate in functional silos, devising their own unilateral strategies and missing many opportunities to improve the performance of the whole organization. We have seen this situation play out in large corporate organizations and smaller businesses. **Chapter 6:** *LANDSCAPE* then explores the wider context of the landscape in which organizations exist and operate, referencing the emerging paradigm referred to as the Values Economy.

CHAPTER 5
SERVICEBRAND

"Building a visionary company requires
1% vision and 99% alignment."
Jim Collins and Jerry Porras[1]

It is likely that the term 'SERVICEBRAND' is new to many people reading this book because it is a word invented by coauthor Alan. It is an evolution of the term 'service brand,' which refers to a brand that primarily represents services rather than tangible products. It focuses on the reputation, perception and overall experience associated with the delivery of services. When developing a service brand, organizations typically focus on factors such as service quality, customer experience, brand promise, employee engagement and differentiation from competitors. Effective service branding aims to create a positive and distinctive brand image that instils trust, loyalty and satisfaction in customers. Perhaps the easiest way to describe the meaning of SERVICEBRAND is "an organization for which the people delivering the service are a central element of the offer or proposition." In the business-to-consumer (B2C) sector, it is easy to think of a traditional SERVICEBRAND, such as a five-star hotel or an airline. Other B2C examples include leisure, healthcare, logistics, financial, legal and others, where a service is provided by the employees of an organization and is paid for by the customer. Arguably, some brands that might previously have been considered a 'product,' in sectors such as technology, automotive, telephone and retail (household goods, clothing, food and drink), are becoming a SERVICEBRAND. This is because it is increasingly challenging for companies in these sectors to differentiate

SUPERCHARGING THE CUSTOMER EXPERIENCE

themselves based on product benefits and features that are relatively easy to replicate, and quickly. The people delivering the customer experience, therefore, become a more important differentiator[2] and one that is not so easy to copy.

Beyond the B2C sector, the SERVICEBRAND term is also relevant in the business-to-business (B2B) sector – for example, from providers of services (legal, financial, property, technology, management consultancy, call centres, etc.) to corporate organizations. It is also relevant in the public sector – for example, healthcare, municipal services, education, transport services and social services. The SERVICEBRAND approach is even relevant for functions in an organization – for example, HR (or People and Culture), Finance, IT, Corporate Real Estate Services, etc., which provide a service to their internal clients.

A SIMPLE CONCEPT

At one level, the approach could not be simpler: focus on delivering a great customer experience and align all facets of the 'way things work around here' with your organization's purpose and values (the heart of the organization's brand identity). It is an elegant way to distil all the various complex aspects of an organization.

"The height of sophistication is simplicity."
Clare Boothe Luce[3]

Over time, alignment is achieved at both an individual and group level, bringing the organization's values to life at all levels within the organization, even extending beyond the organization to other stakeholder groups such as service partner companies. The concept of alignment is central to the approach, and this is why the quote from Jim Collins and Jerry Porras at the start of this chapter is so apt – you can read more about this topic in **Chapter 3:** *Alignment*. In turn, on the one hand, there is symmetry and consistency between the decisions made and behaviours displayed (day in, day out) and, on the other, what the organization states is important. This releases untapped potential, reduces the risk of ambiguity, duplication and waste, and can ultimately result in profound authenticity being displayed across all facets of the organization. A sense of trust can be established with customers and other stakeholder groups. However, in contrast, when employees' behaviour and decisions are not aligned with the organization's values, then these values are not being lived. There is no middle ground. The SERVICEBRAND approach, therefore, facilitates authenticity and improves employees' sense of wellbeing with the resulting positive impact on performance that you would expect. It is also visible to customers and other stakeholders such as service partners and communities.

The importance of the people who represent an organization has increased significantly. The general shift from a product-based reputation to an experience-based reputation[4] has resulted in customers' perception of an organization being based on their personal experience of those representing the organization. Similarly, employees' perception of their own organization is based on the degree of alignment between their personal values and those of the organization, their personal experience of how they are treated and how they see colleagues behaving.

> "Take care of your employees and
> they'll take care of your customers."
> **Bill Marriott[5]**

Articulating your brand identity, including your core values, is a waste of time unless employees understand what the values mean in their day-to-day activities and how the values can change their daily decisions.[6]

FRAMEWORK

The SERVICEBRAND approach consists of a robust, methodical framework supported by a host of interwoven underpinnings, theories and thinking. This combination translates a rich and complex concept of delivering values-aligned customer experience into a simple, easy-to-understand and practical approach. Our experience of working in different cultures, geographies, business sectors and organizations of different sizes has been fascinating. We have worked on six continents (prospects in Antarctica are few and far between!) and visited more than 30 countries. The activities have varied from one situation to another, yet all within the overall consistent framework. The key has been respect – to take the time to explain why the approach is valuable, how it works and what happens in practice, and then to listen and appreciate the intricacies of the individual context and allow local ownership of using the framework as an 'operating platform' in a relevant way.

> "I believe that leaders and leadership teams working together
> in a proper design will run the business more effectively
> than by hierarchical, command-and-control managing.
> But I can't prove that. And there are no models."
> **Marvin Bower**[7]

One of the strengths of the framework lies in its blend of practice and theory – on the one hand, we can say 'what works' and 'what the benefits are' and, on the other, we can answer in some depth 'why' the methodology works. Reading this book will give you an understanding of how the framework brings together several different areas in a layered way to create a powerful customer experience-focused approach. Experience tells us that there is no single silver bullet, and we think of any plan as a spider's web of interconnected activity that provides strength and support.

SYSTEMS THINKING

Systems thinking is a method of critical thinking involving analysis of the relationships between a system's parts to understand a situation to enable better decision-making.[8] This is a major departure from the old way of business decision-making, which broke a system down into parts and analysed the parts separately. Supporters of systems thinking believe that the old way is inadequate for our dynamic world, where there are numerous interactions between the parts of a system that combine to create the reality of a situation. According to systems thinking, if we examine the interactions between the parts in a system, we will see larger patterns emerge. By seeing the patterns, we can begin to understand how the system works. If the pattern is good for the organization, we can make decisions that reinforce it; however, if the pattern is bad for the organization, we can make decisions that change the pattern. Our framework enables this 'whole-organization' view by using its five Elements as an 'operating platform' (rather than being led by the organizational structure).

TWO DIMENSIONS

There are two dimensions that are helpful in explaining how the approach works in general terms to deliver customer experience focused organizational alignment. The first dimension is that of horizontal integration, looking at the relationship between the five Elements: Brand Identity, Employee Engagement, Customer Experience, Systems & Processes and Measurement & Insight – more detailed explanations of the individual Elements are provided in **Chapters 7–11**.

"A company's culture and a company's brand are really just two sides of the same coin. The brand is just a lagging indicator of a company's culture."
Tony Hsieh[9]

Here is a simple flow for thinking about using our approach to supercharge the customer experience:

1. Confirm the objective to deliver a consistent brand-aligned customer experience.
2. Clearly articulate the organization's brand identity (this is the character and personality, including purpose and values).
3. Create a team of brand ambassadors (the right people in the right job so they are motivated and productive, with responsibility and accountability at individual and team levels).
4. Design and deliver a consistent, brand-aligned customer experience (irrespective of time, geography or channel).
5. Support the efforts to align brand identity, employee engagement and customer experience with common operating systems and processes (e.g., cross-organization communication, stakeholder relationship management, transparency and visibility of goals, shared technology platforms) and robust measurement and insight processes (quantitative and qualitative) to assess performance across these areas.

How does this compare with your experience of how organizations work? In our experience, in so many organizations, certainly larger (global) corporates but also small- and medium-sized businesses, the Marketing function owns everything associated with brand identity, HR (or People and Culture) deal with 'people' matters (employee engagement), and Operations delivers the customer experience. The three functions often devise their own unilateral strategies, do not talk to each other, and are then shocked when their approach doesn't work. Strategic alignment across these areas and coordinated execution can create so much value with relatively little effort and/or investment. You can see examples of this in **Part Five:** *Practice*, which brings to life the preceding chapters by examining a variety of mini case studies.

The two Elements of Systems & Processes and Measurement & Insight provide a supporting role. This is an important point because how often have you experienced an organization where one function seems to become overly important? In our experience, common offenders are Finance, IT and Health & Safety to name a few. Of course, all these functions are important, it's just that sometimes, for whatever reason, it is overlooked that their primary function is as a support role, and they only exist because of the core business. The framework can be represented in a two-dimensional format, as in *Figure 1*.

STRATEGY

MANAGEMENT

DELIVERY

CUSTOMER EXPERIENCE

Detailed Standards

Consistency
(Time, Place, Channel)

Relationships

BRAND IDENTITY

Purpose
and Vision

Values

CX Signatures

EMPLOYEE ENGAGEMENT

Leadership

People Processes

Training

Recognition

MEASUREMENT & INSIGHT

Performance	Feedback
Brand	Customer
Employee	Employee
Customer	Service
	Partner

SYSTEMS & PROCESSES

Functions/Org Structure

IT Platforms

Governance

Communication
Framework

Glossary

CX-MINDSET AND EMOTIONAL QUOTIENT (EQ)

FIGURE 1
THE SERVICEBRAND FRAMEWORK

The second dimension of the SERVICEBRAND approach is vertical integration, which involves applying the levels of strategy, management and delivery to each Element individually. For a strategy to be delivered successfully, it needs to be clearly articulated, supported by appropriate management processes and with practical actions and/or tools in place 'on the ground.'

We will use a practical example to explain this. Taking the Element of Customer Experience, imagine an organization with a strategy 'to delight our customers.' The strategy might be supported by a management process of a biannual voice-of-customer exercise combined with a robust internal communication plan focused on celebrating successes and actioning areas for improvement. At a delivery level, there might be a discretionary sum for employees to use when they identify an opportunity to delight a customer. With the approach we use, relevant measurement and insight is applied at all three levels to understand performance, and this might have an outcome dimension (e.g., spend and product range data, social media monitoring or number of new customer introductions). Now think about what the impact would be if any of these three levels (strategy, management and delivery) were not in place: if there were no clearly articulated strategy, no effective review of customer perception or no assessment of the impact of the discretionary fund, the strategy would not be achieved. All three levels need to be in place and if any one of them is missing, then a successful outcome becomes very unlikely.

There is also a three-dimensional interpretation of the SERVICEBRAND approach that shows how the Customer Experience Element is supported by all the other Elements.[10]

"A bad system will defeat a good person every time."
widely attributed to W. Edwards Deming[11]

By using a fit-for-purpose 'operating platform,' leaders can overcome the tensions and trade-offs that are usually embedded in the organizations' histories, structures, capabilities and cultures, to lead themselves to new, higher levels of performance. Sometimes, they will discover that changes in the overall strategy are required at the same time. But, at the very least, they will create customer-centric organizations that complement and enable their strategies. Apart from the effective use of the organizational model itself, a key enabler is maintaining a 'one view' visibility (across the organization and between various initiatives) to create value by realizing synergies and minimizing waste and duplication. As for so many facets of business, being able to navigate a range of areas and achieve a desirable balance is key – for example, where people are informed but not swamped with information, focused on what is important but open to emerging opportunities, and individually accountable but motivated to contribute to the wider team goals.

WHY NOW?

We believe several factors are combining to make our approach even more valuable at this time and in the future than before:

- **Transparency and connectedness**: Social media and general media exposure are more intensive and extensive than ever before. Organizations have nowhere to hide in our super-connected world. This means that customer perception (and that of other stakeholder groups) is shared very openly and quickly, and the repercussions can be terminal. It is more important than ever for every single customer touchpoint to be authentic and positive.
- **The speed of change**: The business world is shifting at unprecedented speed. The pace of change will never be this slow again. This requires more flexible and decentralized working practices that empower employees to solve customer problems there and then. Employees require a holistic understanding of what the organization stands for so they can behave in a way that is in line with the organization's values without having to refer upwards to make day-to-day decisions.
- **Business model innovation**: Several organizations are now part of complex organizational structures that comprise a web of outsourced functions. This development requires leaders of organizations to think very carefully about how their brand identity and values can be delivered consistently to customers when they might sometimes be represented by third parties as part of a virtual organization. We think it is ironic that some organizations that promote the importance of customer experience also seem content to have employees from a different organization deal with their customers.

- **The changing focus of 'control'**: Organizations are no more than the people that represent them. This means it is the organization's stakeholders that control the perception and not the organization itself. For customers, the least senior people (the cashier, the car park attendant, the call centre operator, the porter) and not the CEO can often have the greatest influence on how an organization is perceived.
- **Humans are emotional**: There is an increasing body of neuro-scientific knowledge that outlines the importance of emotion in the human decision-making process. One basis for emotional connection is a sense of shared values. Increasingly, customers (and employees) identify with organizations as a statement about themselves, individually and as a part of the 'tribe' they belong to. Organizational authenticity and being 'real' are increasingly important and this places a sharper focus on values – regardless of what your organization does.
- **Sustainable competitive advantage**: Organizations can no longer compete so easily through the products and services they offer when these can be copied (sometimes very quickly). The one remaining point of differentiation is an organization's 'personality,' displayed through its values and the strength of the trusted relationships built with customers. And this is more enduring than any new product or service, especially given that these have increasingly short life cycles.
- **Measurable difference**: Achieving values-aligned customer experience can result in measurable beneficial outcomes across a variety of balanced scorecard measures, ranging from increased customer satisfaction to more inspired employees, increased employee retention, and increased sales and profit.

PLAN

We use a Velocity workshop to support leadership teams in organizations to create their customer experience plan. Why is it called Velocity? Most people know that velocity is something to do with speed, and those of you who remember your science will know that it is a combination of speed *and* direction. In the past five to ten years in business, there has been a focus on short-term delivery and speed. However, to be optimal, efforts need to be aligned, streamlined and executed with precision to fully support both the short-term needs and the longer-term strategic goals and vision of the organization. There is no point going quickly if you are going in the wrong direction. The Velocity workshop realizes individual and collective commitment to the activity plan. Importantly, the focus is on the future and the possible, as opposed to using historical performance as a base. This is because the modern-day business environment is too dynamic for the past to be of much relevance. Instead, it is future possibilities and achievements upon which judgment will be made. Because the essence of our approach is a 'whole organization' one, these sessions work best when there is representation from across the organization rather than, for example, just members from the customer experience function. In brief, there is a four-step process:

1. Envision the best-case future state using the framework as a structure.
2. Identify what needs to be put in place in each of the five Elements to realize this future state. This is the aspirational wish list. The activities are usually a combination of tools and/or practices already in place in the organization and new initiatives. Over the years, we have developed a toolkit of proprietary interventions that can be considered, ranging from a customer journey mapping tool to identifying CX Signatures to the award-winning 31Practices[12] approach and several others. Initiatives from other sources can also be added if appropriate.
3. Have a practical and pragmatic discussion about what resources are needed (people, finance, tools, expertise – in-house and external), who is going to take responsibility to make the various activities happen, and the timeframe (we recommend an initial two-year plan). This is the plan.
4. Put in place a governance framework so the plan stays on track. This can be self-managed, but some leaders see the benefit of an objective, external 'friendly conscience' to hold them to account.

In preparation for the above, some organizations start with an 'outside-in' assessment to understand how they are performing as viewed through this lens. Others prefer to focus on the future and move to implementation straight away.

This approach has been applied successfully in organizations of various sizes, from single business units to global organizations and internal support functions, in different geographies and in a range of industry sectors. It is a tried-and-tested approach that provides the means for customer-centric, holistic management of the organization (rather than a reliance on the organizational structure) in an aligned way. It allows freedom within a structured framework, is flexible in changing circumstances and helps to anchor all activity in the characteristics of the organization's brand identity. At the same time, we appreciate that it is not a panacea – nothing is. We hope you enjoy exploring the approach, developing the thinking and ideas for your own situation, and applying it all in practice.

If this overview has whetted your appetite for deeper exploration, you might like to jump straight to **Part Three:** *Delivering*, which explores the three core Elements in detail and **Part Four:** *Enabling*, which explains the two supporting Elements. However, please also consider reading the remaining chapter in this part of the book, **Chapter 6:** *Landscape*, which shares why our approach is more relevant now and in the future than it has ever been before because of the emerging paradigm of what is referred to as the Values Economy.

TWO TOP TIPS

- Make decisions in the organization that are aligned with your values and benefit your customers.
- Experiment with how a proven framework could provide you with the guidance to make decisions to improve your customer experience.

WANT TO KNOW MORE?

To explore this area further, you might enjoy the following articles:

Roderick J. Brodie, James R. M. Whittome and Gregory J. Brush. "Investigating the service brand: A customer value perspective." *Journal of Business Research* 62 (2009): 345–355.

Christian Grönroos and Johanna Gummerus. "The service revolution and its marketing implications: Service logic vs service-dominant logic." *Managing Service Quality* 24 (2014): 206–229.

James L. Heskett, Thomas O. Jones, Gary W. Loveman, W. Earl Sasser Jr. and Leonard A. Schlesinger. "Putting the service-profit chain to work." *Harvard Business Review, 2008.*

Dan R. E. Thomas. "Strategy is different in service businesses." *Harvard Business Review, 1978.*

Christian Grönroos. "New competition in the service economy: The five rules of service." *International Journal of Operations & Production Management* 8 (1988): 9–19.

Brand Finance (2023) *Commercial Services 100 report.*

CHAPTER 6
LANDSCAPE

"It ain't what you do
(it's the way that you do it)."
Fun Boy Three and Bananarama, 1982[1]

The reason that our suggested approach is so relevant now and going forward is that we believe the business landscape has changed fundamentally. The topic of values has caught the imagination of people all over the world. 'Values' are increasingly top of mind for a wide range of people, from political leaders to high-profile celebrities and a variety in between, all seeking to win support for their various causes. Values even took centre stage at Paris Fashion Week in February 2020, when several brands focused on strong values-based messaging alongside the style and seduction of their garments,[2] e.g., the Dawei range advocating courtesy and respect. World Values Day[3] takes place in October every year since its launch in 2016 and people in more than 100 countries take part. Values movements such as the Global Values Alliance and The Values 20 Group are emerging at a global level and also at a regional, country level (for example, in the US, Brazil, Canada, Sweden, the UK). As the song lyric above says, it's not so much *what* is done that is the most important factor; what matters more is *how* it is done. This is increasingly important for customers in deciding which organizations they want to be associated with.

Putting values at the centre of everything an organization does is the starting point to create a strong and authentic brand. This is particularly relevant for service organizations, where people are a core element of their proposition. But the focus on values needs to be sincere and authentic rather than a lip-service PR campaign. Witness the negative reaction to the McDonald's marketing initiative of flipping its golden arches upside down on Facebook, Twitter and Instagram in honour of International Women's Day in 2018.[4] It is worth noting that five years later, McDonald's has been making good progress in tackling inequalities and supporting women in the workplace,[5] e.g., for the period 1999–2022, the McDonald's Board of Directors has had six of the twelve directors identifying either as White or Caucasian women (three), Black (two), or Hispanic (one).

Simon Sinek's excellent and popular Golden Circle concept[6] is a good place to start understanding how this shift is happening. Sinek explains that it is not *what* people do that inspires them. Instead, it is the *why* (purpose) and *how* (values) that achieve emotional engagement, and we believe there are several other additional contributory factors (see **Chapter 5:** *SERVICEBRAND*).

THE VALUES-BASED CUSTOMER

Research in this area over several years by Forrester confirms that customers explicitly consider company values – such as employment and manufacturing practices, political and social stances, and commitment to certain causes or beliefs – when choosing products to buy or brands to associate with. Customers now believe that company values go beyond a tagline and are reflected in everything a firm does or says – from its hiring practices to its strategic partnerships, supply chain management and advertising tone.[7] Across generations, 52% of customers consider company values explicitly when making purchases.[8] The phenomenon applies across all income levels and nearly four in ten values-based consumers have an annual income of $50,000 or less.[9]

Three key concepts seem to be driving values-driven customer behaviour. First, in a technology-based, digital world, consumers crave interpersonal interaction. When companies show they care about certain causes or communities, they humanize the brand experience for customers. As a result, consumers feel a genuine sense of connection to the company and believe that they can build an emotional relationship with the brand.[10] By way of example, Pret a Manger, the UK-based international sandwich shop chain, earned much admiration from the British public for its response to the COVID-19 pandemic, during which it donated surplus food to homeless shelters, donated to charity partners and hospitals, and reopened shops based near hospitals. Second, in today's 'post-truth' environment, shoppers naturally gravitate toward the brands that match their own identity.[11] Brands that express a core set of values allow customers to form personal attachments with the company and experience a sense of association. Third, even more than emotional connections, customers today seek meaningful relationships that spark a long-lasting sense of satisfaction and purpose.[12] Brands that champion certain causes or stand for specific issues enable shoppers to feel that their purchases make an impact on their community at large. Brands that act as a platform and allow consumers to follow through on the issues they care about stand out and give customers a feeling of validation. Fairtrade is a good example of this, where customers are willing to spend a 20-30% premium because they approve of the way the products arrived on the shelf.[13]

As you would expect, although consumers increasingly factor company values into their buying decisions, they consider these principles alongside elements such as price, convenience, previous experience and accessibility. We are not suggesting that, in the Values Economy, every single person makes decisions based on values above any other consideration. However, Forrester's research suggests that about one fifth of consumers (across industry sectors) put values first and that the majority of consumers, when they perceive brands and products to be comparable in terms of price and quality, see values as a differentiator that can tip their purchasing decision.

There is also evidence that this values-based approach is growing in number and frequency in the business-to-business arena. In 2020, more than 40 major brands across a variety of industries, including Ben & Jerry's, Coca-Cola, Denny's, Ford, Starbucks, The North Face, Unilever and Verizon, halted their paid advertising on Facebook due to the platform's perceived lack of hate-speech moderation.[14] In another example, one of Boohoo's largest investors dumped most of its stake after describing as "inadequate" the online retailer's response to allegations that workers in its supply chain were being mistreated.[15]

The implications for this more values-based approach are profound. Potentially, what an organization stands for and believes in could become the buyer's primary consideration – above the quality and value for money – of the products or services offered.

KEY DRIVERS

There are many influences on the new business agenda that is emerging. We believe that a fundamental shift is being caused by a combination of three strongly customer-driven factors:

1. The way customers make decisions is changing. Previously, decisions were made on a rational, often financial basis, whereas, increasingly, customers (especially younger ones) are making decisions at a more emotional level, based on what is important to them and to express their opinion and identity.[16]

2. In our super-connected world, social media facilitates transparency and amplifies opinions in what some are calling the age of the naked organization.[17] Authenticity, from the tip to the root, has become the new holy grail. Whereas previously it was possible to invest in marketing and PR to 'tell a story,' now, and increasingly in the future, the publicly shared views of customers (and other stakeholders) hold greater sway. This shift in power means that organizations are no longer what they say they are but are, instead, what others say they are.[18]

3. Organizations no longer 'own' their brands. The role of customers (past, current and potential) as ambassadors for their organization alongside other stakeholders, has, in some ways, replaced the traditional marketing function.

These three factors are all leading to a transformation from traditional, fixed, singular organizational ownership and push marketing to a less rigid, more complex concept of brand co-ownership and pull marketing. A perfect storm of values-driven choices, the shift of power to customer (and other stakeholder) opinion and the concept of shared brand ownership has created a new customer-led paradigm that is referred to as the Values Economy.[19]

> "I am able to control only that which I am aware of.
> That which I am unaware of controls me."
> **Sir John Whitmore[20]**

SO WHAT?

So, what does the emergence of the Values Economy mean for organizations and their customer experience?

Looking from the best-case to the worst-case scenario, you can see for yourself the way you can harness core values for good or ignore core values at your peril. The research from Forrester reinforces what we have known for some time. The key factor common to companies that have delivered sustained high performance – at the top of their market for 100 years or more – is a base of values that is strong enough to provide the employees of the company with a common bond – a purpose beyond profit.[21]

A growing body of research shows that there is a strong link between financial performance and values-driven organizations. In 2001, Eric Flamholtz discovered a strong positive correlation between cultural agreement (a proxy for values or cultural alignment) and a company's EBIT (earnings before interest and taxes). He concludes: "Organizational culture does have an impact on financial performance. It provides additional evidence of the significant role of corporate culture not only in overall organizational effectiveness, but also in the so-called 'bottom line.'"[22] Other studies show that companies with strong adaptive cultures based on shared values outperform other companies by significant margins in the areas of sales, profit, employment and stock price growth, over the long term.[23]

The chair of the UK government-sponsored Employee Engagement Task Force and nonexecutive director of the Ministry of Justice in the UK, David MacLeod, describing the power of living values, comments: "All organizations have some values on the wall. What we found was that when those values were different from what colleagues and bosses do, that brings distrust. When they align, then it creates trust."[24]

> "Authentic brands don't emerge from marketing
> cubicles or advertising agencies. They emanate from
> everything the company does."
> **widely attributed to Howard Schultz[25]**

VALUES IN ORGANIZATIONS

"Stay true to your values.
That's why you were a success in the first place,
and that's how you make incredible things happen."
widely attributed to Rafe Offer[26]

Values are fundamental. Some might call them ethics; others might see them as "how we do things around here" – both are right.

Values often exist implicitly, outside formal organizational processes and mostly under the radar of awareness. The commonly adopted behaviour of people in an organization is a representation of the organization's values and creates the culture: the 'felt experience' that stakeholders have. Values affect how the absolute best-thought-out rational processes operate in practice. Such organizational culture is powerful. As Ivan Misner reminds us, quoting Peter Drucker, "Culture will always eat strategy for breakfast."[27]

Awareness of values at an organizational level helps employees and organizations navigate the complex, ambiguous nature of today's business environment more easily. Articulating core beliefs, traditions and "the way we do things around here" through an explicit set of core values opens things up and empowers employees to make decisions without reference to their line manager for tiny details; ideas flow freely, and creativity and innovation take place.[28] Shared and explicit values offer a level of consistency of experience and engagement that is aligned for a standalone business unit, a region or a global operation.

"Without exception, the dominance and coherence of culture proved
to be an essential quality of the excellent companies [we identified] …
the stronger the culture and the more it was directed toward the
marketplace, the less need was there for policy manuals,
organization charts, or detailed procedure and rules."
Tom Peters and Robert Waterman[29]

HARNESSING THE VALUE OF CORE VALUES

Values are moving from a marketing and PR exercise to becoming the guiding compass for organizations, and customers are voting with their wallets and contactless cards. What opportunities could there be if your organization was a leader in this area in your field or market? Reed Hastings, CEO of Netflix, was an early pioneer. In 2010, he made public a 126-slide presentation on how Netflix maintains a culture of innovation. The company's core values are prominent on its website[30] with clearly defined behaviours and skills. It is serious about its values being core to the company's culture of innovation. Netflix enables its employees to embody the values explicitly at work. The presentation went viral.

A public commitment is a commendable start, but it then requires rigorous follow-through. Well-written values without good execution can lead to disasters such as the collapse of Carillion.[31] Carillion's explicit value statement – "We Care, We Achieve Together, We Deliver, We Improve" – masked the real and self-defeating culture at work. Interestingly, the repercussions continue with director disqualifications taking place five years after the company collapsed in 2018. More recently, time will tell what the impact will be on PwC of the tax leaks scandal in Australia.[32] As we mentioned in **Chapter 1:** *Introduction*, research reveals that there is no correlation between the cultural values a company emphasizes in its published statements and how well the company lives up to those values in the eyes of employees.[33]

Our summary is that there has been much progress in the awareness of the importance and value of values and yet there is much work to be done in organizational values being lived in practice. Ken Blanchard and Phil Hodges estimate that fewer than 10% of organizations have clear written values and many take their work on values no further than words.[34] To create an impact, core values need to extend into the day-to-day fabric of the organization and be a reference for decisions and behaviours at all levels, influencing people daily.

"Values are for living not laminating."
Alan Williams

How do you make sure that your customers' (and other stakeholders') experience of your organizational values is explicit and aligned from the boardroom to the front line?

The tone is set by every employee, not just those at the highest level. Those at the top model what is important and are particularly visible in everything that they do – people take notice of how they behave. Yet, wherever you are, you have influence on those around you.

We need to turn the lens inwardly if the organization is going to behave in line with its core values. What are you doing? If you don't behave as if the core values matter, then others won't either. For values to be really cemented in the organization's culture, everyone must be held accountable for living and demonstrating the values in their day-to-day decisions and actions. Embedding values is a challenge.[35]

Many leadership surveys see corporate values as rhetoric rather than reality,[36] with most employees unaware of their organization's values.[37] And yet, most employees see the potential benefits of having a set of values in the first place,[38] especially if the consequences of living and failing to live the core values are explicitly aligned.

"In the wake of the banking crisis and other corporate scandals, now more than ever, organizational values should be at the forefront of business leaders' minds."
Peter Cheese[39]

The lived values of an organization have a huge impact on reputation and business outcomes. It's also possible to delude yourself and your organization that you're fine and all is well. The way powerful and intelligent people deliberately set aside crucial facts and turn a blind eye to fatal errors and fraud is explored in the book *Wilful Blindness* by Margaret Heffernan.[40] But, where actions cut across the beliefs and traditions expected by core communities of stakeholders, the standards expected in a profession, and the ethical standards and practice embedded in legal systems, disaster can be a very real prospect for all involved.

THE BOTTOM LINE

It might appear obvious, but authenticity is the key. It has become fashionable for organizations to describe themselves as values-driven. Yet, for customers (and other stakeholders, e.g., employees, service partners, local communities, investors, members, citizens) of some, if not many, of these organizations, there is a disconnect between the aspirational words and the experienced reality. Values are now mainstream; they are no longer about a framed plaque on the wall. Values are the guiding compass and are most effective when they consciously inform every decision taken and how employees behave. In the Values Economy, the successful organizations will be those that deliver a values-aligned customer experience and create a sense of shared values with all stakeholder groups. The framework we describe in this book enables this whole organization approach.

But ... sustained success requires sustained effort; leaders need to lead – in practice – to bring alignment. To use our variation on the popular adage: practice makes more perfect. By this, we mean that (effective) practice results in improvement and, at the same time, there is always room for further improvement.

"In theory there is no difference between practice and theory.
In practice, there is."
widely attributed to Yogi Berra[41]

TWO TOP TIPS

- Pay attention to every detail in the customer journey because your customers can communicate their thoughts and feelings to millions of people all around the world in a heartbeat.
- Identify and close the gaps between the officially stated values of your organization and the way things are done in practice.

WANT TO KNOW MORE?

To explore this area further, you might enjoy the following books and articles:

Anjali Lai. "The values-based consumer: A Technographics® 360 report using survey, social listening, and qualitative data." *Forrester.*

Ed Mayo. *Values: How to Bring Values to Life in Your Business.*

David Allison. *The Death of Demographics: Valuegraphic Marketing for a Values-Driven World.*

Patrick M. Lencioni. *The Advantage: Why Organizational Health Trumps Everything Else in Business.*

David Gebler. *The 3 Power Values: How Commitment, Integrity, and Transparency Clear the Roadblocks to Performance.*

Richard Barrett. *The Values-Driven Organization: Unleashing Human Potential for Performance and Profit.*

Tanya Meck. "What the new business landscape means for brands this year." *Forbes.*

"50 examples of strong company core values." *Qualtrics.*

PART THREE
DELIVERING

The third part of the book explains in detail the three core Elements of our approach: **Chapter 7:** *Brand Identity*, **Chapter 8:** *Employee Engagement* and **Chapter 9:** *Customer Experience*. We describe what each Element is, look at the component parts and explore how the Elements can be aligned to create the most effective and impactful customer experience.

CHAPTER 7:
BRAND IDENTITY

"Your brand is what people say about you
when you are not in the room."
widely attributed to Jeff Bezos[1]

The terms 'brand,' 'branding' and 'brand identity' are sometimes used interchangeably. The first Element of our framework is Brand Identity, and we refer to this as the collection of all the brand elements that a company creates to describe its personality and character. Brand identity is what makes an organization instantly recognizable to different stakeholder groups (customers, employees, service partners, local communities, etc.), creates the connection with these stakeholders and determines how the organization is perceived. Some leaders in organizations think that their brand is simply the name and logo. Of course, the name and logo are important parts of the visual identity. Yet there is so much more to an organization's complete brand identity. It consists of intangible elements such as the organization's purpose and values, as well as tangible elements such as visual identity and tone of voice. Ultimately, we think Jeff Bezos' description above perfectly captures what a brand is.

THE FACE OF THE ORGANIZATION

When asked the question, "Who is responsible for the organization's brand identity?" we imagine that many people would answer "the Marketing department, the Marketing Director" or similar. This is hardly surprising, when many organizations operate this way. But an organization's brand identity is too important to be owned by one function. This is especially so now, where any shortcomings can be communicated to millions in a heartbeat. Have you ever seen an expensive advertising campaign for a hotel brand on television and yet, when you drove past one of the properties, the external signage needed repair? Or a brand-new car showroom where there were boxes of brochures in the corner because the display racks hadn't arrived? Or a new website extolling the company value of 'excellence' where there were spelling mistakes in the copy? Or a customer service agent who told you something completely different from what you were told by the in-store service people?

> "A brand is the set of expectations, memories, stories and relationships that, taken together, account for a consumer's decision to choose one product or service over another."
> **Seth Godin[2]**

You can see that from a customer's perspective, every single outward-facing detail of the organization forms the brand identity, from the experience with employees (or even outsourced employees) to the built environment to the digital experience. Everything counts – just think about how important customer service employees' uniforms are as a visual representation of the brand. And it goes even further than this. Are customers the only stakeholders who are influenced by the organization's brand identity? Not at all. We've already covered how the brand is now co-owned by the various stakeholders. How is the organization's brand identity presented to employees, service partners and local communities? Consistency in messaging is key and, in the Values Economy, there is no place for organizations that try to present one face to one group of stakeholders and a different one to others.

COMPONENT PARTS

In practical terms, brand identity is much more than a logo.[3] We see it as a combination of purpose or vision, values, brand attributes, unique positioning, CX Signatures (explained later in this chapter), visual identity and tone of voice.

The starting point is to identify and articulate the organization's purpose and values. The brand purpose or vision captures what the brand desires or promises to accomplish (usually for the buyer). The organization can use *positioning* and *differentiation* to communicate the brand's purpose and ultimately enrich the brand's identity.[4] And this can transcend the functional to also express the brand's higher purpose (its reason for being, or why it exists). The higher purpose suggests emotional and social benefits for the customer from choosing that brand. A key point here is to capture the unique essence of your organization and then bring this to life in practice. This area is of particular importance to employees because there is evidence that a personal commitment to an employer's core values is the top driver of employee engagement[5] (see **Chapter 8:** *Employee Engagement*). Directly related to this, close alignment between individuals' values and those of their organizations leads to a number of positive organizational outcomes, including a reduction in staff turnover.[6] A strong purpose and values set the tone for the organization's tribal purpose and code of conduct, which ultimately creates the organization's culture and is a highly visible, integral part of the customer experience.

Philip Kotler's six-step branding conceptual model is an easy-to-understand guide to developing a brand; the first three steps – brand purpose, brand positioning and brand differentiation – all help in creating an effective brand identity, step four.[7] The last two steps – brand trust and brand beneficence – are of particular relevance in the context of the Values Economy. Professor Kotler describes brand trust as customers believing that the brand will deliver what it claims and brand beneficence as creating value for the benefit of others.

In **Chapter 6:** *Landscape*, we highlighted that, in the Values Economy, customers are making decisions based less on a rational, financial basis and more on a deeper, emotional level. Brands, therefore, need to target the hearts and wellbeing of customers as well as their minds. The concept of emotional marketing has been described in several books, and marketers such as Howard Schultz of Starbucks, Richard Branson of Virgin and Steve Jobs of Apple have demonstrated great examples of this approach via (respectively) Starbucks' concept of a 'third place for drinking coffee,' Virgin's 'unconventional marketing' and Apple's 'creative imagination.'

In the past, it was commonly accepted that organizations owned their brand identity. The marketing function usually took the lead, decided what the brand identity was, and then used marketing and/ or public relations campaigns to pump out this message to target audiences. In the Values Economy, this is no longer the case and an organization's brand identity is now co-owned by the various stakeholder groups (e.g., customers, employees, service partners, local communities and investors). In the future, we believe that the most successful brands will not be focused on direct control of brand messaging. Instead, they will invest energy in being true to their brand identity, led by their purpose and values. They will then focus on enabling their customers and other stakeholder groups to communicate how they feel about the brand, effectively acting as the marketing department.

> "A brand is no longer what we tell the consumer it is
> – it is what consumers tell each other it is."
> **widely attributed to Scott Cook[8]**

This new thinking about the function of marketing in the business-to-consumer (B2C) arena is made more relevant by the role of social media in a digital world, where information flows more freely and faster than ever before in networked communities. We talked previously about the double-edged sword this creates: on the one hand, organizations with a clear and consistent brand identity that is experienced as authentic will be lauded and, on the other hand, inauthentic brands might not survive. Honesty, originality and authenticity will become prerequisites to achieve sustained performance. At the same time, we are mindful of the impact of 'fake news;' false reports or misinformation shared in the form of articles, images or videos that are disguised as 'real news' and aim to manipulate people's opinions.

WHAT ABOUT BUSINESS TO BUSINESS?

Research shows that business-to-business (B2B) brands drive more emotional connections than B2C brands, and by some distance.[9] While it may seem surprising at first, this high level of connection with B2B customers makes a lot of sense. When a personal consumer makes a bad purchase, the stakes are relatively low because most purchases are relatively low value and often returnable. If not, the consumer might require an explanation or even accept that a purchase was a waste of money. Business purchases, on the other hand, can involve huge amounts of risk: responsibility for a multi-million-dollar project that goes wrong can lead to poor business performance and even the loss of a job. A business customer will not buy unless there is a substantial emotional connection to help them overcome this risk.

CX SIGNATURES

We use the invented term 'CX Signatures' to describe a distinctive pattern, product or characteristic by which an organization can be identified, usually by its customers. At the most basic level, this is a logo, icon, mark, brand or emblem – please note that there are subtle differences and sometimes similarities between these logo-related terms.[10] If you receive your coffee in a cup with the Starbucks logo on it, you can be in no doubt which coffee shop brand you have visited. There are also more subtle ways to reinforce an organization's brand identity through the customer experience, making use of the five senses. Consider the following examples:

- Hearing: Ritz-Carlton's, "It's my pleasure, Sir/Madam." You will never hear alternatives such as, "No problem," "OK," etc.
- Sight: the use of the colour orange by easyJet for employee uniforms and airport vehicles.
- Smell: Apple's signature scent captures the essence of the brand – innovative, vibrant and modern.
- Taste: Colgate's unique and patented toothpaste taste.
- Touch: the weight and texture of a Moleskine notebook.

CX Signatures play an important part in delivering a uniform brand voice (i.e., a selection of words, an attitude and the values of the brand). They are a way to convey the distinctive brand personality to the external audience.

The Element of Brand Identity is the starting point for our framework. Once there is clarity about all aspects of the brand identity, this is then used to inform every facet of the organization, focusing on the employee and customer experiences, which we cover in the next two chapters (**Chapter 8:** *Employee Engagement* and **Chapter 9:** *Customer Experience*). This 'brand triangle' ensures the organization's brand identity is 'alive' and aligned at multiple levels: purpose- and values-led decisions and behaviour of employees representing the organization; a uniform brand voice, across channels and stakeholder groups; and a range of reinforcing CX Signatures. Customers consistently experience the brand with the same tone, the logo is always used in similar ways, and the typography and colours are consistent. The brand has its own style, which enables the stakeholder groups to differentiate it from the competition and to relate to it on a deeper, emotional level.

AUTHENTICITY

In **Chapter 1:** *Introduction*, we describe authenticity as the new holy grail for organizations. However, the increasing interest in this concept brings with it some complexity. What is authentic? Handcrafted goods, local coffee shops and micro-breweries have become all the rage (the number of operating craft breweries continued to climb in 2022, reaching an all-time high of 9,552).[11] It is interesting to consider that an important part of the brand identity of these independents is often to criticize the big chains. And yet, taking the coffee shop sector as an example, in the 1990s, it was the big chains that created the market that has resulted in the opportunity for the smaller businesses to exist now. And what happens if a large corporate organization acquires one of these 'artisan' businesses? Does this mean they are no longer authentic? In the UK, Harris + Hoole became a source of controversy for Tesco when customers, initially enticed by the independent feel of its coffee shops, found the chain was owned by a retailer with a reputation for crushing smaller local competitors.[12] Perhaps the sale of Ben & Jerry's to Unilever is an example of how smaller independent companies can maintain their brand identity after a change of ownership.[13]

"If people believe they share values with a company, they will stay loyal to the brand."
Howard Schultz[14]

Some organizations advertise their products as 'real' or 'authentic,' but this is the traditional (or perhaps old-fashioned) approach to marketing, where messaging is used to 'persuade' the audience. The more progressive organizations stand behind their convictions, align their marketing efforts with their core values and are an authentic brand, building a loyal and growing customer base.[15] Our question for marketers is, "Would you rather be a master of persuasion or a master of authenticity?"

TWO TOP TIPS

- Consider how customer-facing employees' remuneration packages could reflect the importance of their role as custodians of your organization's brand.
- Strive for brand identity consistency – every touchpoint, every day, everywhere.

WANT TO KNOW MORE?

To explore this area further, you might enjoy the following articles and books:

On Brand (2021). *"What is brand experience?"*

Steven Poole. "Why are we so obsessed with the pursuit of authenticity?" *New Statesman.*

Hannah Trivette. *"How a strong brand identity can bring in customers."*

Robert E. Quinn and Anjan V. Thakor. "Creating a purpose-driven organization." *Harvard Business Review.*

PwC. *"Your personal brand workbook."*

Neil Gains. *"Brand esSense: Using Sense, Symbol and Story to Design Brand Identity."*

Alberto Gallace and Charles Spence. *In Touch with the Future: The Sense of Touch from Cognitive Neuroscience to Virtual Reality.*

CHAPTER 8
EMPLOYEE ENGAGEMENT

"Always treat your employees exactly as you want them
to treat your best customers."
Stephen R. Covey[1]

Chapter 6: *Brand Identity* covered the first Element of our approach. A key question following from this is: "How is the organization's brand identity going to be represented and brought to life?" If you have read **Chapter 5:** *SERVICEBRAND*, you might remember that this word is described as "an organization for which the people delivering the service are a central element of the offer or proposition." The people delivering the service and representing the brand, therefore, play a fundamental and crucial role – this is why they warrant so much attention, as stated in Stephen Covey's quote above.

We define the second Element of our approach, Employee Engagement, as referring to people who represent the organization (directly employed and outsourced service partner employees as well as contractors and part-time employees) showing passion for delivering excellent service to customers. When this is in place, there is evidence of decisions being made at all levels of the organization in the interest of the customer and there is a general understanding of how the whole organization needs to support the representatives who engage directly with customers. There is a widespread misconception that employee engagement is the same thing as employee satisfaction, but a satisfied employee isn't necessarily an engaged employee. An engaged employee puts their full heart and mind into their work, whereas an employee who is merely satisfied or 'happy' may be doing the bare minimum to remain employed.

"Highly engaged employees make the customer experience.
Disengaged employees break it."
Timothy R. Clark[2]

REPRESENTATIVES VS. EMPLOYEES

The point about including everybody who represents the organization is important. If an organization's employee engagement efforts are limited to full-time employees, we believe this is a fundamentally flawed approach because not all the people who represent a company are full-time employees. Sometimes they are employees of the outsourced service partner companies that manage the company's computer systems, call centre or other functions, and some are temporary workers or contractors. Still others are part-time workers who are employed in line with demand. Significantly, all these representatives who are not directly employed full-time employees often perform customer-facing roles where their behaviour has a direct influence on the perception of the organization and its brand – the receptionist in a corporate office, the car park attendant, the food server at an industry awards venue, the call centre handler, the delivery person or the IT engineer. The outsourced services sector continues to grow rapidly.[3]

Our approach encourages 'one view' of the organization in its entirety and an appropriate response. Sometimes, the challenge is made on employment law grounds that it is not possible for the parent organization to be involved in how its outsourced service partner organizations manage their employees. While this is a complex area with some risk, in our experience, it is possible to achieve mutually beneficial outcomes for all parties where there is a strong will and creative thinking is applied. We think the situation can be summed up by a question we posed to the HR director of a bank: "Why would the bank's HR leaders have no interest in the level of engagement of the 1,500 corporate real estate services people around the world who are involved in delivering the bank's office services every day and, in effect, represent the bank's brand identity and values to its employees?"

WHY BOTHER?

In this chapter, you will read about some areas relating to employee engagement generally and other more specific suggestions.

Engaged employees are the starting point for many good outcomes for an organization. Research shows that there is a correlation between employee engagement and customer experience performance – 74% of employees at companies with above-average customer experience in their industry feel highly or moderately engaged, as opposed to only 31% at other companies.[4]

It's no accident that employees of organizations that are leaders in the field of customer experience are almost 2.5 times more engaged than employees in other organizations.[5] When compared with disengaged employees, highly engaged employees are more than three times as likely to do something good for their employer, even if it's not expected of them; almost three times as likely to make a recommendation about an improvement at work; more than 2.5 times as likely to stay late at work if something needs to be done; and more than twice as likely to help someone else at work. Companies with highly engaged workforces outperform their peers by 147% in earnings per share.[6] In **Chapter 1: Introduction**, we stated that employees now co-own the brand with other stakeholder groups, and recent research puts the importance of front-line employees in stark perspective: 38% of consumers want to hear from employees on the front line of brands' communications, followed by 30% who want to hear directly from the CEO or founder.[7]

> "It's the people on the front line who are ultimately defining the reputation of the business. And the reputation of your business, let's face it, is really the brand."
> **Shane Green**[8]

The impact of the COVID-19 pandemic has left its mark in this area and, even some years later, how we feel about work and employment remains both profound and still in flux. According to Gallup's State of the Global Workforce 2023 Report,[9] 2022 saw a widespread resurgence in jobs and the percentage of employees thriving at work reached a record high. At the same time, though, the majority of the world's workforce is 'quietly quitting' (when employees continue to put in the minimum amount of effort to keep their jobs, but don't go the extra mile for their employer). More than half of employees expressed some level of intent to leave their jobs and employee stress remained at a record level. The report highlights that the quiet quitting employees know what they would change about their workplace and that engagement has 3.8 times as much influence on employee stress as work location.

For many people, the pandemic forced a reassessment of what matters, including the role of work in their lives. People have chosen to change careers, move countries, shake up their lifestyles or opt out of work entirely, a phenomenon referred to as the Great Resignation.[10] There has also been a significant increase in employee activism.[11]

WHAT IS ENGAGEMENT?

A single agreed-upon definition of 'employee engagement' does not exist and definitions from benefits professionals, industry bodies, HR consultants and academics vary considerably. However, there is broad agreement that engaged employees are typically motivated to contribute greater discretionary effort for their employers and that a balanced psychological or emotional contract between employers and employees helps to make this happen. Engagement comes from feeling good, passion for the organization, meaningful work and attaching part of one's identity to one's job. And this is all down to some neurotransmitters and a hormone. The programmes in an employee engagement strategy can be designed to help the brains of employees generate dopamine (anticipation of reward), serotonin (feeling good, wellbeing) and oxytocin (bonding, feeling connected to others) to create good feelings for the organization.

"This is about how we create the conditions in which employees offer more of their capability and potential."
David MacLeod[12]

One definition of employee engagement is, "a workplace approach resulting in the right conditions for all members of an organization to give of their best each day, committed to their organization's goals and values, motivated to contribute to organizational success, with an enhanced sense of their own wellbeing."[13]

Analysis conducted by The Conference Board identified 26 common drivers of engagement among 12 leading engagement research companies – eight of which were common to all:[14]

- **Trust and integrity:** How well do managers communicate and 'walk the talk'?
- **Nature of the job:** Is it mentally stimulating from day to day?
- **Line of sight between employee performance and company performance:** Do employees understand how their work contributes to the company's performance?
- **Career growth opportunities:** Are there opportunities for growth within the business?
- **Pride about the company:** How much self-esteem do the staff feel as a result of being associated with their business?
- **Coworkers/team members:** How much influence do these people exert on the employee's level of engagement?
- **Employee development:** Is the company trying to develop the employee's skills?
- **Relationship with one's manager:** Does the employee value relationships with managers, and is there trust and credibility between the levels?

David MacLeod and Nita Clarke's "Engaging for Success" report proposes four key drivers of employee engagement: strategic narrative (leadership), engaging leaders, employee voice and integrity.[15]

We know that employees increasingly attach more importance to a sense of meaning and fulfilment than a monthly pay packet[16] and also want their voices to be heard. Weber-Shandwick estimates 38% of employees report that they have spoken up to support or criticize their employers' actions over a controversial issue that affects society.[17]

A NARROWER PERSPECTIVE

While there may be neither an agreed-upon definition of employee engagement nor an agreed-upon set of drivers, research in the area covers a lot of common ground and there are subtle differences in the way these ideas are perceived and reported. Our interpretation of the term 'employee engagement' is narrower than some other perspectives because certain aspects are dealt with in other Elements of our suggested approach (e.g., purpose and values in Brand Identity and communication framework in Systems & Processes). The Element we call Employee Engagement is concerned purely with people and people processes throughout the employee experience or journey, from the point of first engagement until the point of leaving, or even after this if you consider how some alumni networks keep people connected after their official engagement has ended.

In **Chapter 7:** *Brand Identity*, we noted that a global study found that personal commitment to an employer's core values is the top driver of employee engagement and,[18] in our experience, the following factors can create a remarkable positive impact.

RECOGNITION

Recognition can provide a sense of accomplishment and makes employees feel valued for their work. Recognition not only boosts individual employee engagement but also has been found to increase productivity and loyalty to the company, leading to higher retention.[19] Other studies have shown that 37% of respondents would be encouraged to produce better work more often by more personal recognition.[20] Organizations with highly effective recognition programmes have 31% lower voluntary turnover than organizations with ineffective recognition programmes.[21] The key word here is 'effective' because you might well know of or have heard about recognition programmes that have not been successful, and there are important factors to consider when putting a programme in place.

We strongly believe that recognition works best when it is just that and is not confused with reward. This view is supported by a study showing that 82% of employees think it's better to give someone praise than a gift.[22] When working with clients, we recommend a focus on intrinsic motivation and spreading this, rather than extrinsic motivation.

The key is to align the recognition programme with the core values of the organization. This brings the values to life by making a direct connection between the behaviour being displayed and the values. It provides a great opportunity for storytelling about the specific behaviour and the values and, over time, this helps to build the 'heritage' of the organization. Ultimately, it creates social validation (dopamine and serotonin) and engenders employees' personal commitment to the organization's core values. This combination of two already powerful drivers of employee engagement creates a turbocharged effect.

> "There are two things people want more than
> sex and money — recognition and praise."
> **widely attributed to Mary Kay Ash[23]**

Many recognition programmes we have seen result in an individual or team being honoured publicly in some way, and this is all well and good. However, a focus on the act of recognition and the recipient misses the point because it is far more important to celebrate and share the behaviour that warranted the recognition. In this way, other employees appreciate what behaviour is desirable and might be inspired to follow suit. For this reason, it is also important to be specific about what behaviours are being recognized. An example that comes to mind is a person in housekeeping at a five-star hotel in London whose job was to clean and polish the marble floor in the reception area. She talked about "my floor" and how she wanted it to sparkle and greet every guest. She was never sick or late and served the hotel loyally for many years. It was her display of ownership, pride, customer focus and dedication that was recognized.

The type of behaviour that is recognized is also important. Many, if not most, recognition programmes are based on 'going the extra mile' or doing something out of the ordinary. The intention is well meant but it has a significant weakness. Why? We asked a group of hotel company employees to consider how they spent their time at work, split down by opportunities to go the extra mile versus day-to-day routine tasks. The answer was 20% extra mile and 80% routine. So why would a recognition programme be limited to 20% of what employees do rather than include the 80% of their time spent on routine work? This applies equally to the area of customer experience.

Recognizing remarkable achievements and accomplishments catches the imagination and can help create a positive, inspiring environment, but we recommend also taking the opportunity to recognize more seemingly mundane performance that is sometimes overlooked. Is the contribution of the person from housekeeping above less worthy of recognition than a sales executive's single quarter of spectacular results? This is why we think values-based recognition is so powerful.

Another critical factor is timing. How often is recognition purely retrospective, where somebody is only recognized after the event? Taking the example above, just think about how much more value could be created by announcing at the beginning of the year that there is going to be a Customer Experience Award and, every month, nominations according to specific criteria will be requested to select the best example of internal or external customer service. Then, the 12 monthly recipients will be considered to identify the annual Customer Experience Award winner. This way, everybody in the company knows about the recognition scheme and can strive toward it for a 12-month period, creating much more energy than a retrospective award. The other aspect of timing in recognition is timeliness: showing people that their great work has been noticed at the time is important because delay can cause a reduced perception of sincerity. This is especially important for informal recognition, which can complement any more formal, structured recognition process. Team leaders have a critical role to play in this area.

The role of hierarchy is an interesting area in relation to recognition. On the one hand, peer-to-peer recognition can free managers from being the gatekeepers of praise.[24] There is also evidence that peer-to-peer recognition can result in marked positive increases in customer satisfaction and a positive impact on financial results compared to manager-only recognition.[25] On the other hand, we know that personal recognition received from a very senior person instils an enormous sense of pride. One of Marriott's most prestigious awards is The Chairman's Award, which is given to Associates who have saved lives (the brand refers to its employees as Associates; see **Chapter 12:** *Hanbury Manor*). We know recipients who have kept their personal letter from the company's chairman, Bill Marriott, for many years, sometimes on display at work or at home.

EMPLOYEE EXPERIENCE

In **Chapter 9:** *Customer Experience*, you will be able to explore the concepts of customer experience management and customer journey mapping; we believe that these approaches are just as relevant to employees as they are to customers. This is because employees are organizational stakeholders in the same way as customers. In both cases, the objectives from an organization's perspective are similar: attract and retain, engage, make productive, and create advocates of the organization. The term 'employee experience' and the abbreviation EX is being used increasingly in a similar way to the way that 'CX' was adopted in the field of customer experience.

> "I have always believed that the way you treat your employees
> is the way they will treat your customers."
> **widely attributed to Sir Richard Branson[26]**

The customer journey mapping approach can be applied to employees throughout the employment life cycle. *Figure 2* shows our suggested 11 stages of the EX (employee experience).

1. Awareness, sourcing and recruiting
2. Pre-boarding
3. Onboarding (orientation and initial training)
4. Compensation and benefits
5. Learning and personal development
6. Communication, involvement and feedback
7. Reward and recognition
8. Performance planning, feedback and review
9. Career advancement
10. Retirement, termination or resignation
11. Alumni

FIGURE 2
THE 11 STAGES OF THE EX

Opportunities for improvement can be identified in operations, policies and procedures, programmes, and even specific touchpoints to provide a seamless, engaging and valuable employee experience by evaluating the employee journey through two lenses: the employees' points of view and the organization's brand identity perspective. The alignment between brand identity and employee engagement is a fundamental feature of our approach because, just as for customers, the employee experience does not exist in a vacuum. The experience is more relevant and meaningful when it is rooted in the organization's brand identity. Finally, if employees have first-hand experience of the organization's brand identity, they are better equipped to represent this when dealing with customers.

To use a practical example, imagine you have been invited to attend an interview at a tech start-up famous for its (very expensive) disruptive products and services, commitment to hiring the brightest and highest-performing people, public disregard for the status quo and core value of 'difference.' You arrive in good time and introduce yourself, but the receptionist is preoccupied and does not seem to be expecting you; 30 minutes later, you are shown into a poorly lit internal office with an unpleasant odour and a chair that wobbles; 15 minutes later, an unkempt man enters the room, seeming quite disinterested, hands you a badly photocopied application form and tells you to complete it by the time he returns in one hour. How are you feeling about your experience of this organization?

Now imagine if this was handled differently: instead of being invited to the company office, the interviewer wants to meet you somewhere local to where you live that you really enjoy visiting; you are asked to use a $20 dollar budget to 'make a difference' to the meeting. How do you feel about your experience now? This is the value that can be created by consciously reflecting the brand identity in the employee experience. This way, employees experience the benefits of the brand and values first-hand and are better equipped and motivated to reinforce and interpret them with customers. It also helps to cultivate a distinctive culture in the company, which in turns helps attract and retain employees who fit the culture and are more likely to thrive in it.

The traditional approach to developing an experience strategy begins with needs-based segmentation; in this case, grouping employees into clusters based on their wants and needs. Employees don't all want the same development opportunities, rewards and involvement. They have different levels of interest in communicating and participating, and they value different kinds of compensation and reward. To achieve the best results, companies can provide experiences designed to appeal to these different segments. A robust values-based approach simplifies the exercise because groups of employees, albeit diverse (in terms of seniority, gender, ethnicity, religious beliefs, etc.) are attracted to work with and are motivated by a common set of values.

LEADERSHIP

"It's not that these employee-focused initiatives are unimportant.
It's just that your immediate manager is more important."
Marcus Buckingham and Curt Coffman[27]

The relationship with the immediate line manager might be the strongest of all drivers of employee engagement,[28] so focusing on this relationship potentially creates the most positive impact. Leadership is a broad heading and includes topics such as empowerment,[29] listening[30] and trust.[31]

Specifically, we believe in the power of both informal and formal one-to-one communication between a leader and a member of their team who reports to them. The informal communication helps build the personal relationship, and more formal meetings provide structure and focus. The frequency of the meetings might vary depending on the level of seniority, the size of the team and personal preferences. Meeting monthly is a good guideline. In addition, we have experienced the importance of leaders honouring the time scheduled (rather than postponing or cancelling) because this demonstrates respect and shows that the employee is valued.

There are signs that the impact of the COVID-19 pandemic has caused significant changes to effective leadership styles. We do not believe that this is a new phenomenon but that it is, instead, an acceleration of a trend that already existed. Having said this, the qualities of pragmatic hope, empathy, authenticity, lightening the burden and clarity of purpose[32] have never been more important parts of a leader's toolkit to engage team members in a meaningful way.

OTHER FACTORS

In addition to the above, there is a range of other factors – including pride in the company's products and services, having a voice, employee welfare,[33] work environment,[34] career opportunities and fairness – that can all play important parts in achieving employee engagement.

Finally, we want to highlight the hybrid working environment, where employees split their time between working remotely and working in the office, which has become increasingly relevant in recent years caused, or at least accelerated, by the impact of the COVID-19 pandemic. We still see leaders in some organizations who seem to think that there should be a return to pre-pandemic norms with everybody working in the office from Monday to Friday. However, the majority of employers recognize that hybrid working is not a fad but is, instead, a new emerging paradigm for workers whose output is not dependent on place. There are undoubtedly implications for customer experience, e.g., a call centre operative working from home with a dog heard in the background could be perceived as less professional and it is more of a challenge to monitor service standards 'in the moment.'

Ultimately, there is no magic bullet for creating highly engaged teams with a focus on delivering a great customer experience. Employee engagement requires focused and consistent effort from everyone, from executive leadership to mid-level managers to front-line employees. Each organization has its own unique set of circumstances and, by definition, requires its own unique solution. Continuous, small, data-driven actions based on employee feedback (formal and informal) can lead to significant, and sometimes remarkable, measurable improvement.

TWO TOP TIPS

- Ask employees how to improve the customer experience, listen to suggestions and implement them.
- Do recognition well because it might be the best return on investment you ever make.

WANT TO KNOW MORE?

To explore this area further, you might enjoy the following articles and books:

David MacLeod and Nita Clarke. "*Engaging for success: enhancing performance through employee engagement.*"

World Economic Forum. "*What is The Great Resignation and what can we learn from it?*"

Achievers. "*The case for employee recognition.*"

Peter Drucker. "*They're not employees, they're people.*"

Jeanne Meister. "Employee activism is on the rise: workers protest return to office." *Forbes.*

Antonio Pangallo. "The 5 employee experience trends redefining work in 2024." *Qualtrics.*

Anthony J. Rucci, Steven P. Kim and Richard T. Quinn. "The employee-customer-profit chain at Sears." *Harvard Business Review.*

Gallup 2023. "*Report the Voice of the World's Employees.*"

Blink. "*Frontline Employee Engagement in 2023.*"

CHAPTER 9
CUSTOMER EXPERIENCE

"There is only one boss. The customer."
Sam Walton[1]

Our approach has the primary objective of helping leaders of service sector organizations to design and deliver a great customer experience. Without customers there is no business, so we agree with Sam Walton (also mentioned in **Chapter 2:** *CX Evolution*) above that they are the ultimate boss. Think of the Customer Experience Element as the outcome and what is enabled or facilitated by the alignment and coordination of the other Elements in the framework. We define customer experience as the cumulative total of what a customer feels (experiences) across all touchpoints, across all customer experience channels and across all stages of the customer life cycle. The customer experience is made up of three parts: the customer journey, the brand touchpoints the customer interacts with, and the environments the customer experiences (including the digital environment). The term 'customer' is just as relevant to sectors where the terminology is not commonly used (e.g., healthcare – patients; clubs or associations – members; local government services – citizens; charities – donors; etc.) as it is to traditional business-to-consumer (B2C) environments.

"It is not the employer who pays the wages.
Employers only handle the money ...
It is the customer who pays the wages."
widely attributed to Henry Ford[2]

Chapter 2: *CX Evolution* summarizes how the concept of customer experience has evolved over time and in this chapter we will explore some of the tools that can be used to support the CX efforts. As we have stated all through the book, however, the tools or 'content' is not what is most important. Instead, it is how these tools are applied in the context of a specific organization with its unique situation that will determine whether a relevant and impressive customer experience can be delivered.

"Content without context is toast."
Alan Williams

In terms of delivery, research has found that standout customer experiences are fuelled by new, cross-functional collaborations across organizations. Customer experience can no longer be driven by the frontline sales representative or even a dedicated customer experience team — everyone in your organization has a role to play.[3] This is a fundamental principle of the approach we recommend, to align the whole organization in the service of delivering an excellent customer experience. And this is what can supercharge the customer experience.

CUSTOMER EXPERIENCE MANAGEMENT

The way in which organizations control and deliver all aspects of the customer experience is called customer experience management (CEM), defined as, "the practice of designing and reacting to customer interactions to meet or exceed customer expectations and, thus, increase customer satisfaction, loyalty and advocacy."[4] Good CEM can create tangible business value by strengthening brand preference through differentiated, valued experiences, which improves customer loyalty and advocacy. This can result in incremental sales from existing customers and new sales from new customers introduced by word of mouth, as well as reduced costs through customer retention and word-of-mouth introduction of new customers.

"Customer experience is the new marketing."
Steve Cannon[5]

Boundaries in CEM are increasingly irrelevant. CX is not industry-specific. Greater geographical mobility and broader horizons mean that people experience new and different customer experiences in different geographies, in different channels or at different times. People's expectations in one area flow into others. By way of example, the internet has increased expectation of instant service more generally; if people receive good service in a different country, from a different service provider or in a different channel, similar levels of service are expected elsewhere and from others.

CEM execution can also vary from one customer segment to another, depending on customers' needs and wants.

EFFORT

While much of the CX narrative centres on delighting the customer, there is another school of thought. In 2010, researchers found that reducing the amount of effort required for a customer to get their problem solved is a higher indicator of customer loyalty than delight.[6] By acting on this insight and removing obstacles for the customer, they found that companies can reduce customer service costs and attrition rates. Indicators of high-effort activities include customers switching channels to get their problem resolved, repeating information, generic service and getting transferred to a different agent. Similarly, other research indicates that, "96% of customers with a high-effort service interaction become more disloyal compared to just 9% who have a low-effort experience. Disloyal customers are likely to cost the company more – they spread negative word of mouth and cease future purchases."[7] This factor is particularly relevant because the customer experience is increasingly digital, and there is evidence that one in three consumers (32%) say they will walk away from a brand they love after just one bad experience.[8]

> "In the world of internet customer service, it's important to remember your competitor is only one mouse click away."
> **widely attributed to Douglas Warner[9]**

CUSTOMER JOURNEY MAPPING

One of the most helpful tools for CEM is customer journey mapping, used to understand and define the customer experience. There are many variations of this technique, and our aim is to highlight some points for you to bear in mind if you think this might be a useful initiative. Start by considering the end-to-end journey of the customer, even if this includes areas over which you have little or no control. If you are a train company, the local car park is part of your customers' experience. It will affect customers' perception of your offer (even if it is provided by a third party) and might have an impact on your business (e.g., the car park is always full, is badly maintained or is prone to vandalism and there is another train station close by).

At each stage of the customer journey, all the senses need to be considered to design and implement the optimum customer experience. In a banking client's office, we discovered that mailroom employees wheeled a trolley through the reception area, where important visitors were awaiting their host. The trolley had the loudest squeaky wheels you can imagine and clearly this did not support and reinforce the smooth, sophisticated image the bank wished to portray. In **Chapter 7:** *Brand Identity*, we highlighted some examples of how the senses can be used to emphasize the uniqueness of a branded customer experience.

> "You've got to start with the customer experience
> and work back toward the technology,
> not the other way around."
> **Steve Jobs[10]**

It is also important to think about what you want the customer to think, do and feel at each stage of the journey or at key touchpoints. Using the example of a car hire collection, welcoming a customer back lets them know that you know they have used the company's services before and makes them feel valued as a returning customer. If an upgrade is available, this could be offered as a reward for their previous loyalty. The car hire company representative can politely enquire about the customer's plans and perhaps be able to offer suggestions and tips about the local area. They can also confirm the vehicle return details and offer best wishes for the customer's time with the car.

PERSONAS

Customer personas are fictional representations of your ideal customers based on real data and insights. They help you understand their needs, goals, preferences and behaviours so that you can tailor your products, services and interactions accordingly. There are four ways that customer personas can help you improve your customer experience and achieve better outcomes: uniting your teams around a shared understanding of customers and their expectations; segmenting customers into distinct groups for delivering tailored messages and offers; recognizing gaps and opportunities in the customer journey and devising solutions to address them; and measuring and optimizing your CX performance based on feedback and data from your persona segments. As with any tool, using customer personas has its benefits and limitations, and it is good to remember that this approach is a guide rather than an absolute solution.

To create effective customer personas, organizations need to understand their customers, and this is often achieved through research and analysis such as customer surveys, interviews, feedback and reviews, analytics and metrics, and market research. With this information, profiles can be constructed that detail each persona's demographics, psychographics, pain points, goals, motivations and behaviours. Additionally, each persona can be given a name, a photo and a quote that encapsulates their perspective and brings the persona to life to assist internal communication. In our experience, care needs to be taken in not becoming obsessed with demographics. A less scientific approach, which can often be valuable, is to tap into the knowledge of front-line employees who have a wealth of information about different types of customers at their fingertips.

Once the personas are created, they can be used to inform and guide the CX strategy in several different ways: solving your personas' problems and adding value with new products, features and services; communication content and campaigns that appeal to the personas' interests; user experience improvements to enhance the personas' satisfaction and loyalty; and segmented targeting of messages.

In the real dynamic world, things change, sometimes rapidly. Personas, therefore, need to be updated regularly to remain accurate, relevant and of value. This involves using new data and feedback to review, validate, modify or remove existing personas and communicating this to the relevant people in the organization.

DETAILED SERVICE STANDARDS

When the decision has been made about the customer's perception of the journey, then it is time to put this into practice and make it a practical reality. In our experience, a key tool to help deliver a consistent, desired customer experience is to put in place detailed customer service standards and operating procedures. These can include more subjective and less tangible standards, such as 'anticipating the needs of customers by putting ourselves in their shoes and proactively seeking to meet their needs.' They can also include more objective, tangible standards, such as answering a telephone within three rings. Finally, operating procedures are helpful in ensuring the desired customer service standard is delivered by the person responsible (e.g., specific distances between the cutlery handle and edge of the table or a detailed method and nominated materials to clean a wooden coffee table). The reason these procedures are important is to ensure that the customer receives the desired experience time and time again. If the people who are delivering the service standard do not know how to do this, there will not be consistency of delivery. We know a senior vice president in a hospitality company who placed great importance on service standards and a mindset of attention to detail. He asked the department managers to involve all members of their team to document every single task they performed in minute detail, "so that if somebody landed from Mars, they would be able to follow the instructions."

> "Details make perfection,
> and perfection is not a detail."
> **widely attributed to Leonardo da Vinci[11]**

To give you some perspective, take a moment to consider how many steps are involved in a simple task like making tea (with milk and sugar): go to the cupboard, open the door, take out a mug, close the door, put the mug on the counter, go to the kettle, take it to the tap, open the lid, turn on the tap ... and so on. How many steps did you count? Perhaps 50, 60 or more? Now imagine applying this approach to every single task in each department of a hotel. It was a painstaking job.

However, the exercise resulted in every employee becoming more consciously aware of their tasks and the detailed standard that was required and expected. Other organizations have recognized the weakness of creating unwieldy detailed written documents and used videos to demonstrate how tasks should be performed. It also helps if employees know the reason *why* they are doing what they are doing.[12]

CONSISTENCY

This topic might not sound as exciting as some of the others we have already touched on, but we think that the opening to a McKinsey article sums it up well: "It may not seem sexy, but consistency is the secret ingredient to making customers happy."[13] A consistent experience across all brand touchpoints is a key driver of brand trust[14] and the payoff for companies that focus on consistency can be considerable because consistent brands may be worth 20% more than those that aren't consistent.[15]

> "In the game of customer experience …
> consistency will always trump delight."
> **Jake Sorofman[16]**

In fact, we think that consistency is a 'magical' ingredient in making customers happy. Why magical? Because it is so rare. Why so rare? Partly because our brains are hardwired for instant gratification. In the field of behavioural economics, this is known as the 'immediacy effect.' Basically, your 'present self' trumps the actions of your 'future self.' It might be an urban myth, but there is a story about Walt Disney's board members being in conflict over whether to sell their customer experience training to other companies. Some board members felt that this would be selling their secrets and would risk them losing their competitive edge. Others maintained that nobody would have the discipline to put what they learned into practice. Who was right? Well, 80% of companies in a survey believed they provided a superior proposition while 8% of their customers agreed with them.[17]

We think your own personal experience will support these findings: consistently good customer experience is rare.

"A lot of people have fancy things to say about customer service, but it's just a day-in, day-out, ongoing, never-ending, persevering, compassionate kind of activity."
Christopher McCormick[18]

Consistency is also rare because customers use a variety of channels, times and locations to interact with a company. This creates clusters of interactions that make the individual interactions less important than the customer's cumulative experience. Research from McKinsey identified three keys to consistency: delivering consistency across customer journeys (irrespective of time, geography or channel), forging a relationship of trust with customers through consistency, and fulfilling promises supported by strong, ongoing marketing communications to reinforce those experiences.[19]

"Every day, you're only as good as your last show."
(widely attributed to Oprah Winfrey[20])

PROBLEM RESOLUTION

In the real world, things do not always go according to plan and some-times customers are unhappy about the service they have received. The model in *Figure 3* (attributed to Disney) was used by Marriott Hotels and we have not come across anything better.

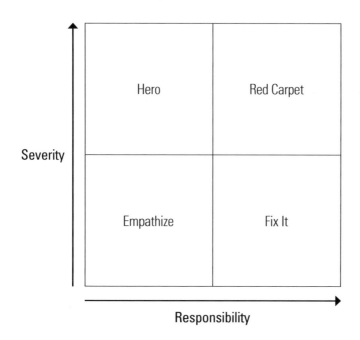

FIGURE 3
PROBLEM RESOLUTION MODEL. ATTRIBUTED TO DISNEY

The quadrants, determined by the organization's level of responsibility and severity of the problem for the guest, are used to guide an appropri-ate response. Here are some examples to bring the theory to life:

- **Empathize (low severity, low responsibility):** for example, a con-ference event organizer complains about the rain limiting the out-door activities.
  "I can understand how disappointed you are, especially when the forecast was for a sunny day. I can offer ... "

- **Fix it (low severity, high responsibility):** for example, a shopper returns a shirt because a button is missing.
"Would you like a replacement shirt or a refund?"
- **Red carpet (high severity, high responsibility):** for example, the host of a dinner party has wine spilt on their jacket by a member of the restaurant service team.
"We are so sorry for this accident and will arrange for the jacket to be dry cleaned or give you the money if you would prefer to do this yourself. Also, we would like to offer you a bottle of wine, with our compliments, the next time you dine with us."
- **Hero (high severity, low responsibility):** for example, a hotel guest left their passport in their room and has departed for the airport.
"We found your passport in your room and one of our team will bring it to you at the airport."

In all cases, the key is that the severity of the problem is viewed from the guest's perspective. This is variable according to the individual and the circumstances.

"Your most unhappy customers are
your greatest source of learning."
Bill Gates[21]

The LEARNT model is also valuable when dealing with an unhappy customer, using the following process:
- **Listen:** rather than quote process or justification for the situation
- **Empathize:** show some understanding of how the other person is feeling
- **Apologize:** be sorry that the other person has had this poor experience – this does not mean accepting fault
- **React:** deal with the issue and solve the problem
- **Notify:** whoever in the organization needs to know to prevent a reoccurrence

At a client workshop, an attendee suggested adding T for 'thank' – thank the person for raising the issue because this gives you the chance to resolve it. The LEARN model, therefore, became the LEARNT service recovery model.

Sometimes things do not go as planned with a customer experience. However, when this happens, the best organizations will react in the right way. It is said that a customer who has had a complaint resolved successfully is more loyal than a customer who has not had a problem in the first place.[22] Think of complaints as a gift because they are a great opportunity to correct the situation immediately at hand, address shortcomings and create a strong sense of loyalty. They also provide the opportunity to understand if more general improvements need to be made to prevent any reoccurrence.

The complexity and importance of the Customer Experience Element are reflected in this chapter being longer than most of the others in this book. We have shared some key topics rather than conducted an exhaustive exploration of the whole area, and we trust this has highlighted some helpful points and areas of interest.

TWO TOP TIPS

- Constantly remind yourself and all colleagues that without customers, your organization does not exist.
- Design the customer experience that you want to create and explore all the CX tools at your disposal.

WANT TO KNOW MORE?

To explore this area further, you might enjoy the following articles and books:

B. Joseph Pine II and James H. Gilmore. "Welcome to the experience economy." *Harvard Business Review.*

Chris Hurn. "*Great customer service never ends: Joshie the Giraffe Part 2.*"

Katherine N. Lemon and Peter C. Verhoef. "Understanding customer experience throughout the customer journey." *Journal of Marketing* 80 (2016): 69–96.

Rohit Kapoor. "How data is humanizing customer experiences." *MIT Sloan Management Review.*

Mercer Smith. "*107 customer service statistics and facts you shouldn't ignore.*"

Bruce Temkin. "*The human experience cycle.*"

Kevin Neher et al. "Prediction: The future of customer experience." *McKinsey.*

"How To Use Journey Maps To Kick-Start A Customer Experience Transformation." *Forrester.*

"Designing exceptional customer experiences." *YouWe.*

"CX Landscape report 2023." *CallMiner.*

Customer Experience Live Show UK 2023 Intelligence Report.

PART FOUR
ENABLING

The fourth part of the book explains in detail how the three core elements covered in **Part Three:** *Delivering* are supported by the other two Elements of the framework with **Chapter 10:** *Systems & Processes* and **Chapter 11:** *Measurement & Insight*. We describe what these two Elements are and look at the component parts. This part of the book encourages you to consider how these two Elements support the areas of Brand Identity, Employee Engagement and Customer Experience in your organization.

CHAPTER 10
SYSTEMS & PROCESSES

"Systems and processes are essential to keep
the crusade going, but they should not
replace the crusade."
Simon Sinek[1]

Organizations are complex adaptive systems. They consist of interconnected, interwoven components or sets of things that work together as part of a mechanism or interconnecting and dynamic network to achieve an overall goal. If you take away or change a component, it affects the whole system. Ralph Stacey, an eminent figure in the field of complexity, points out that all human systems are 'self-organizing' and not open to control.[2] Interactions between humans are cocreated and emergent, with multiple possible outcomes at each point of engagement. A complex environment consists of any number of competing factors, combinations of agents and potential outcomes.[3]

The components of an organization's system can be viewed in different ways. One perspective is that they are a collection of different functions where, for example, the HR team is one component, the service delivery team another, the outsourced supply chain another and so on. These functions are interdependent, so if there is a high-performing service delivery team but the HR processes and procedures are not working well, then the level of performance of the whole organization is reduced.

"Systems are not sexy –
but they really DO drive everything we do!"
widely attributed to Carrie Wilkerson[4]

Systems & Processes is the fourth Element of our suggested approach. We think of this as the organization's infrastructure: a collection of 'assets' that assist in the strategic alignment and coordinated execution of the Brand Identity, Employee Engagement and Customer Experience Elements. We define the Systems & Processes Element as the arrangement of resources, operating processes, communication framework, technology infrastructure and governance to enable and support delivery of a brand-aligned customer experience. The term 'resources' includes people, functions, information, finance, property and equipment.

The focus on an alignment and support role is critical because, otherwise, there is a risk that areas within systems & processes will achieve a disproportionate level of importance, to the detriment of brand identity, employee engagement or customer experience. Can you relate to the following quotes?

- "Your details cannot be located because the system needs a case number."
- "I cannot serve you with a cup of hot water because it is against the company health and safety policy."
- "Do you have a reservation?" (in an empty restaurant)
- "Unless you have your booking reference, you will not be admitted to the event."
- "The delivery day cannot be changed, so if nobody is at the address it will be delivered the following day."
- "I can only issue you with a uniform when the approval form is received from your department manager."
- "To collect your train ticket, you must have the credit card you used to pay for it."
- "Your query will be dealt with by the foreign exchange team – I am unable to transfer you and they do not make outgoing calls so please call this number ..."
- "I do not know why you were able to make a reservation for those dates because our arrival date is always a Saturday."

In all these examples, for whatever reason, the organization's systems and processes are not helping to achieve the best outcomes and, in some cases, present an active obstacle. Many organizations have issues like this and others: people are swamped with processes, systems require a lot of maintenance, and meta-work (work about work – e.g., meetings, project planning or progress reviews) can take more time and effort than the work that needs to be done. But systems and processes can be done well:[5] Amazon is quite rightly lauded for the ease of their return process for faulty goods.

Using our approach helps maintain a focus on what is important (aligned brand identity, employee engagement and customer experience) and enables you to keep in check the component parts within the Systems & Processes Element. In Simon Sinek's words above, they do not replace the crusade.

> "A cardinal principle of Total Quality escapes too many managers: you cannot continuously improve interdependent systems and processes until you progressively perfect interdependent, interpersonal relationships."
> **Stephen R. Covey[6]**

PROCESSES

A process is a series of tasks that is completed to accomplish a goal. A business process, therefore, is a process that is focused on achieving a goal for a business. Anything from making a coffee at a coffee shop to building a sports car on an assembly line uses one or more business processes. There's an input, some work sequences and an output.

Organizations use processes every day to accomplish their mission. The better the processes, the more effective the organization. Some organizations see their processes as a strategy for achieving competitive advantage because a process that achieves its goal in a unique way can be a differentiator. A process that eliminates costs can allow an organization to save money or pass on the benefit to customers with lower prices or enhanced services.

"If you can't describe what you are doing as a process,
you don't know what you're doing"
W. Edwards Deming[7]

Generally, processes address effectiveness, whereas systems address efficiency. Improved systems can increase the speed of execution. If you're working quickly but not seeing the benefit, your processes probably need to be improved. As a rule of thumb, processes are a good place to start.

We encourage you to consider a common format for processes to be documented so that there is alignment across the organization, consistency over time and familiarity for everybody using them.

BENEFITS

Effective systems and processes enable organizations, their customers and employees in several ways.

To begin with, the discipline of developing a system provides a focus on what the main purpose or outcome of the system is supposed to be. It is only when there is clarity on what the specific outputs need to be that a system can be designed to achieve that. Effective business systems have clear, well-defined outputs and are constructed just to deliver those. Our approach is to consciously gear systems and processes toward delivering a brand-aligned customer experience.

Consistency is another core pillar. Having a system that everyone understands and works with means that the same task is being done in the same way each time. A consistent process is likely to give consistent results. Developing consistent quality in products or services, costs and profit provides a sense of security to all stakeholders. Clarity is also key. A precise and detailed description of a process gives everybody involved the same level of understanding of what is expected, what they need to do and what the required output is. If everyone is clear on each step, then they are more confident performing the tasks and there is less requirement for supervision. The secret is to make sure that consistency does not become a barrier to improvement. Consistently suboptimal is not a good place to be!

"Ninety-four per cent of problems in business
are systems-driven and only 6% are people-driven."
W. Edwards Deming[8]

A continuous improvement approach ensures that systems and processes are always being reviewed and developed so that they remain fit for purpose and appropriate for the steps in a certain order. Over time, practical experience, new situations and changes in the operating environment, such as technological developments, mean that a system needs to be developed to remain effective and optimal. Having a clear system makes it easier to review which step or steps need to be changed or updated, making them quicker, simpler or cheaper. The learning gained from the practical experience of one person can be embedded in the system to benefit all users for the future. This also gives the opportunity to look at other systems in the organization and identify areas where they can be streamlined or merged, or have redundant steps removed.

Effective systems give leaders in organizations confidence and assurance that things are going as expected and planned. They provide a way of controlling the key aspects of the business. The systems can be monitored and reviewed instead of trying to manage and control every activity. Also, because the systems and processes are replicable and scalable, this approach is particularly beneficial for growth situations such as acquisitions as well as new locations, business units, products or services. It is also easier to make changes at scale.

"Most companies have good people.
The companies that win over the long term
have the best processes."
widely attributed to Peter Drucker[9]

COMMUNICATION FRAMEWORK

Some people are surprised to see a communication framework in the Systems & Processes Element, perhaps because it could be argued that it is neither a system nor a single process. We view the communication framework as a critical part of any organization's infrastructure. It is a tool for planning communication with all stakeholder groups: customers, employees, service partners, investors, peers, local communities, etc. Leaders can use a framework to achieve effective and efficient communication, build a better understanding of the organization and ultimately enhance the organization's reputation.

In our experience, communication in organizations can develop in an organic way with little overall design or structure. There also tends to be a focus on internal communication with less outward-looking communication (see **Chapter 3:** *Alignment*), even at a function or department level. How does this relate to your organization?

Communication in the workplace is important because it boosts employee morale, engagement, productivity and satisfaction. Communication is also key for better team collaboration and cooperation. Ultimately, effective workplace communication helps drive better results for individuals, teams and organizations.[10]

The communication framework is designed with the following dimensions in mind: the parties involved (originator, target audience and whether they are internal or external); the messaging purpose, style and content; the delivery channels (email, cloud, meetings, intranet, newsletter, etc.); and the timing and frequency.

> "The great enemy of communication,
> we find, is the illusion of it."
> **William H. Whyte[11]**

The first step is to identify the various stakeholder groups and describe the attitudes you want them to have about your organization. This should be strongly influenced by the brand identity (see **Chapter 7:** *Brand Identity*). Researching the various stakeholder groups to understand their communication preferences can assist this stage of developing the framework. For example, we once received feedback from a Europe-based team saying that they would welcome emails being written in simple English to respect colleagues for whom English was a second language. When you have described these aspirational attitudes, the various parties (originator and target audience) involved in different communication types can be identified.

For the messaging itself, it is always important to consider the purpose so as to keep on track. Why is this communication taking place? Many readers will be familiar with attending a meeting that does not seem to add value but takes place 'because it happens every month.' We know of a senior bank executive who frequently prowled the floor of meeting rooms in the bank's London office, joined groups uninvited and asked the question, "Are you getting something from this meeting?" This is one way to avoid the all-too-prevalent 'meeting for meeting's sake' culture!

The style of the messaging will be led by the brand identity – for example, a wealth management company with a focus on personalized service might choose to send invoices signed by its CEO, whereas a Swiss watch manufacturer might strive to deliver its invoices on the same day as delivery to emphasize its timeliness. Both examples demonstrate how the customer experience can be enhanced by providing a brand-aligned context.

Finally, there is the content – in other words, what is being communicated – and here the power of language and tone can make a big difference. Marriott Hotels refers to its employees as associates (see **Chapter 12:** *Hanbury Manor*). In Marriott's Spirit to Serve training programme, delivered to all associates, there was a section on the power of using positive words and avoiding negative words. We also heard about a train company where there were poor customer satisfaction results and, upon investigation, it was discovered that front-line service employees were referring to passengers as 'human freight.' Words can change your brain.[12]

The range and variety of delivery channels for communication are vast, and many tools are specifically designed to facilitate communication between various stakeholders. These can offer convenience and efficiency ... if they are used. We know of an international life insurance company that made a conscious decision to direct specific types of communication through one chosen channel and enforced this until it became the norm. Another example is the use of shared directories and collaboration tools so that groups of people can access and work on documents. We recommend making conscious choices about how these tools are used rather than allowing a more organic, haphazard approach.

Finally, consider what level of control and understanding your organization has over the communication to your customers. What might the impact be of handling a customer call in a professional and helpful way? On the other side of the coin, what might the impact be of the same call being handled in a careless, abrupt manner? Is it enough to wait for the measurement and insight data or could more be done to ensure the desired standards are in place at source? See **Chapter 8:** *Employee Engagement* and the reference to hybrid working in this context.

ORGANIZATIONAL STRUCTURE

An organizational structure is described as a system used to define a hierarchy within an organization. It identifies each job, its function and where it reports to within the organization.[13] A structure is then developed to establish how the organization operates to execute its goals.

There are many types of organizational structures. There is the more traditional functional structure, the divisional structure, the matrix structure and the 'flatarchy' structure. Each organizational structure comes with different advantages and disadvantages, and each might only work for organizations in certain situations or at certain points in their life cycle.

Many leaders find it increasingly difficult to operate within outdated or dysfunctional structures.[14] We believe this is because traditional organizational structures tend to encourage a silo mentality and are too 'fixed' for the dynamic environment in which organizations now exist. The approach we use provides a whole-organization view and allows the organizational structure to be designed and developed accordingly to suit the current and emerging context.

We are also supporters of the inverted pyramid view of the organization, with the leaders at the tip at the bottom supporting the rest of the organization and the customer-facing people at the base at the top.

IT INFRASTRUCTURE

The term 'IT infrastructure' is defined by the ITIL Open Guide[15] as a combined set of hardware, software, networks, facilities and so on (including all the IT-related equipment) used to develop, test, deliver, monitor, control and support IT services. Associated people, processes and documentation are not part of the IT infrastructure.

In the context of an operating organization, we are concerned with how the IT infrastructure can support the operating processes throughout the organization to make them as efficient and as effective as possible. It is a fascinating area, because technology continues to provide service sector organizations with game-changing advancements to support their customer experience, brand identity and employee engagement efforts.

Think of a 360-degree tour of a conference centre, an online learning service, same-day delivery, or AI-informed personal preference offers. IT infrastructure has also helped create new service businesses such as Airbnb, Uber and Deliveroo. At the same time, however, there are common issues with IT systems not 'talking' to each other within an organization and the pace of change being so rapid that a fit-for-purpose system today becomes outdated in a short period of time.

> "In order for any business to succeed, it must first become a system so that the business functions exactly the same way every time, down to the last detail."
> **Richard Harshaw**[16]

If the impact of technology on customer experience is of interest to you, you will enjoy **Chapter 17:** *Digital*.

TWO TOP TIPS

- Clarify to support functions their role in supporting the alignment of the Elements Brand Identity, Employee Engagement and Customer Experience.
- Put in place systems and processes in your organization that benefit the customer.

WANT TO KNOW MORE?

To explore this area further, you might enjoy the following articles and books.

Theodore Levitt. "Production-line approach to service." *Harvard Business Review.*

Andre Schwager and Chris Meyer. "Understanding customer experience." *Harvard Business Review.*

Andrew Filev." Differentiate yourself through operations: A roadmap to excellence." *Forbes.*

Colin Mitchell. "Selling the brand inside." *Harvard Business Review.*

Joao-Pierre S. Ruth. "That DOS Won't Hunt: Hard Rock's Andre Gowens on Streamlining CX." *Information Week.*

John Seddon. *Freedom from Command and Control: A Better Way to Make the Work Work.*

CHAPTER 11
MEASUREMENT & INSIGHT

"You must get involved to have an impact.
No one is impressed with the won-lost record of the referee."
John H. Holcomb[1]

To have an impact means to have a marked influence – a strong effect on someone or something. Impact is often associated with measurement and reward in organizations, and the phrase, "What gets measured gets done," has been attributed to Peter Drucker, Tom Peters, W. Edwards Deming, Lord Kelvin and others. It is true – impact is only seen historically, after the fact.

Measurement & Insight is the fifth (and final) Element of our approach and is applied equally to the previous four Elements: Brand Identity, Employee Engagement, Customer Experience, and Systems & Processes. We define Measurement & Insight as the efficient and effective use of data to inform future development of the organization at all levels, including collection, interpretation, communication and decision making. The purpose of the Measurement & Insight Element is to understand what impact the organization has delivered in each of the different Elements of the approach and to enable decisions that will create the most value in the future.

BE CAREFUL WHAT YOU ASK FOR

In the decades to come, when organizational management from the 1970s to the 2010s is looked back on, it is likely that 'metrics' will be a key topic. We think that the use of measurement-based approaches such as KPIs (key performance indicators), SLAs (service level agreements), incentivized pay schemes and others might be viewed as, at best, misguided and clumsy and, at worst, crude and ineffective.

We are strong supporters of measurement and insight as an aid to decision making and accountability, which is why you are reading this chapter about the final Element of our approach. Measurement and insight in themselves are not the issue. The digital revolution has made it much easier and cheaper to measure multiple dimensions of an organization's activities, and this has led to what has seemed like an almost obsessive, simplistic application on the basis that it is 'the answer.' But metrics are a support to, rather than a substitute for, thinking. It is the simplistic way in which they are applied by organizations' leaders that can cause issues, and sometimes catastrophic damage. Measurement is immensely powerful – either for good or ill – and the outcome is dependent on the level and quality of leadership involvement, just like in the quote above.

Consider these two examples of measurement intended to deliver the best customer experience:

- **Case 1:** A call centre was focused on the speed with which calls were answered. A standard was set that calls must be answered within three rings, and this was measured and reported on. The call centre operatives received bonus payments for meeting the standard. Then somebody pointed out that while the targets were being met and bonuses paid, there were many customer complaints about the poor quality of the service. Further investigation revealed that call centre operatives had a single-minded focus on meeting the three rings standard ... and, in order to answer incoming calls, they were cutting off existing calls mid-conversation!
- **Case 2:** A bus company chose to actively manage the timeliness of its service by putting in place a performance indicator stating that drivers would not be late at more than 10% of bus stops. To meet this targeted measure, bus drivers missed out stops completely to catch up time rather than miss the target.

Research in the financial services sector shows that it is difficult to have high rates of risk policy compliance in the presence of profit-based payments. Employees are likely to believe that profit-based payments signal the true priorities of the organization, and they modify their behaviour accordingly.[2] It is, therefore, easy for measurement and reward programmes to result in actions and behaviours counter to what you are aiming to achieve.[3] It is also possible to get it very right when you consider more carefully what the core purpose is. Zappos' call centres measure time per call, but they reward satisfaction and loyalty measures.

> "Cutting the deficit by gutting our investments in innovation and education is like lightening an overloaded airplane by removing its engine. It may make you feel like you're flying high at first, but it won't take long before you feel the impact."
> **Barack Obama[4]**

The American Nobel Prize winner for economics, Joseph Stiglitz, observes that, "What we measure affects what we do. If we have the wrong metrics, we will strive for the wrong things,"[5] – or, in other words, if you don't measure the right thing, you don't do the right thing. The notion that you can't manage what you don't measure is a trap. Deciding what to measure is so much more important than the measuring itself.

We are in favour of a broader approach to measurement and insight, and we admire the way that, if used as intended, the balanced scorecard has stood the test of time since it was proposed in 1992.[6] This holistic, multidimensional approach is how we apply measurement and insight, with sustained great customer experience as the final objective.

MEASURING AND SUSTAINING BEHAVIOUR

The call centre and bus company examples above demonstrate the risk of overreliance on simplistic measurement by numbers. Impact also needs to be assessed at a less quantitative, more qualitative level. A combination of carefully considered metrics or quantitative measures (to provide direction) and a collection of qualitative data (e.g., narrative, story and open comments) clarifying the impact on individuals and groups of stakeholders provides a much richer picture of impact and the context within which this happens.

While stories might not seem 'measurable' by numbers, management educator Henry Mintzberg proposed starting "from the premise that we can't measure what matters."[7] Mintzberg suggested that this gives leaders the best chance of realistically facing up to their challenges. Stories are a particularly fruitful way of communicating.

To build awareness of what impact has been made, here are some core principles to consider:

- **Reflection:** To see the impact that you have had so far, look behind you and notice what kind of footprint or impression is left: on colleagues, peers, your profession, people you interact with, teams, departments or organizations you have led. This process of reflecting back is key to learning and to moving forward, to create new meaning and understanding as to how to act in the future.[8]

- **Feedback loops:** Organizational processes for exploring impact, resetting goals and agendas at a systemic level previously suffered from a significant time lag between the point in time when the measurement was taken and the review process, with a six-month timeframe commonplace. This situation has been turned on its head by technological advancement and it is now possible to receive feedback at any frequency, daily or even hourly – also known as real-time.[9] The challenge has become how to generate interest in providing responses and avoid feedback fatigue. There is also a need for balance between quantitative and qualitative feedback. For example, it is good to know that 70% of customers feel that your organization's employees are doing their best to deliver a great customer experience and even more helpful to receive comments about what these employees could do better. This is why this Element of the approach is called Measurement & Insight.

Sometimes the simplest techniques work best, and technology is making this ever easier.

- **Rewarding success:** This final step in habit formation – reward – has been clearly documented by behaviour specialists over the decades. Perhaps two of the most well-known scientists are Ivan Pavlov,[10] with his work on conditioning, and B. F. Skinner,[11] whose experiments around reinforcement are well documented.

> "Reward is the most important part [of a habit]
> – that's why habits exist."
> **Charles Duhigg[12]**

Money can and does motivate people to work, yet large performance-related bonuses can reduce the level of personal interest in tasks and potentially undermine performance. While some progressive employers have started to take note of discoveries by the behavioural sciences, a larger number could probably benefit from a deeper understanding of employee motivation in order to redesign working patterns and payment schemes in ways that could improve both job satisfaction and productivity. We are complex beings who are rarely driven by only one type of motivation. Different goals, desires and ideas tell us what we want and need.

Edward Deci and Richard Ryan suggest that people have three psychological needs: to feel autonomous, to feel competent and to feel related to others.[13] Payment, according to Deci and Ryan's research, does not fulfil these needs. Overemphasis on financial reward undermines autonomy and, therefore, intrinsic motivation.

"I am not suggesting that they [people] should not be well paid for doing their work," says Deci. "I am saying we need to get out of the place of thinking that the way to motivate is to give them incentives for specific tasks. We need to think about how to make the workplace one in which people will get their needs satisfied and in which they will perform well."[14] In our experience, financial reward can be a highly effective short-term motivator and can play an important part in an overall performance strategy. However, when people are engaged at a deeper, more personal, more emotional level as part of a community, they value their own contribution and commit discretionary effort

– we focus on how values-based recognition is such a strong driver of emotional engagement in **Chapter 8:** *Employee Engagement.*

PRACTICAL APPLICATION

To finish this chapter, we share some ways in which we have seen the Measurement & Insight Element applied. We share examples from each of the Elements of our approach and not just the customer experience examples. As you are reading through them, ask yourself, "What is the benefit for the customer experience of having measurement and insight on this other Element?"

We often favour a Net Promoter Score[15] style of measurement because of its simplicity and challenging scoring system. A mix of surveys, one-to-one interviews, small group interviews and focus group sessions can be used to capture the data, and these can be conducted by phone, video or in person. It is critical to use the data to make decisions about what to do differently, to action these decisions and to tell the respondents when the actions have been completed. This makes the respondents feel that their feedback is valued and that the leaders of the organization have listened and care. It creates a sense of trust and increases the likelihood of feedback being received in the future. The measurement and insight activities need to be conducted with authentic intention, because if they are not, this will be noticed, and the respondents might treat further requests for feedback less seriously or not respond.

Finally, we have found that the ambition regarding response rate has an important impact. When Alan was the managing director of a five-star hotel (see **Chapter 12:** *Hanbury Manor*), he received the annual employee opinion survey from the parent company. In the briefing material, a target response rate of 66% was indicated. Alan put it to his leadership team that this was, in effect, stating that it was acceptable not to hear the opinions of a third of the employees. The team agreed on a new 100% response target and achieved 95%. We feel that low response rates are often a result of a lower level of ambition by the organization's leaders. Another key driver is the strength of the relationship between the stakeholder and the organization, including how connected they feel. If the relationship is strong, respondents are far more likely to provide feedback.

We trust that you will find these examples helpful even if you think something slightly (or altogether!) different will be more suitable for your organization.

BRAND IDENTITY

The purpose is to understand how well recognized the brand is, determine the level of unprompted awareness of the brand compared to a group of peer brands, and learn how well the brand is understood. These measurement and insight exercises can be conducted with all stakeholders to provide a 360-degree perspective:

- **corevaluescore survey:** perception of the way the organization's values are being lived
- **Brand recognition:** familiarity with the organization's visual identity
- **Brand awareness:** comparative awareness versus peer group of brands
- **Brand understanding:** the degree to which the brand is understood – what it does, scale, delivery model, etc.

EMPLOYEE ENGAGEMENT

The purpose is to understand the level of engagement of the people who represent the organization and provide them with a 'voice.' We recommend that this includes full-time and part-time employees, employees of outsourced service partners, and contractors. Potential exercises include the following:

- **Engagement survey (periodic assessment):** This can be an annual exercise or occur more frequently. We know of an organization where there is a daily 'pulse' measurement.
- **Pulse surveys:** Advancements in technology mean that it is now possible to conduct impromptu or planned surveys with targeted questions as often as you want to.
- **Forums:** These can be a highly effective way to capture feedback from employees and give the authority to take action.
- **Skip-a-level meetings:** Employees meet with their team leader's team leader. When Alan was in corporate leadership roles, he found this to be the most informative and enjoyable meeting format.
- **Suggestion scheme:** This involves providing employees with the opportunity to put forward their ideas and suggestions for improvement. This can be more formal and structured or less formal.

Both can be effective. It is important to consider the administrative resources required to manage the submission process, assess the suggestions and provide feedback because if there are not sufficient resources in place, the scheme may quickly lose credibility.

- **Performance review process:** This works best when employees lead (i.e., the employee rates their performance and justifies this to their team leader). Ideally there should be regular, structured review sessions throughout the year and an annual review because the employee/line manager relationship is such a key driver of employee engagement (see **Chapter 8:** *Employee Engagement*).

CUSTOMER EXPERIENCE

The purpose is to understand customers' perspectives at several levels and provide them with a 'voice.' This includes understanding the characteristics they look for in a company, product or service; finding out what they think of the organization generally; learning what they enjoy about your products or services and what could be improved; creating a benchmark against competitors; and understanding the degree of loyalty and advocacy. Potential exercises include the following:

- **Customer satisfaction survey:** Just as with the employee engagement survey, this is a periodic assessment. It can be an annual exercise or be carried out more frequently. Some organizations attempt to receive feedback after every interaction.
- **Feedback sessions:** This involves creating opportunities for customers to give their opinion. These can be more formal and structured sessions with a focused topic, a customer 'panel' format, or less formal – for instance, some hotel groups have cocktail parties for their regular guests to enable them to meet with the hotel general manager.
- **Listening box:** We have used this idea with several organizations. The core principle is recognition that customer-facing employees are the ears of the organization. It is a simple process of recording what employees hear customers saying about the organization.
- **Relationship calendar:** For business-to-business environments, we have seen the benefit of proactive and structured management of the client relationship. Some companies in this area have dedicated relationship managers to put in place a line of communication separate from the operational delivery relationship.

The approach involves periodic structured feedback sessions with the relevant people and the same principles apply as were mentioned previously: capture the information, decide what to do differently, implement, and tell the client when it is completed.

- **AI:** Mining customer insights from thousands of customer journeys with the help of traditional analytic tools is time-consuming and laborious. AI-enabled analytics sifts through larger and more complex data and thereby uncovers consumer behavior. Customer insights platforms are gaining traction with a host of APIs and development kits. These platforms can offer real-time touchpoint integration with minimal investment. Soon, your personal device will know more about your emotional state than your own family!

SYSTEMS & PROCESSES

The purpose of measurement and insight in this area is to understand whether systems and processes are effective or can be improved.

One potential exercise is assessments. These can be specific (e.g., focusing on finance) or general (e.g., focusing on a collection of core processes across the organization). We have found that a combination of self-audit, peer audit, and central or external assessment all using the same structure creates the best sense of ownership and robust insight. A good example of this is the Marriott Brand Standards process, which combines an incognito hotel visit to assess the guest experience with an assessment of core operating processes across the hotel departments.

The above are specific examples of measurement and insight that you can consider. You might feel that you wish to use some or many of these, and it will be important for the best outcome to make sure that they 'fit' with your organization. A sensitive and robust communication plan will need to be put in place from the outset to explain the purpose (why), approach (how) and detail (what). It is all too easy for such an initiative to be misinterpreted by people in the organization and for them to 'play the system,' which is self-defeating.

TWO TOP TIPS

- Make decisions based on the measurement and insight being captured or stop capturing it.
- Resist the temptation to focus on the scores, because it's the feedback that helps you improve.

WANT TO KNOW MORE?

To explore this area further, you might enjoy the following articles and books.

"Theories of motivation." *Saylor Academy.*

Courtney E. Ackerman. "Self-determination theory of motivation: Why intrinsic motivation matters." *Positive Psychology.*

Andrew Gori. "10 customer experience KPIs." *Zendesk.*

André A. de Waal. "The future of the balanced scorecard: An Interview with Professor Dr Robert S. Kaplan." *Measuring Business Excellence* 7.

"Drive seamless digital customer experiences with composable UX." *Gartner.*

PART FIVE
PRACTICE

This part of the book brings to life the preceding chapters by sharing a collection of carefully selected mini case studies. In some of these examples, our approach has been used explicitly and, in others, we have used our lens to gain a structured view of an organization's CX performance.

We have either had personal experience of these organizations or have interviewed employees or people with detailed first-hand knowledge.

We share real experiences with you, using the lens of our suggested model to identify areas of best practice, benefits and challenges that have been faced. This practical, operational perspective brings to life the thinking we share throughout the book. The CX principles and methodology remain the same whether you are in a single business unit in any country or for a global organization. It is industry-sector agnostic. The framework accommodates varied contexts, and we explore the implications using examples from quite different industry sectors, geographies and stages of maturity. We summarize key takeaways for each situation.

Our deep gratitude goes to our connections in these organizations for making this part of the book possible.

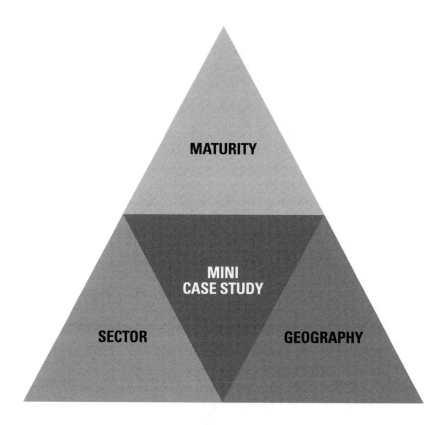

FIGURE 4
A RICH VARIETY OF MINI CASE STUDIES

The mini case studies featured are:

- **Chapter 12:** Hanbury Manor is a five-star hotel and country club and one of the first places where our approach was implemented.
- **Chapter 13:** EMC was an enterprise storage business acquired by DELL. This mini case study is focused on the Europe, Middle East and Africa Global Real Estate Function (GREF).
- **Chapter 14:** Nordstrom is a North American retailer renowned for its level of customer service.
- **Chapter 15:** BT Group is a leading global communications services company, providing a wide range of services including broadband, mobile and fixed-line telephony to millions of customers worldwide.

See *Figure 4* for a representation of the key components that support each case study.

CHAPTER 12
HANBURY MANOR

Hanbury Manor Marriott Hotel and Country Club is a five-star hotel with 161 bedrooms, a championship golf course, a leisure spa, restaurants and bars, set on a 200-acre estate, 25 miles north of London in Hertfordshire, UK. Between 1997 and 2002, coauthor Alan applied the SERVICEBRAND approach in his role as managing director. During this period, annual revenue was £12-16 million, and the guests and members were looked after by a team of about 160 Associates (Marriott refers to associates - the terms 'staff', 'employees' and 'workers' are never used and Alan decided to capitalize the word to denote extra importance and respect).

THE BUSINESS LANDSCAPE

Hanbury Manor was the only five-star hotel in a portfolio of Marriott hotels managed by Whitbread plc. There were a couple of other stakeholder-related factors that added a level of complexity. First, the property was a joint venture between Whitbread plc and a local property company, Poles Ltd, and the hotel was operated as part of the Marriott brand. Second, the golf and leisure club membership part of the business had originally been set up as a separate limited company with board member representation from the golf and leisure members, the hotel management company and the local property owner company.

Whitbread had instigated a change of management to turn around the performance of the hotel, which had been underperforming financially and had experienced poor results for the Associate Opinion Survey and Guest Satisfaction Survey. In addition, there was some sensitivity around the brand in the eyes of the local property owners because they perceived Marriott as a primarily four-star rather than five-star brand.

BRAND IDENTITY

The development of the brand identity was applied at several levels because, in addition to positioning the overall hotel and country club brand to meeting planners and individual guests, there were also several sub-brands (e.g., the golf and leisure club, the fine dining restaurant and the informal restaurant positioned with the local community).

From a commercial point of view, the opportunity was identified to attract a larger proportion of residential meeting business. There would be two main advantages if this could be achieved: first, these guests stayed at the hotel for two or three nights with breakfast, lunch and dinner as well as evenings spent in the bar, so the average spend per head was relatively high compared to a corporate business guest or independent traveller; second, the spend for a residential meeting for 20–30 people was several thousand pounds, so the cost-of-sale ratio was very healthy. The hotel's location 25 miles north of London also provided several benefits for meeting planners: it offered an alternative to central London locations because of the short journey from London, it was a far more attractive and relaxing environment, and it was competitive on price because London hotel rates were considerably higher than the local price point. The venue also benefitted from the Marriott brand, providing a sense of security and confidence in globally recognized standards. This powerful combination helped create the brand position of London's Favourite Hotel and Country Club.

A conference brochure focused on the country club elements and the outside spaces as well as the extensive and flexible meeting space. If a CEO or senior leader was working with their senior leaders to devise a three-year strategy for their business, imagine the extra value that could be created if they could be more productive because of the environment they were in. For example, they could have an afternoon break to enjoy home-made lemonade in the walled garden rather than another cup of coffee in a London meeting room with no natural daylight.

This single strategy to position the brand to attract residential conference business was a key reason for the financial turnaround of the business and resulted in a second major decision. The owners' newfound confidence resulted in an investment to increase the number of bedrooms from 96 to 161. This was a game-changer for the potential profitability of the business.

The venue hosted the English Open professional golf tournament on the European Tour for three years, which strongly supported the golf and country club positioning nationally and internationally. The golf course, designed by Jack Nicklaus II, was frequently cited as one of the top courses in the UK.

We also remember hosting a heat of *Pop Idol* in the leisure club dance studio and arranging for a large golf course banner to be strategically placed before television filming started!

At a local level, an open day was organized in support of local charities. A range of activities was showcased including golf lessons, a putting competition, a tennis demonstration, a cookery class, a cocktail demonstration, a sculpture exhibition, a photography competition and others. The local community welcomed the opportunity and 2,400 people visited the estate, helping to raise £600 for a local charity.

You might remember from **Chapter 7:** *Brand Identity* that a core principle of the approach we use is that the brand identity should be reflected in the areas of employee engagement and customer experience. An employee recognition programme was introduced (see **Chapter 8:** *Employee Engagement*) and this was called the Golden Apple Awards in celebration of the orchards on the estate. In the area of customer experience, departing guests were presented with their bill accompanied by a small sachet of poppy seeds with a message on the outside: "'To remember your stay with us.'" Tom Angus, Head Gardener." This simple idea was very well received by guests, and it had particular impact because poppies are perennial, so they provided a reminder of the hotel every year for guests who had planted them.

Marriott and Ritz-Carlton used the Daily Basics programme, which was a set of 22 service-based behaviours, consciously practiced by Associates all over the world each day in rotation. As an example, one of them was along the lines of "We acknowledge guests when within ten feet." This was the equivalent of bringing organizational values to life, and a few years later it was the inspiration for creating the award-winning 31Practices approach.[1]

The informal restaurant overlooking the 18th hole of the golf course was refurbished as part of the bedroom extension project and the opportunity was taken to reposition it with a contemporary English menu using local produce. It was renamed Oakes Grill in honour of some of the old trees on the estate.

EMPLOYEE ENGAGEMENT

This was a critical focus area because, when Alan took up his post, Associate turnover was high and morale was low. One of the first decisions made was to improve the environment and food provided for Associates at meal breaks. The small room used for breaks was renamed and decorated over a weekend.

Full advantage was taken of Marriott's expertise and resources, and the Investors in People (IiP) framework was used to provide a structured approach. To eliminate any risk or temptation for managers to be motivated by the IiP award itself, the HR director was sworn to secrecy about the initiative. A central element was the Spirit to Serve programme, a series of four modules each lasting four hours and delivered face-to-face by members of the hotel senior leadership team. The content focused on positive mindset, behaviour and personal impact, and the style was fast-paced, interactive and experiential. Apart from the learning, there was great benefit in Associates, who might not normally interact, spending time together and engaging at a more personal level.

A creative approach was applied just as much to this area as to the brand identity and customer experience. The key question was, "How can the Associates be engaged, energized and made to feel special?" A range of initiatives was put in place demonstrating that a positive impact can be achieved without necessarily involving significant financial investment.

The employee focus started at the beginning of the employee journey, when Alan welcomed all new Associates with three requests:
- Give yourself a pat on the back – you are the best person we saw for this job. That is why you are here.
- If you need to break the rules to make a guest happy, do it. Then tell your team leader, quickly.
- If you cannot enjoy yourself working in a beautiful setting like this, there is no hope for you. Enjoy your time with us.

As explained above, the Golden Apple Awards were put in place with nominations each month and the monthly recipients were considered for an annual award. One year, the hotel celebrated its 10th birthday (it had previously been a convent school) and Alan requested donations of complimentary stays from peers at Marriott hotels all over the world, to be given away at the Christmas party. It was a memorable night with more than 100 free stays raffled (Associates were responsible for funding flights). For the Annual Golden Apple Award, the prize was a week in Hawaii, a week in San Francisco and a week in LA, including flights. Steven, from the concierge team, was stunned to receive his award and remarked: "Hawaii – I don't even know where that is." From the day he returned from his trip, he could often be heard telling guests about his experience when he took them and their luggage to their rooms.

In addition to the Christmas party, all Associates were invited to attend a Christmas lunch. The senior leadership and management teams served the meal in one of the meeting rooms and then performed a short cabaret performance. On Christmas Day morning, Alan visited the hotel (with two young children) to thank the Associates who were working that day. Another example was the first day of the new millennium, when individual photographs were taken of Associates in their work setting as a souvenir of the landmark day.

Various team-based activities were organized, including a summer sports day, a football tournament with other Marriott hotels and a blind date evening with employees from a local hotel. Other simple ideas were well received, such as allowing Associates to use the swimming pool and golf course at quiet times.

There was a consistent focus on encouraging Associates to reach their potential and celebrate success. Examples included a six-month work experience exchange for a greenkeeper supervisor with their counterpart at the renowned Augusta National Golf Club in the US, part-funding an MBA programme for a member of the senior leadership team, funding of a chef for a competition entry, supporting a waiter who reached the final of Young Waiter of the Year, and the administration assistant who was a finalist in a PA of the Year Award.

There was also a focus on performance supported by a robust approach with clearly aligned objectives being set, followed by regular reviews to monitor performance, recognize achievement and take corrective action if needed. A twist was the addition of a personal objective that was monitored in the same way as the business objectives

– for one member of the team, this was to replace all the skirting boards at his home! Tried-and-tested Marriott processes, such as daily short-take training sessions, also helped ensure consistent standards were delivered.

CUSTOMER EXPERIENCE

To understand the magnitude of the challenge in this area, on his first day in the role, Alan asked to see all complaint letters (yes, this was a different era!) addressed to the managing director in the past 12 months. It was a shock to discover that there had been 600! That was more than one letter of complaint every single day. Issues ranged from poor Associate attitude to unsatisfactory accommodation standards to below-standard housekeeping to complaints about food quality.

It was important not to allow this 'poor service' narrative to continue, so a conscious decision was made to stress how important it was to receive feedback. When feedback is received, action can be taken, whereas when there is no feedback, no action is taken. The focus was on preventing any issue being repeated by making whatever changes were necessary. At the same time, compliments received were publicly celebrated to positively reinforce the desired behaviour. Individual senior leaders and managers were held personally accountable for their areas and people, and for correcting the specifics of any issue. Some areas, such as tired bedroom decor, were an ongoing challenge, but it is remarkable how this becomes much less of an issue when the service delivered is genuinely warm and efficient.

Marriott introduced a corporate meetings product at this time called Meeting Edge, and this helped put in place detailed service standards in this area. An enhancement introduced at Hanbury Manor was to confirm the purpose of the event in order to brief the service team. It is important to adjust your behaviour accordingly if you are serving a health and safety training course or a redundancy counselling session (for example).

Other initiatives included the creation of a guest services function and business centre, which involved bringing the switchboard team into a public area, wearing the hotel front-of-house uniform. This was combined with an initiative called At Your Service, where guests could call one number irrespective of their request – for example, room service, an extra pillow, a restaurant reservation or booking a taxi (previously there had been a list of separate numbers in the bedrooms).

In the golf and leisure club, generally high standards of service were already in place and being delivered consistently. The meticulous attention to detail in the presentation of the golf course by the greenkeeping team was particularly impressive and they were identified as a benchmark for other departments to aspire to. Service innovations were also regularly introduced (e.g., locker room laundry service for golf members).

SYSTEMS & PROCESSES

There were three key components in this area that provided the foundation for much of the improved business performance that followed. The design of the organizational structure was one of the first decisions made. Most of the roles were already in place and reporting lines were reconfirmed with some minor changes. A two-tier management structure was also introduced: the senior leadership team, responsible for the strategic direction of the business, and the management team, responsible for operational delivery. The concept of a focus on leadership rather than management was a new experience for the hotel team.

At the same time, a comprehensive communication framework was introduced for all stakeholders. At a hotel team level, this comprised the following meeting schedule:

- **Quarterly senior leadership team:** to review performance and develop strategy
- **Monthly management team:** to share successes and identify operational improvements
- **Weekly events:** to preview the events and conferences for the following week and address any issues from the current week
- **Daily stand-up briefing:** to focus on the day ahead (e.g., arrivals and departures, notable events, occupancy and member events) and address any issues from the previous day (held in a different location each morning)

There was also a Direct Line monthly forum where Alan invited junior members from each department to have lunch or afternoon tea. There were just two items on the agenda: (1) How can we deliver better service for our guests and members? and (2) How can we make this a better place for us all to work? These were the most enjoyable and informative meetings, and they lacked management 'interpretation.'

At an individual level, there was a structured calendar of monthly one-to-one meetings to provide a more formal review of activity and performance.

A similar framework of quarterly review meetings was put in place for the owners (Whitbread plc and Poles Ltd) and the golf and country club company board. An annual general meeting and a new annual report for members were also put in place.

The hotel benefitted greatly from several systems and processes provided by both Marriott and Whitbread. These ranged from the installation of a computerized meeting booking system to a revenue management tool to a daily health and safety system to nominated suppliers to operational processes. One system that did not have a positive impact was a suggestion scheme set up by the Whitbread hotel division managing director. When the scheme was launched, Alan challenged his team to fully contribute with their suggestions without realizing what the consequences would be. The central administration was totally under-resourced relative to the volume of suggestions received and this had a counterproductive impact. It was a good lesson that if you are going to ask for any input from employees, you must be prepared to respond and use the suggestions.

MEASUREMENT & INSIGHT

This was another area where being part of a Marriott and Whitbread portfolio was beneficial. Robust, tried-and-tested measurement and insight processes were in place, ranging from the balanced scorecard approach to running the business to centralized assessment of key processes such as health and safety (a process involving daily inspection called Safety Matters), conference booking, revenue management, etc.

BRAND IDENTITY

There was little formal measurement in this area, but very positive feedback was received from guests, colleagues, peers and Associates about the London's Favourite Hotel and Country Club concept. The golf course was frequently listed as one of the top courses in the UK and the hotel was awarded the prestigious AA Hotel of the Year award.

EMPLOYEE ENGAGEMENT

Marriott used an annual Associate Opinion Survey (AOS), which was treated very seriously. There was an incident reported in which a hotel general manager was disciplined for being 'overenthusiastic' in gaining positive scores. We think that one of the AOS questions was inspired: "The general manager knows my name" (with a yes/no answer). This was such a strong statement of an Associate-centred business. It might have been an urban myth but there were stories of hotel general managers being fired if the answer to this question was below 80%.

Due to the hard work by everybody at all levels of the hotel, and support from colleagues at Whitbread and Marriott, Hanbury Manor received the award for the most improved AOS in the world (out of 3,000 hotels at that time).

CUSTOMER EXPERIENCE

Marriott operated an in-room Guest Satisfaction Surveys (GSS) system. Results were issued to all hotels monthly, but this information had never been shared at Hanbury Manor. At an early meeting, members of the senior leadership team were asked to indicate where Hanbury Manor was placed on a global GSS league table of Marriott Hotels. With one exception, they were all under the impression that the hotel was in the top 10% whereas, in fact, it was in the bottom 10%. Facing the unpalatable truth was a critical wake-up call and the starting point of what would prove to be a great success story. The transparent use of the GSS results and other guest feedback was a key tool in being able to improve the service and results. For a time, a 5pm Friday meeting was held for any manager to explain their response to any issue that had received lower than a rating of 8.

The Marriott Brand Standards inspection process provided another source of data. This consisted of an incognito visit for two or three days and nights to assess the guest experience. The inspector then announced themselves and proceeded to assess several core processes and service standards (see below).

Due to the hard work by everybody at all levels of the hotel, and support from colleagues at Whitbread and Marriott, Hanbury Manor received the award for the most improved GSS in the UK portfolio.

Surveys were also used as part of the Meeting Edge offer. Golf and leisure club members were surveyed to identify areas for improvement, but the most important source of feedback was given directly by the members to the golf and leisure Associates.

The various ways in which measurement and insight were captured demonstrate the benefit of applying an appropriate process rather than a one-size-fits-all approach.

SYSTEMS & PROCESSES

The Marriott Brand Standards inspection included a review of core operating processes and was a great asset. The format of the Brand Standards report was adopted at departmental level for weekly self-assessments to firmly establish and embed the required standards. There were also some challenges with the process because the format had been designed for primarily newer, city-centre hotels. For example, a 100-year-old oak floor in the Oak Hall did not meet the standard, "The floor is free of marks and scratches," and there was no recognition of how the informal restaurant terrace overlooking the 18th hole of the golf course added to the guest experience.

KEY 'CX IN CONTEXT' INSIGHTS

- How our suggested approach can support sustained performance
- Practical examples of how customer experience initiatives are so much more powerful when aligned to the brand identity and with similar efforts in employee engagement, and need not be expensive to implement
- The value of proactively seeking input from customers and customer facing employees

CHAPTER 13
EMC GREF

Before the acquisition by DELL, EMC was a global leader in information technology as a service, operating in 86 countries, with manufacturing plants in the US and Ireland. In Europe, Middle East and Africa (EMEA) region, EMC occupied 125 buildings in 49 countries supporting approximately 12,000 EMC employees. The EMC EMEA GRE&F (Global Real Estate and Facilities) function (incorporating real estate, facilities operations, environmental health and safety (EHS), compliance and security) had a small number of directly employed senior employees and operated an outsourced service delivery model with several different regional service partner companies and more than 300 employees. This model was in keeping with EMC's longstanding culture of outsourcing. The company's cofounder, Richard Egan (the 'E' in EMC), believed that the business wouldn't be successful without support from supply chain partners. The entire EMC GRE&F function continued to embrace Dick's philosophy through EMC's facilities management outsourcing arrangements, where service providers were treated as partners and integrated into the EMC structure.

THE BUSINESS LANDSCAPE

The mentality within the EMEA RE&F function was very much "let's not have anything go wrong" rather than "what does excellence look like?" Attention wasn't always focused on the customer experience. There were around a dozen supply chain partners across the region engaged individually by the EMC leadership team, with no sharing of collective vision, no consistent standards, strategy or roadmap. There was also a silo mentality and the different areas within the RE&F team – real estate, facilities operations, environmental health and safety (EHS), compliance and security – rarely thought beyond their own responsibilities. This made the team appear disjointed from the EMC internal customers' perspective.

At the same time, the core EMC business was shifting, with a need for improved compliance, risk mitigation and agility, together with cross-functional and regional coordination. EMC wanted to deliver facilities management industry best practice to enable and enhance the core business's performance and support the attraction and retention of the best employees.

One of EMC's core values was Customer Experience First, and this was front of mind in a decision to introduce the hospitality sector's service culture into the EMEA RE&F function in order to create a One Team approach to service delivery. The aim was to design and implement a culture of service excellence, innovation and sustainability across the region. The plan was to achieve this through trusted, industry-leading service teams and partnerships delivering exceptional service to emotionally engage EMC employees. A senior executive, Bruce Barclay, was recruited from outside EMC to lead the initiative, largely due to his background in five-star resort hotels and property management.

The concept of our approach (see **Chapter 5:** *SERVICEBRAND*) was introduced and because there had already been previous success in creating a common operating platform for the Finance function, the benefits of extending the approach into operational service delivery were readily understood and anticipated. This fundamental shift in service delivery was introduced so that the RE&F function could provide the EMC internal client with a consistent and predictable service outcome at a predictable cost.

Our approach was adopted for the transformation project and an appropriate brand was applied (see Brand Identity below). There was also a tweak to the generic approach with Finance as an additional standalone Element, i.e., Brand Identity, Employee Engagement, Customer Experience, Systems & Processes, Finance, and Measurement & Insight.

BRAND IDENTITY

EMC's core values and mission had been well documented, serving as the backbone to EMC's success. The starting point was for the RE&F leadership team to hold a series of workshops to adapt the core EMC values into a set of values specific to the RE&F function and create a universal strategy and roadmap. There were 10 EMC values, which was not an ideal situation and some compromises were made to remain aligned with the core business and avoid possible criticism of maverick behaviour.

A shift in service partner thinking was needed. The historic model of disparate service partners seeing themselves as working alongside competitors for one client was not sustainable and would never deliver the results that the core EMC business required. The solution was to create a one-team culture that resulted in the entire group (from external supplier partners and internal employees) feeling part of one business family working together to reflect and enhance the client brand. The 'One Team' managed the integration of the real estate, facilities operations, environmental health and safety (EHS), compliance and security functions owned by the RE&F leadership team based in Ireland.

A One Team brand logo was launched and embedded into a geo-wide branding initiative and was gradually disseminated throughout all sites so the logo was visible on everything from email signatures to presentation templates to signage across the EMC property portfolio. This was a highly visible change from a situation where individual service partner organizations used their own company branding or no branding at all. As the project developed the One Team brand was developed into a 'Facilities as a Service (FaaS)' brand to achieve alignment with the Global RE&F function. The principle throughout was the same: a bold, uniform visual identity that made a strong statement about mindset and consistency, both to everybody involved in delivering the various RE&F services and also to the customers receiving the service (i.e., EMC employees and visitors).

EMPLOYEE ENGAGEMENT

A key challenge in establishing a one-team mindset was that the wider group of RE&F leaders were geographically spread and were even employed by different organizations. To create the sense of one cross-border team, an inaugural leadership summit was organized where 34 members of the EMEA RE&F team spent inspirational and interactive time together. The event in Paris included keynote speeches, working sessions, and discussion of the mission and values, the roadmap and the One Team approach. The structure of the One Team operating platform was introduced and explained, and the group generated ideas about how it would be implemented and work in practice. These ideas were prioritized and the top 15 agreed upon. Nine of the 15 ideas were implemented within six months and the rest within the next six months.

The impact of time spent together was valued highly by the attendees. Several of the service partners acknowledged they were skeptical about the approach until that point, suspecting it was a covert way of making suppliers accountable rather than improving outcomes.

Signs of how beneficial the One Team approach would be was already evident at this first event. The attendees were encouraged to photograph and video parts of the conference at will and the footage collected was edited to produce a conference video. This was produced at no cost, without external resources, and had the additional benefit that the team had collaborated in its making. A copy was sent to each attendee as a gift souvenir of the event.

The feedback from this first summit was so overwhelmingly positive that the leadership summit became an annual event, hosted by a different service partner in a different location each time and improved year on year. In advance, a social media guide was distributed to encourage the attendees to engage with the online community and stay in touch, sharing best practice post-summit. On arrival, attendees were given welcome bags including books, a 'mission impossible' community task, and motivational materials. By the end of the third year, there was a true sense of belonging, togetherness and camaraderie in the group, which is extraordinary considering that the service partners were direct competitors.

At the second leadership summit, in Frankfurt, an awards programme was introduced to much anticipation and excitement. The awards recognized individual and team achievement in areas that were aligned with the EMC values: living the values, customer service, improvement and teamwork. The programme was announced nearly one year before the event, along with the criteria for entry. This was to ensure that there was a focus on these specific areas in the regions, and submissions were invited for review by an independent judging panel made up of industry experts outside of EMC to bring further credibility to the process. Great care was also taken to highlight the whole team effort and all the entries. All entries were celebrated as winners and one entry was selected to receive the award. Based on the success of the inaugural awards event, the following year a brand was developed for the programme. At the Cork summit, these much-coveted awards were named the 'Greftas' (Global Real Estate and Facilities Team Achievement Awards). GREFTY trophies were presented to the submission considered to be the most deserving by the panel of judges. Best practice highlighted through the GREFTA program drove innovation and continuous development of business enablement solutions and service excellence. One powerful example of the impact of the awards programme was that service partners even nominated their competitors for the awards. The end goal of delivering an excellent service had transcended competitive adversarial behaviours and people pulled together to collaborate.

CUSTOMER EXPERIENCE

Consistency of the EMC employee and visitor customer experience across the region was a key focus of the initiative. The aim was for employees and other stakeholders who visited different offices throughout the region to have a consistent 'EMC' experience. One way in which this was achieved was by creating consistent service standards, job roles and descriptions, so a corporate receptionist in London had the same job description as one in Frankfurt. The job profiles were rewritten to fit in with the RE&F vision and values. Although the job descriptions were owned by the different, individual service providers, it is testament to their commitment to the programme that they were enthusiastic about streamlining this area. It was also a pragmatic, practical approach and it was understood that, naturally, there would be some cultural differences between locations, e.g., between the corporate reception dress code in London and the one in Dubai. However, the way the visitors were greeted, and the importance of their arrival experience was a priority, and so there was a strong focus on the areas that could be consistent, regardless of location, e.g., unprompted use of a visitor's name by the receptionist.

The regional teams were also encouraged to launch initiatives locally to the EMC employees and there was a combination of core cross-region activities together with locally driven events. An annual event calendar was devised to provide the core content well in advance and allow the addition of local activity to be scheduled accordingly. Events were as varied as a celebration of World Values Day or Customer Experience Day in all properties to a night-time charity run or a wellbeing week at individual locations. As with the example of the recognition programme above, there was a conscious effort to align the theme of all events (core or local) with the EMC values and the services provided by the RE&F function.

The One Team approach encouraged and trusted the local teams to introduce ideas to delight customers. For example, in London, the service partner company installed a bike rack and bikes (at their own cost) for use by everyone working at the building, to encourage use at lunchtime to ride into the local park, or for getting to the shops instead of using a car or public transport. Other examples of what were called 'wow moments' for EMC employees from various service partners, outside their contracted scope of work, included Valentine flowers/cupcakes, free herbal plants for Global Earth Day, free bicycle service (repairs/check), ergonomic tips, free fruit during flu time to improve health, etc.

The response from EMC employees was highly positive with very positive feedback and there was the sense of a ripple engagement effect, albeit this was a challenge to quantify.

SYSTEMS & PROCESS

The use of the branded operating platform, to which all the service partners were associated, ensured consistent systems, processes and standards across the region. It helped the team coordinate all activities from high-level strategy through management practices to delivery on the ground, maximizing synergies and minimizing duplication and waste.

ONE TEAM WORKING GROUPS

Following the first leadership summit in Paris, the different service partners expressed a desire to work together outside their contractual agreement to improve service delivery.

Total Customer Experience (TCE). The core EMC business had a history for its excellence in providing 'Total Customer Experience' and had won international recognition and awards for TCE. The EMEA RE&F team adopted key elements of this programme in its own service delivery to focus on the customer experience of the EMC workplace. Once again, there was a secondary benefit in terms of the perception by the EMC TCE senior leaders and wider community of the EMEA RE&F function.

Communication. Ongoing communication was identified as an important part of maintaining momentum for the One Team programme, and there were several initiatives in this area. There was an overarching communication framework including everything from region-wide activities such as the annual summit, newsletter calendar and quarterly review calls to more local meetings and communications.

A regional EMEA newsletter was introduced to update the teams about progress, and this supplemented an existing global RE&F news-letter. As with the events calendar, a two-level approach was taken with a region-wide calendar for publication, core content generated centrally and space for locally relevant content to be inserted and local publication/distribution.

A One Team planner provided a calendar to accommodate and help schedule both region-wide and local tasks. An internal communica-tion intranet system tool was also made available through the firm's Community Portal 'Inside EMC.' This provided access to common resources as well as providing a place to collaborate and share ideas through blogs and forums. It was believed to be an industry first, where competitive companies could come together, across geographies and from different perspectives to learn, offer new ideas and look for best practice models to achieve one common goal.

These initiatives meant that people from diverse locations and cultural backgrounds were engaging with each other in the working group and sharing ideas regularly. It was also a highly efficient way of working because there was ready acceptance and adoption of what the One Team colleagues in the working groups had recommended to be done. There were numerous examples at the Cork summit of the working groups transcending national borders and corporate compet-itiveness for the greater goal of service excellence to EMC.

MEASUREMENT & INSIGHT

It was recognized at an early stage that it was critical to put in place a range of quantitative and qualitative measurement processes to sup-port ongoing development. As an example, although regular feedback had been received about the EMC internal client's perception of the RE&F service, it was generally informal. It was important that the EMC business unit managers, who were cross-charged with the RE&F costs, could see the value of the RE&F function and in turn support the team with their long-term strategy. A first-ever full customer survey, to managers and EMC employees, revealed that overall the RE&F team was doing a good job, but highlighted areas for improvement, which were fed back to the service partners. In this way, objective feedback identified what customers were finding frustrating in the workplace, and it was possible to put in place proactive solutions to address the issues. As an example, in response to reported difficulties with meeting room availability, meeting room booking software was implemented to manage the space in a better way. This had a positive impact on the organization in terms of ease of use and time efficiency. The branded customer experience survey became an annual event, helping to ensure that the R&EF team constantly captured accurate customer opinions and was equipped to deliver a focused, appropriate and relevant service. Strategically, it provided valuable insight into what investment was required to further enable the business. Some of the data from the second survey of 3,620 respondents was as follows:

- Eighty-five per cent of respondents stated that they were satisfied with their office environment, a 5% increase year on year.
- When asked, "Would you recommend your current office to your peers?" 65% agreed that they would or already had done so, a 7% increase year on year.
- Ninety-nine per cent of respondents stated that they understood the function of Global Real Estate and Facilities and 98.2% felt that they were kept up to date and informed by the EMEA RE&F teams.

The developments in the RE&F function also assisted EMC in its aim to be in the Top 25 Great Places to Work globally. In the results from the first survey, EMC was ranked 18th at a global level, and seventh for best multinational workplaces in Europe, with high rankings across individual European countries including first in Spain. Compared to the previous year's results, scores improved year-on-year in 19 areas, with 83% of people saying, "EMC is a great place to work." The following year, there was another significant increase in RE&F performance and customer appreciation. Finally, the improvement in direct, local response to EMC internal client issues resulted in achievement of zero escalations from 18 in the year before the programme began.

This approach to capturing measurement and insight was also applied in other areas. For example, after the first year of the programme, a survey was conducted with the service partners employees to build a picture of how they felt about their roles, the One Team programme and the Leadership Team based in Cork. Unfortunately, the budget was not available for this to become an annual exercise like the customer experience survey.

There was also a specific survey following each of the first two leadership summits and the feedback was used to inform development of the following year's event/programme. The Net Promoter Score (NPS) scores from attendees at the first summit were as follows:

- Impact of Summit – very high impact 94%
- Commitment to the One Team programme – very high at 91%
- Delegates at the summits confirmed the value of face-to-face time with each other, understanding the importance of being able to pick up the phone to share best practice, no matter where they are based, with whichever supplier.
- A cohesive and trusted culture positively affected the way supply partners worked together and solved problems.

In each case, care was taken that the measurement and insight was meaningful, consisting of quantitative measures and qualitative data so that informed decisions could be made. Data was always used to make decisions, rather than collected for the sake of it.

FINANCE

The area of finance was included as an additional standalone Element in the operating platform rather than be included in the Systems & Processes Element because there was a strong focus on this area from the EMC core business. Work was done to bring spending across all the various elements of the RE&F function under a single global cost model. The main objective was to prove that savings could be achieved with centralization, which would improve buying power as well as provide useful operational data to inform better business decisions, for example, why one office was more expensive to run than another.

One major challenge was to achieve overall responsibility for the ownership of all spending aligned to the RE&F function. Equipped with this information, the RE&F leadership was able to show how much it was costing EMC to process invoices – $195,000 per month. By consolidating this procedure, instead of processing thousands of invoices each month, each service partner submitted just one invoice per month, with every commodity clearly identified under the contract. Over a two-year period, this saved EMC more than $4.6 million.

For all of the above achievements, what could be more fitting than to leave the final words in this chapter to a 'customer?':

"From a sales perspective, we've seen the GREF team flourish over the past 18 months. They provide a consistent high-quality service to our sales teams across the region and we see them as a trusted advisor to the business. The team plays a significant part in EMC's business growth, and I believe the work they do every day plays a critical part to the overall success of EMC's 'Best Place To Work' rankings, which inspire and motivate our employees and help attract top talent into the company."

Adrian McDonald, President, EMC EMEA

KEY 'CX IN CONTEXT' INSIGHTS

- Our suggested model is just as powerful when applied to an internal function and supply chain as it is when applied to a commercial corporation or any service-focused organization.
- The balanced scorecard nature of the remarkable impact on the business across all areas of the operating platform, from internal customer satisfaction to employee engagement and retention to cost savings.
- The scalability and flexibility of the One Team approach allowed the EMEA RE&F team to better respond to the needs of the business and integrate employees of EMC acquisitions more efficiently, reducing risk.

CHAPTER 14
NORDSTROM

Nordstrom, Inc. is an American luxury department store chain founded in 1901 by John W. Nordstrom and Carl F. Wallin. It originated as a shoe store and evolved into a full-line retailer with departments for clothing, footwear, handbags, jewellery, accessories, cosmetics and fragrances. Some stores feature home furnishings and wedding departments, and several have in-house cafés, restaurants and espresso bars.

As of January 2023, Nordstrom operates 368 stores, including nearly 100 full-line stores, in 44 US states employing 60,000 people (full-time and part-time employees). The corporate headquarters and flagship store are in the former Frederick & Nelson department store building in Seattle, Washington; a second flagship store is located near Columbus Circle in New York City. Its subsidiaries include the 247-store off-price Nordstrom Rack division, two clearance stores, five Nordstrom Local service hubs and the members-only online store HauteLook. There is also a comprehensive online service across the portfolio. In 2022, the company had $15.5 billion revenue in the year and profit of around $500 million.

Somebody who possibly knows Nordstrom nearly as well as the Nordstrom family is Robert Spector, the author of *The Nordstrom Way* book series, who has interviewed three generations of the Nordstrom family and is an international keynote speaker on the Nordstrom culture of service. We invited Robert to collaborate with us for this mini case study and have been fortunate enough to receive his insight into the company for this chapter.

BUSINESS LANDSCAPE

The retail sector in North America is experiencing an ongoing transition. Some of the top retailers have achieved stability and, at the same time, there have been bankruptcies. The emphasis on understanding what consumers really want continues to expand the gap between the leaders and everyone else. Developing this level of insight has never been more important, especially with the convergence of supply chains, digital technologies and other innovations.

There was already an uncertain economic outlook with the possibility of recession – and then COVID-19 arrived and the aftershock continues. It seems clear that the best-placed retailers are those with a strategic plan that can handle adjustments when and as needed, focusing on four factors critical to success: clarity of purpose and value proposition, a war chest for strategic investment, embracing technology and automation, and looking beyond brick-and-mortar outlets to embrace partnerships and innovation.

BRAND IDENTITY

Delivering a great customer experience is at the heart of the Nordstrom business model. The company's mission is: "To continue our dedication to providing a unique range of products, exceptional customer service, and great experiences."[1] When asked about the company and its goals, Erik B. Nordstrom, Chief Executive Officer & Director, stated, "Above all, our number one goal remains focused on improving service for customers so that people feel even better about the time they spend with us."[2] In summary, customer experience is the brand.

Values are also of paramount importance. "Values define who we are, and if they change, we become something else," says Pete Nordstrom, President and Chief Brand Officer (as quoted in Spector's latest coauthored book).[3] "Practices are ways of doing things that express our values. Practices may serve us well for long periods of time, but they're not values, and therefore can be changed without changing our culture."

According to Spector in his forthcoming book, the Nordstrom narrative is a culture story built on nine nonnegotiable values: trust, respect, loyalty, awareness, humility, communication & collaboration, competition & compensation, innovation & adaptation, and give back & have fun.

Operating against trend, Nordstrom provides little in the way of a formalized training programme. When asked who trains Nordstrom salespeople, Bruce Nordstrom, then Chairman Emeritus, answered: "Their parents."[4] Or their grandparents or guardians – whoever instilled them with a set of values. According to Spector, the Nordstrom Way can be summed up in three operating strategies:
- Stay true to the values of the culture
- Attract people who share the values of the culture
- Teach and coach based on those values

With those values as the foundation, Nordstrom creates a culture of innovation and adaptation to stay relevant. Another core element of the Nordstrom brand is the two pillars of community and environment. There is a publicly stated ambition to "leave the world better than we found it" and this involves Nordstrom supporting the many people and communities it serves and respecting the environment by reducing the company's environmental impact and conserving resources where possible. Nordstrom's mission, vision and core values are clear. The company uses these driving principles to model its brand and business based on customer service, quality and value, and social and environmental impact.

This approach has resonated internally within its company culture and externally with its loyal customer base. It is a great example of our approach being applied in practice: alignment of brand identity, employee engagement and customer experience.

EMPLOYEE ENGAGEMENT

The goal is to first attract and then retain people who share and abide by the Nordstrom values because it is understood that only those kinds of people will be happy working for the company. As Bruce Nordstrom says, "We can hire nice people and teach them to sell, but we can't hire salespeople and teach them to be nice. We believe in the philosophy of 'hire the smile, train the skill.'" And Jamie Nordstrom, President of Stores, tells students that they should "join a company whose values align with yours."[5]

Every Nordstrom employee (whether they work on the sales floor or in a support position) is focused on making people feel good, and the culture is centred on creating an environment where employees feel supported and empowered to do just that. Employees are encouraged to work as though it is their name on the door, thinking of themselves as an entrepreneur whom Nordstrom is providing with the tools (store, merchandise, technology) to build their own business. Then, they do what they feel is right to build lasting relationships with their customers and provide them with an outstanding experience in keeping with a long-term view of the lifetime value of the customer. Employees are empowered to do what it takes to make customers feel good and have just one rule in all situations, which gives them the freedom and flexibility they need to make that happen: use good judgment.

RECRUITMENT

When Nordstrom is recruiting, it looks for people with enthusiasm and a belief that service is a noble endeavour. Candidates are interviewed by five to six managers and asked about the best customer service experience they have had (given and received). This question aligns the recruitment process with the central role that customer service plays in the Nordstrom brand identity. The strategy of empowerment works well with millennials, who want to work for an organization with values that align with their own, and also provides a clear path to progress.[6] Instilling a sense of such empowerment involves placing trust in employees to use their initiative to do the right thing. It is a strategy that clearly works for the retailer because it has "better-than-average morale and retention" rates, especially among millennials.[7]

This use of 'good judgment' is something that Nordstrom encourages its employees to take beyond the workplace. When employees are out in the community for a coffee, having dinner or being a customer of some other business, they are encouraged to make connections at every opportunity with people who have the attributes to become Nordstrom employees. The same applies to employees' use of social media. Once again, this plays into the millennial desire to feel empowered by the company that they work for and, importantly, it is backed up with clear learning and development opportunities that Nordstrom provides exclusively to its employees. An engaging set of values and a culture of community in which career paths can be mapped out at any stage of employment has proven to be extremely attractive to the millennial generation.

There is also a robust campus programme where Nordstrom leaders connect with students as they start to think about their career choices. The starting point is an internship programme and the active 'promote from within' culture offers attractive career options.

RECOGNITION AND REWARD

There is a strong emphasis on recognition (manager to worker and peer to peer), with several creative and meaningful ways to celebrate and thank employees when they work hard and succeed. It is a wide-ranging approach, including less visible and celebrated roles such as tailors.

There are frequent Recognition Meetings where Nordstrom managers reinforce, recognize and reward employees for outstanding sales achievements while also rallying the troops and generating excitement about the stores' performance. The meetings are built on four pillars: sincere, specific appreciation; competition to be the best; delivering something fresh every time; and reinforcement of what Nordstrom is all about. Sometimes, the employees singled out for praise will be surprised to find their parents, spouse or children in the room for the announcement – secretly arranged by management – and this can produce an emotionally charged occasion. There is also an event to celebrate all previous winners to which even ex-employees are invited.

High performance is recognized by the elite 'million-dollar club,' consisting of the company's top-performing employees who bring in more than $1 million in sales to the company. These various schemes make employees feel like owners of something they care deeply about rather than just moving parts in a large, faceless machine.

Nordstrom's employee retention strategy is based on providing the best pay and employee benefits possible. The company is known for its range of small, but unique, employee benefits and this sets it apart from its competitors. Benefits include health insurance (e.g., dental and vision), employee profit share, matched contribution to retirement savings plan, paid time off (four to five weeks per year), paid maternity leave, commuter benefits, assistance to employees who are undergoing legal processes and a 24/7 anonymous suicide hotline.

Employees also receive exclusive discounts on all Nordstrom products before anyone else, with an additional 20% discount. All-stars (the most prestigious award given to employees who go beyond expectations to aid and support not only their consumers but also their fellow teammates) and managers receive 33% discounts. Furthermore, once a year, Nordstrom discounts everything by 40% for all employees and provides exclusive access to new products before they go into retail. However, perhaps most important of all to employees is that Nordstrom's pay is unmatched in the industry.

CAREER DEVELOPMENT

There are still some areas of the company that have a more traditional, specialist one-track career path, but, generally, a more tailored approach has evolved to developing the path that best aligns with the employee's capabilities and interests. There is more of a focus on recruiting people who can embrace change from diverse backgrounds (to reflect the changing customer demographic). Roles across teams and in different areas over time equip employees with broader knowledge and experience, which is especially helpful for larger projects.

A typical career path is to start as an intern or selling employee and from there move into an assistant manager position; a department manager role is next and then a divisional retail merchandiser role. This is where employees usually make a choice about moving into the merchant division to participate in buying roles or go down the route of store leadership, which would move them into a Rack store manager role. The options start to open up at this point in an employee's career and the path becomes less defined and more focused on the individual employee's desire and strengths.

PERFORMANCE MANAGEMENT

Hand in hand with the human, caring approach sits a laser focus on business performance. Employee performance is assessed first and foremost on sales results, then on customer service and then on teamwork. Competition is used to drive performance (for example, keeping a list of sales per person per hour) and top salespeople can earn $200,000 per annum. People who perform less well are initially offered help and further training, then moved to a nonsales role. If this does not allow them to perform to the required standard, they are fired.

CUSTOMER EXPERIENCE

Nordstrom's customer service is legendary, and there is plenty of supporting evidence, whether it is a story about searching through vacuum cleaner bags to return a customer's lost diamond, driving a customer's forgotten bags to the airport before their flight, selling a single shoe or helping mall shoppers carry purchases from other stores to their cars. One of the most well-known Nordstrom customer service stories is about a man who wanted to return a set of tires that had been purchased at a store that had occupied the same space prior to Nordstrom moving in. After some discussion, the Nordstrom store manager decided to allow the customer to return the tires there.

All these stories are examples of how the company gives employees the empowerment referred to earlier in this chapter and the autonomy to make their own decisions instead of having an expensive and time-consuming authorization process. Similarly, employees are encouraged to create and make use of their client lists – they personally notify customers of special events and sales through mail or email and send handwritten thank-you notes to new customers.

This genuinely customer-centred behaviour from employees is supported by some quite simple processes, such as the way returns are dealt with by the salespeople (so they can be seen as the hero in the customers' eyes). In Nordstrom stores, customers are asked, "How much time do you have?"; in Racks, there is a streamlined process involving the customer signature, scanning the receipt and taking the goods, with no questions about the reason for the return.

This unconditional approach recognizes that time and convenience are the most important issues for customers and creates a powerful psychological difference compared to customers' experiences with most retailers. Returns history is also tracked to identify those customers who are not always acting with integrity!

Two more small, yet powerful examples from Nordstrom stores are that there is a concierge by the main entrance so customers can drop off or pick up items, and in-store curators hand packages to customers face-to-face rather than over the counter, creating a much more personal customer experience.

There is a general underpinning philosophy that consumers are statistics, whereas Nordstrom customers are people, and they are all individuals. Nordstrom employees are encouraged to develop a relationship with a customer to create trust, which leads to loyalty. Then, as the relationship is being developed, they move on to the sales stage.

The position taken by Nordstrom on the public acclaim for its level of customer service is worth noting. The company rarely discusses its commitment to please customers, apart from suggesting it still has a lot to learn. There is a refreshing 'work really hard at it every day' approach rather than a sense of the company trying to stake a claim to customer service expertise.

A SEAMLESS BLEND

In addition, while these stories are generally from store settings, it is important to emphasize that Nordstrom is always aiming to improve customer service and deliver a great customer experience – but this aim does not mention clothes or shops. You might be surprised to know that those slick, well-stocked, full-line, regular-price stores that anchor the local upscale shopping centre account for only 38% of Nordstrom's annual sales. The balance comes from Nordstrom Direct (online and catalogue) and the Nordstrom Rack clearance stores. This is the company staying true to the strategy of improving customer service and not being confined to doing this in traditional Nordstrom shopping stores.

The Nordstroms say they are channel agnostic: they don't have a channel strategy; they have a customer strategy. They think of the customer having an imaginary seat in the boardroom and are always seeking to make life easier for the customer, not the organization.

In this new omnichannel world, Nordstrom is reimagining the role of the physical store, which is now digitized and complements the online channel.

The company is seeking to seamlessly blend the sensory experience of the physical store and the personalization and convenience of online shopping, continually adding value to the customer experience to be relevant and attractive to customers.

Shoppers can buy items they see on Pinterest and Instagram with just a couple of taps on their phones, via apps such as Like2Buy. When they visit Nordstrom locations, they will see items that proved popular on Pinterest prominently displayed, sometimes with a distinctive red Pinterest tag. Another example is the in-store payment process that follows the online lead: Nordstrom's technology enables customers to make payments from anywhere without visiting a register to avoid the need to queue. Another application of technology is a 3D foot-scanning sizer to match the perfect shoe without the need to try on several pairs.

Sales associates are connected with customers outside the four walls of stores with an employee app featuring a style board, which allows personal stylists to send clients product suggestions based on the items they recently purchased. This is the technology-assisted version of having a favourite salesperson call you with a hot tip. Similarly, employees can access digital store layouts and chain-wide product information and inventory so they can lead shoppers in the right direction. There is also a partnership with eBay to test drive a 'fitting room of the future' that turns a full-length mirror into an interactive touch screen that can be used to search for other items, scan product reviews or call for a sales associate. These digital tweaks all amount to a repositioning that could help Nordstrom attract younger shoppers – and keep them as they get older and wealthier.

Nordstrom took the concept of self-service one step further than its competitors by adding self-service return bins where customers can drop off returns, including online purchases, and get credit almost immediately. The retailer also offers 'Scan and Shop,' a feature on the Nordstrom app that allows customers to take a picture of an item, upload it to the app and find similar items online. By offering the ease and convenience of returns and frictionless integration with its online store, Nordstrom is giving its customers more reasons to shop in-store.

Beyond technology-assisted service, Nordstrom is constantly experimenting with new retail concepts, finding better ways to serve its customers. Nordstrom Local stores carry no new merchandise. Described as service hubs, the local stores offer on-site tailoring services, handle online pick-ups and returns, and even have seating where customers can relax, have a drink or work. Nordstrom Local's unique combination of services and subtle but effective brand awareness make it a standout example of experiential retail. Pop-ups have been another experiment, as has the high-growth area of selling second-hand apparel, with the 'See You Tomorrow' concept. "We want our customers to feel good not only about what they're buying but how they're buying it," says Olivia Kim, Nordstrom's Senior Vice President, Creative Merchandising.[8]

SYSTEMS & PROCESSES

You will have seen from the examples in this chapter, under the 'Customer Experience' heading above, that Nordstrom is embracing technology in its drive to deliver the best possible customer service. In fact, about 30% of its capital expenditure is earmarked for developing its internet infrastructure. The key point, though, is that any technological advancement put in place is always for the benefit of the customer rather than for any other reason.

The systems and processes in the organization are there to support the Nordstrom salespeople and customers. As an example, the merchandising team has been adapted to be more responsive to regional preferences, while at the same time leveraging the company's size and expertise on a national level. The perpetual inventory management system enables a salesperson to track down an item for a customer from anywhere in the company in the time it takes to ring up the sale.

Even the supply chain is viewed from the perspective of delivering quality customer experiences. The company recently set out to create a system that can evolve with changing customer demands and help customers engage with the brand on their own terms. One size does not fit all, which means the supply chain needs to be customizable for each customer. The approach involved three opportunities in flexibility, space and operational simplicity. With these opportunities in mind, Nordstrom's revamped supply chain leverages in its existing physical space, as well as new technology such as robotics and automation, to quickly deliver products to customers. Nordstrom's customizable supply chain now helps deliver great service whether a customer wants to pick an item up in store, browse the racks to find the perfect item or have it delivered to their home. This is a great example of how the supply chain is viewed as a crucial aspect of systems and processes that exist to support the customer experience.

Communication is another key factor and there is a participative style of management at Nordstrom. Communication flows freely between employees and managers within a structure and it is normal practice for senior leaders to ask the sales teams for recommendations. The tone is set by the Nordstroms, who frequently communicate about customer service matters. The store manager is the kingpin in much the same way as a hotel general manager. There are individuals responsible for specific merchandise categories and operations, but all company-wide decisions are made by committees and require a consensus of the family members. Another example is the daily morning meeting huddle, where department teams gather for 15 minutes to talk about anything relevant from the day before or about the day ahead, any known customer visits, customer service feedback (positive and negative) and Nordstrom news.

MEASUREMENT & INSIGHT

This area is focused on, guess what: the customer!

A primary source of feedback is still from the customers and salespeople. There is a hunger throughout the organization to receive customer feedback, whether this is a compliment or disappointment. At the same time, Nordstrom avoids the trap of 'data processing' and always remembers that the feedback is from a person. There is a response to the customer and the information is passed on to the service delivery teams that are responsible for celebrating success and fixing any issues. Salespeople are regularly consulted and there is more formal market research (for example, inviting shoppers and asking what they think about new ideas). Ultimately, however, when all is said and done, there is an unwavering belief that 'sales is the truth.'

Nordstrom's innovative approach to data helps the company to understand its customers and create personalized experiences.

Each online customer has a profile with their style preferences and purchase history. That information is used to make product recommendations and let customers know when their favourite brands are available. Once again, though, data is seen as a supporting tool rather than an end in itself, and an example is that feedback from salespeople (rather than printouts) is used to make decisions about inventory levels because they are closest to what is happening.

In the last decade, Nordstrom has transformed the way that data is used to drive stronger outcomes for the business. The starting point was a recognition that marketing expense was outpacing sales, and yet the rate of customer acquisition was declining at the same time. The approach to measurement and insight was recentred on the customer to measure what really matters.

Previously, there were silos of channels and silos of merchant activity. The marketing and analytics teams were organized by search, display, social and email. Each merchant within the brand portfolios was looked at separately: Nordstrom Rack versus Nordstrom.com versus brick-and-mortar stores. As a result, the value back to the business was not fully understood. Action was taken to restructure the internal teams and organize them around customer profiles. At the highest level, the business goals are to attract new customers and nurture existing customers, regardless of channel or merchant. The individual channel teams were replaced with two marketing teams – a customer acquisition team and a customer retention team. Acquisition is about profitable investment informed by insight into future trends and how to reach a new generation of customers. Retention is about growing the lifetime value of current customers by increasing trips and spend – for example, Nordstrom Rack customers now have visibility of the sales promotions (such as anniversary sales) of the full-price channels.

Another area of change has been the way that marketing effectiveness is measured. Previously this was done solely through last-click return on ad spend but it was realized that the state of marketing today is too complex to rely on a single measurement solution. Now there is a focus on four key signals: a media mix model, multi-touch attribution, last-click and experimentation. This provides a holistic view of the customer and helps improve understanding of the effect of incremental marketing.

The information captured can then be used by the relevant expert teams to decide what actions to take to drive growth based on the business outcomes agreed. This is a huge task because there are potentially tens of millions of customers and prospective customers, and so many possible drivers of customer lifetime value beyond the obvious number of visits and spend (e.g., introducing the customer to a new category or new brand, encouraging the customer to try a 'buy online and pick up in store' feature, engaging with a stylist, enrolling in a loyalty club or downloading the app). Being able to assess these potential actions is invaluable and helps drive marketing campaigns and also calculate the appropriate level of investment in them.

By reorganizing around the customer, the mindset has shifted from one of last-click return on ad spend to one of incremental marketing. As a result, expenses are now in line with sales, efficiency has increased and the rate of acquisition has gone up.

EMPLOYEE ENGAGEMENT

Nordstrom has been listed in *Fortune* magazine's 100 Best Companies to Work for over 23 years. It is ranked by *Forbes* as one of the Best Employers for Diversity and is a certified Great Place to Work. Nordstrom employees have also featured regularly since 2011 in the "Happiest Company in America" annual survey by job satisfaction–focused web resource CareerBliss.com.[9]

SYSTEMS & PROCESSES

Measurement and insight in this area are carried out through observation and supervision by the store managers to ensure consistency of operating processes and, ultimately, the customer experience. On the digital front, Nordstrom was one of four brands in the retail category that attained Genius status in a ranking of overall digital IQ in four areas: site and e-commerce skills, digital marketing, social media and mobile strategies.[10]

POST-COVID-19

Nordstrom shut its stores in March 2020 in an effort to limit the spread of COVID-19 while keeping its apps and websites open. The company said it would provide pay and benefits for store employees during the period.

Action was also taken to manage the financial impact. In 2020, Nordstrom suspended its quarterly dividend and pulled its outlook for the year. There was a restructuring of its regions (including closure of 16 stores), support roles and corporate organization to save $150 million in costs and, reportedly, landlords of premises were informed that the company would only pay half of its occupancy costs for the rest of the year.

Nordstrom stores reopened with a revamped shopping experience and safety as the priority: a limited number of customers and employees were allowed on the salesfloor at one time; shoppers were supplied with a disposable mask upon entry and asked to maintain a distance of six feet away from each other; employees underwent health screenings; fitting rooms were sanitized between each use; items were held for a period of time after being tried on or returned; at the cash registers, there were plexiglass screens; and payment could only be made by card. There were shorter opening hours, and high-touch services and customer events were paused or adapted. But the attention to customer service remained, with managers briefing colleagues to 'smile with their eyes' when they greeted customers while wearing masks. The company encouraged customers to shop online via their websites and apps during the pandemic, and collections and returns were carried out in kerbside pickup spots.

Subsequently, a decision was made to close the whole Canadian business (stores and online) with chief executive officer Erik Nordstrom saying the company "... entered Canada in 2014 with a plan to build and sustain a long-term business there ... Despite our best efforts, we do not see a realistic path to profitability for the Canadian business." Since it entered into the market, Nordstrom had not been able to deliver a profit, so the challenges of the pandemic might have made this decision to exit the market much easier to make.

The company is exploring new formats and business models such as its Nordstrom Local concept stores, which offer services like alterations and styling without carrying inventory on site. These stores allow Nordstrom to provide a high-touch customer experience while minimizing the risk and cost associated with traditional retail operations. In retrospect, this latest move might be seen as yet another innovation in honour of Nordstrom's single-minded commitment to delivering a great customer experience, irrespective of the channel.

KEY 'CX IN CONTEXT' INSIGHTS

- The textbook application of our approach, where there is a focus on alignment of brand identity, employee engagement and customer experience, supported by systems and processes, and measurement and insight
- How Nordstrom has adjusted the delivery of the customer experience to suit changing tastes and demographics while staying true to its high-level purpose and values over time
- The longevity of the humble, "work hard every day" ethic of Nordstrom founder Johan (John) Wilhelm Nordstrom in spite of the adulation the company has received about the level of customer service it provides

CHAPTER 15
BT GROUP

BT Group is one of the world's leading communications services companies that provides products and services in around 180 countries, supporting international and multinational organizations, with its headquarters in London, employing nearly 100,000 people and has an annual revenue of over £20 billion. In the United Kingdom, BT Group provides mobile and fixed broadband services to more than 30 million consumers and one million businesses and public sector customers. There is also a strong presence in mainland Europe, with offices supporting customers. The Americas region is run from an office in Dallas, Texas, that supports other offices across that region. With other offices in Asia, the Middle East and Africa, BT Group supports customers and organizations with a range of telephony, communications, next generation networking, cloud and security services.

BUSINESS LANDSCAPE

The organization sits in a very competitive marketplace across its mobile, broadband and TV products, with companies like Virgin Media, Sky, Three, O2, Vodafone and TalkTalk providing similar services.

In 2016, BT Group faced a major reputation crisis when it received the annual "Daily Mail Wooden Spoon" award for the major UK company providing the worst customer experience.[1] The award was a wake-up call, highlighting the urgent need to revamp the organization's customer experience strategies. The company was criticized for its poor service quality, long response times and lack of customer-centricity.

To make matters worse, this was the second year in a row that BT Group had been awarded the Wooden Spoon – and the third time in the previous four years.

The subsequent negative publicity surrounding the award had severe consequences for BT Group. The company's brand reputation suffered, leading to a decline in customer trust and loyalty. In addition, potential new customers were hesitant to subscribe to BT's services due to the widely publicized customer experience issues. The CEO and senior executives responded immediately and decisively. They publicly acknowledged and apologized for the shortcomings and committed to a comprehensive plan to transform the organization's approach to customer experience. Coauthor Dave has been a keen observer of developments over the following seven years and explores this period using our approach.

BRAND IDENTITY

BT Group is predominantly known for its expertise in communication and connectivity services, such as fixed-line and mobile telecommunications, broadband and digital services. As part of this customer experience transformation and brand refresh since 2016, the values were refreshed to guide interactions with customers and shape its overall approach to providing services to "personal, simple and brilliant." These values reflect BT Group's commitment to putting customers at the centre of its operations, simplifying its services and processes, and striving for excellence in everything it does. They were introduced to signal a renewed focus on customer satisfaction, streamlined operations and innovative solutions.

Since 2016, BT Group has focused on transforming from a typical telecommunications company into a modern-day tech firm, with a view that the solutions they provide are integral to modern life. The company website states, "Our purpose is as simple as it is ambitious: we connect for good." The vision or ambition is, "To be the world's most trusted connector of people, devices and machines." One of the biggest problems that the organization faced was overcoming the public and customer perception. There were many skeptics that were waiting to see if there was any action behind the apology and plan to improve.

Others were still haunted by their past experiences and would need time to see that they could once again trust BT Group. In October 2019, the organization launched its biggest brand campaign in 20 years called "Beyond Limits." It revealed the company's ambition to help families and communities across the UK, and companies in Britain and around the world. The campaign reflected the changing nature of BT Group and its focus on improving connectivity, with an ambition to set a new standard for customer experience and provide essential skills training for 10 million people and businesses. The organization also refreshed its visual brand identity at this time, with a new logo and advertising campaign. According to their website, "it's not just a change of the brand's symbol, but a symbol of the brand's change."

EMPLOYEE ENGAGEMENT

To drive lasting change, there was recognition of the need for a major cultural shift within the organization and its tens of thousands of employees. The company emphasized the importance of a customer-centric culture by encouraging employees to prioritize customer satisfaction in their daily work and decision-making processes, and by conducting extensive internal communication campaigns to ensure that all employees were aware of the transformation efforts and their role in the process. Employees were empowered to take ownership of customer interactions and problem-solving. Frontline staff were given the authority to make decisions that would lead to faster issue resolution and better customer satisfaction, reducing the need for escalations – one part of the business specifically springs to mind. One of the cloud contact centre products designed their team to best support their customer base, changing their entire ethos in the process, using continuous improvement to do so. Customers ended up paying for specialist support that took them directly to the team that would solve any incidents – cutting out the gatekeepers in the process.

This employee empowerment was significantly aided by an initiative that was already running within the organization, called 'continuous improvement.' Teams and units within the different areas of business were proactively looking at how to be more productive and more efficient, by assessing the current state of processes and how they actually work, rather than how they may be documented. A huge part of the continuous improvement drive in BT Group was understanding the voice of the customer across the different interactions that teams were having with external customers. If that team wasn't externally facing, then it was critical to understand how the team contributed to the value stream,[2] how their work contributed to the product or service that end customers would be purchasing and using. For a lot of teams and individuals, this was a change in mindset and approach that was new to them, but the continuous improvement framework is heavily based on creating a customer-centric approach that is led by employees. Teams were, and still are, actively encouraged to engage with customers up and down the value stream, including other teams that may be internal to BT Group to ensure that the value stream is as effective as possible.

Continuous improvement requires sponsorship from senior managers, and so this sponsorship was leveraged to ensure that all levels of leadership were aligned in their commitment to transforming the customer experience. The senior leadership team made it clear that improving customer satisfaction was a top priority and that all employees, from frontline staff to executives, had a role to play in the transformation journey. Reward and recognition are vital too. Creating a bottom-up approach requires the sponsors and management to actively ensure that employees are recognized – whether that is suggesting an innovative idea or being a part of the implementation of that improvement.

CUSTOMER EXPERIENCE

BT Group faced widespread criticism for the quality of its services after the 2016 award of the Wooden Spoon. Customers reported frequent network outages, slow broadband speeds and unreliable phone connections. These service disruptions not only frustrated customers but also impacted their daily lives and business operations. The call centres were notorious for long wait times and difficulty in reaching a customer service representative. This led to customer frustration and further exacerbated the negative sentiment. BT's services and pricing plans were often perceived as complex and confusing.

Customers struggled to understand their bills and the terms of their contracts, leading to misunderstandings and disputes.

There was a significant digital transformation initiative aimed at enhancing customer self-service options and accessibility. The website and mobile app were revamped, making them more user-friendly and informative. Additionally, the introduction of chatbots and virtual assistants enabled customers to get quick answers to common queries, freeing up customer service agents for more complex issues. To address the lack of transparency and customer communication, a strategy of proactive communication was put in place. The organization started sending regular and proactive updates to customers about planned maintenance, service disruptions and account-related information. This approach helped manage customer expectations and reduce frustration caused by unexpected interruptions, while showing an immediate change in approach to handling service-affecting issues. In some cases, the issues weren't noticeable to customers yet and this was through the efforts of proactive monitoring of services to track performance, highlighting any degradation to service.

Complex procedures were simplified, reducing the need for customers to navigate convoluted processes when seeking assistance or resolving problems. The continuous improvement tools, containing an array of problem-solving techniques, were central to this effort and the focus on streamlining internal processes to ensure faster response times and issue resolution continues today. It is deeply rooted across all areas of the business and is still growing and evolving. There are other methodologies that are contributing to the fundamental customer experience programme, such as Agile[3] and DevOps,[4] but continuous improvement is seen as the foundational mindset to empower teams to take the required action.

This customer experience transformation saw the birth of many different CX teams across the organization, embedding and educating the principles of customer experience within operational teams. This has arguably led to the current three-point strategy for the company, designed to grow value for all stakeholders:

1. Build the strongest foundations
2. Create standout customer experiences
3. Lead the way to a bright, sustainable future

The way that this strategy is formed shows how seriously BT Group are taking their customer experience programme. The first point is to build the strongest foundations. If you were to try and create stand-out customer experiences without having the foundations in place, you're essentially just attempting to 'do' customer experience. Strong foundations are critical to not only executing customer experience strategies well but ensuring that the mindset of customer experience becomes embedded within the organization. This strategy indicates that BT Group have learned a lot in the past few years since they have embarked on their customer experience journey.

Finally, to demonstrate the commitment to improved service quality, service guarantees were introduced. These guarantees ensured that if a customer experienced prolonged service outages or repeated issues, the company would offer compensation or other remedies. Such guarantees not only increased customer confidence but also incentivized BT to maintain service excellence.

SYSTEMS & PROCESSES

A transparent communication campaign was launched to keep customers informed about the changes that were underway. The company shared its commitment to improving customer experience and outlined its strategy to address the issues identified. Regular updates were provided through various channels, including social media, press releases and direct customer communications. Recognizing that customers have different preferences for communication channels, support options were extended. In addition to traditional phone support, customers could now make contact using email, chat, social media and even video calls. This multichannel approach provided customers with more flexibility in how they sought assistance. You will discover more about this in the Measurement & Insight section of this mini case study. Recognizing that addressing the customer experience challenges required substantial investments, the organization allocated significant resources to fund the transformation initiatives. This included budgeting for the implementation of specific CX teams across critical areas of the business, that go beyond just 'customer service.'

The continuous improvement initiative has driven major improvements in how problems or opportunities are tackled across the entire organization. One example of this is the strategic decision made in 2019 to move service management processes to a single platform (Servicenow). The drive for this came from a realization that some teams had been siloed for so long that they were using legacy systems that had long seen their support contracts expire. There were 56 active tools performing similar functions across the organization and 76 different ways of implementing service processes. There was no doubt that the move to a singular system was the best option ... but it was far from simple. Specialist teams and squads were assembled to ensure that the transition was as efficient as possible, with the correct level of training for employees to ensure they could seamlessly service customers' issues and implement changes to products or services.

The investment in ServiceNow has been significant and continues to grow as more opportunities are identified with more teams using the system. The automation possibilities and capabilities have identified more than 10,000 manual tasks that can be eliminated, creating quicker and more efficient processes that benefit both the customer and the organization. From an employee point of view, the implementation process has been engaging. Reducing from 56 tools means that teams need to change their ways of working, which directly impacts the working of employees. This can have a positive or negative effect on behaviour, with the possibility of emotions running high. Gaining the buy-in from employees has been vital and there has been a concerted effort to involve employees when their processes are being prepared for transition. A key part of this process is engaging the subject matter experts, understanding how they carry out the task today in the current system, and how it can be mapped to the new platform – with little or no interruption. This early engagement has helped engage employees and also creates reassurance that their expert views of a given process are listened to and understood before any development takes place. This is an ongoing process to migrate all teams and processes and the potential improvements are remarkable: there could be a 50% reduction in the effort required to deliver service requests and it is possible to make 20 times the number of changes into customer services in a given time period, compared with using earlier systems.

The structure of the employee engagement survey also provides regular measurement and insight on the strategic customer experience programme and consistency with employees. Employees know that they have formal opportunities to tell the organization and management structure how they are feeling, with completely anonymous feedback. This is crucial, as it provides psychological safety and prevents 'witch hunt'-type chases across the business to find out who may have said what. There is a strong sense of the 'who' isn't important, it's the 'what' that counts.

The entirety of this customer experience transformation and continuous improvement initiative required investment, both in time and finances; employee training programmes, process improvements and the development of new customer service platforms are just a few of the investments made to ensure customers are kept informed.

MEASUREMENT & INSIGHT

An in-depth assessment of the customer experience landscape within the company began in 2016, involving extensive data analysis, customer feedback surveys and direct interactions with customers to identify pain points, recurring issues and areas that needed improvement. This thorough analysis provided part of the foundation for the subsequent transformation efforts.

It has been an incredible transformation journey since 2016, which would not have been possible without the robust and complex measurement and insight framework that has been embedded. There is detail and granularity across the organization; horizontally, vertically and geographically.

BRAND IDENTITY

An early decision was to introduce the Net Promoter Score measure for the organization, its business units and major products and services. The business units of BT Group are Business, Consumer, Digital, Networks and Openreach, all of which underpin the three major brands of BT Group – BT, EE and Plusnet. The major products and services that now use NPS as a measure are pay monthly and pay-as-you-go mobile, fixed broadband and TV. We'll explore the details of how this system works under the Systems & Processes subheading.

In 2023, all three brands won USwitch awards – EE won fastest mobile network, BT won most reliable broadband and Plusnet was the best broadband provider. This highlights the brand transformation that BT Group has been through in the past seven years. From winning Wooden Spoons to winning industry-recognized awards that reflect the service the organization provides. The brand identity has also improved when it comes to complaints to the UK regulator, Ofcom. There were 10 complaints per 100,000 customers for BT Broadband, a rate that continues to be better than the industry average. For EE mobile, there were two complaints per 100,000 customers and for EE broadband there were seven complaints to Ofcom per 100,000 customers – both are second-best in the industry. A year earlier, at the 2022 UK Customer Experience Awards, BT Group were winners for 'Best Customer Experience' and 'Best Customer Experience in the Crisis.'

In recent years, the organization has posted some impressive statistics around customer experience, highlighting the improvement and investment in their journey so far. In the end of financial year results as of 31 March 2021, BT Group reported the 19th successive quarter-on-quarter growth of its NPS results. That is nearly five years of continuous NPS growth that started in 2017, where it grew five points over that financial year. In the 2018 financial year, the NPS result grew by 8.3 points, in 2019 it grew by 6.5 points, another 5.5 points in 2020 and 7.8 points growth in 2021. In the third quarter results reported on 31 December 2021, BT Group recorded its highest-ever NPS score. This growth in scores has been driven by a motivation to improve the customer experience, not driven by improving NPS results. This is highlighted by the result at the end of the 2022/2023 financial year, where the BT Group NPS result fell by one point "due to cost of living challenges and industrial action affecting consumer brands and the wider telecoms market." Within the first quarter of the very next financial year, the results reported on 31 June 2023, the NPS result for BT Group was 23.7. This is up 1.8 points year-on-year, suggesting that progress on improving the customer experience has been resumed.

EMPLOYEE ENGAGEMENT

After empowering employees, it is vital to measure their engagement by gathering data and comments. This is achieved with a formal internal employee engagement survey twice a year, with many areas of business running other pulse surveys in between to ensure that suggestions are actioned where possible, utilizing the feedback of their employees to make improvements. Questions such as, "Is it easy and straightforward to get things done?" creates a lot of suggestions and ideas to improve productivity and efficiency. The employee engagement survey asks a variety of questions and creates detailed results that can be broken down from an organization-wide view, all the way down to an individual team of six or more people. The survey records the results of the following:

- Employee engagement
- Employee wellbeing
- Diversity
- Inclusion
- Leading our people
- Team manager scores
- Ethical business
- Empowered employees

Arguably, the most important results are 'Enabling outstanding Customer Experience' because this is what everybody in the organization is working toward. Does the individual answering the survey believe that they have the support to do the right thing for the customer? Do the processes help the individual provide great customer service? The breakdown includes the results from the previous survey to see the change in score, as well as providing a year-on-year view.

Leaders throughout the organization also hold regular 'town halls' or 'all hands' meetings, both face-to-face or by phone. There are always opportunities for questions at the end of these sessions, where on the phone there is active conversation or answers provided and it is reviewed face-to-face after the event. Either way, all feedback is collated and analysed by the leadership teams to see what employees think and if there are any improvements that can be explored. This loop is then closed when an improvement is made and some internal communication is sent out, or it is addressed at the next event.

Feedback from the twice-yearly employee surveys is also highlighted by leaders during these events, either creating discussion or indicating the steps that will be taken to implement improvements.

CUSTOMER EXPERIENCE

Customer feedback was actively sought and integrated into the improvement efforts. The company encouraged customers to provide input through surveys, feedback forms and direct interactions. This feedback helped identify areas for improvement and validate the effectiveness of implemented changes by informing customers of the changes that had been made, truly closing the feedback loop.

As well as the NPS measures that take place in Consumer and Business, there is also customer experience work that constantly takes place in the Networks division of BT Group. Here, the performance of the networks is measured predominantly through NPS and customer satisfaction, or CSAT. In Networks, mobile and broadband network performance is measured proactively through surveys that are sent via text message. As an example, here are the questions that are asked around EE network performance, using a scale of 0 to 10, where 0 is not at all and 10 being extremely likely:

- How likely are you to recommend EE based on the quality of your experience when using the network in the last month?
- How satisfied are you with the ability to make calls wherever you are and then maintain the call without being cut off?
- How satisfied are you with the consistency of speed when using the internet on your phone?
- How satisfied are you with having good signal at locations where you mostly use your phone?

These questions are asking customers if they would recommend the service, the quality of voice calls, the internet speed and the coverage they receive on their phone. Customers that receive this text will not be targeted for another survey until six months have passed. One standout improvement on the back of this feedback in the Networks division utilizes the data gathered to understand the key drivers for customers to call contact centres. Using this data and analysing customer sentiment, one of the biggest reasons and key themes identified was customers impacted by changes on mobile masts by the organization.

Internal conversations took place with the appropriate teams that plan and implement these changes, with a simple question in mind: "How can we do change differently?" This led to a host of ideas and plenty that have been implemented, such as the time of day to implement changes, the time of day that service is resumed, analysing the status of masts and even understanding the changes that other providers may be planning that would potentially interrupt service. The insight that came from customers has driven improvement to processes, and the organization is now starting to see fewer calls regarding change into the contact centres, driving improvement in the relevant CX metrics as a result.

SYSTEMS & PROCESSES

The organization leveraged customer data to provide personalized support and recommendations. By analysing customer behaviour, usage patterns and preferences, the company could offer tailored solutions that catered to individual needs. This approach not only improved issue resolution but also demonstrated a deeper understanding of each customer's unique requirements. There was then a direct connection to the systems and processes at all levels of the organization so improvements could be made.

The major products and services of BT Group (pay monthly and pay-as-you-go mobile, fixed broadband and TV) track customer experience on a monthly basis and drill down into the key drivers behind each product. For each of these products, customers are surveyed on four components of the product, with drivers beneath that so that the organization can track and measure performance monthly. The components and their respective drivers in the area of Systems & Processes are:

- Value – price paid, right plan, rewards and benefits, clear pricing
- Connectivity – outdoors, indoors, travelling, voice quality, internet speed
- Personal – recognition, empathy, brand affinity
- Ease – website, app, store, call centre

Every one of these components and key drivers has their own score, and they aren't just measured by BT Group. They are all measured by competitors and tracked monthly to see how each product ranks in comparison to other organizations. This insight alone provides great detail on a number of different measures that are important to the vast customer base. On top of this, channel satisfaction is measured for each of the products. The channels that are measured are call centre, retail and digital interactions. Overall satisfaction is tracked as an NPS measure for each channel, which is consistent across all major competitors and allows comparison. These include measuring the wait time, if the staff cared, if staff were clear and easy to understand, if the interaction achieved what the customer needed and finally, first contact resolution (FCR).

Online chat is another channel that is used and measured for fixed broadband and TV products, that follows the same satisfaction and key driver system. Once again, there is monthly competitor comparison across each of the channels and products. This measurement and insight process can be worked back to the improvements that have been and continue to be made by BT Group. The organization has invested significant time, effort and money into ensuring that customer experience is at the heart of what they do across all products and services. While the organization appreciates that scores enable comparisons to competitors and provide a benchmark, the real motivation is to provide standout customer experiences.

The customer experience strategy has stood the test of the last seven years very well. There have been three CEO changes in recent years, as well as numerous changes to other senior leadership positions at other levels of the business across its different customer-facing units. Customer experience is still the priority; there hasn't been a wholesale change of direction, and everyone has bought into the vision, contributing to the progress that the organization has made so far and continues to make.

KEY 'CX IN CONTEXT' INSIGHTS

- The importance and power of senior executive sponsorship and public declaration in encouraging collective commitment and accountability
- The first attempt at alignment might need to be adapted as time goes on
- The value of designing an all-encompassing measurement framework to facilitate internal and external benchmarking

PART SIX
FUTURE

The final part of this book helps explain why values-driven alignment is the key to delivering a consistently excellent customer experience and highlights some relevant topics to pay attention to. This is a crucial part, because throughout the book we have highlighted the importance of applying a structured framework to create an effective CX solution for your particular context rather than thinking of it as an 'oven-ready' application.

Here, the perspective is the broader system and landscape that leaders and organizations find themselves in, now and in the future. We highlight key topics that we believe will have an impact on most organizations for you to consider when you are planning the development and implementation of your customer experience strategy. We believe these topics are already relevant in organizational environments in the 21st century, are specifically relevant for the area of CX and are magnified by the new paradigm we call the Values Economy. Our intention is that by sharing these subjects, we will enable you to develop your insight into how and why you could implement a CX approach to create maximum value for your organization from an informed but practical, operational perspective.

In the first of three chapters, **Chapter 16:** *Behaviour*, we explore the emotion and behaviour patterns of employees and customers, and the relationship between the two.

Chapter 17: *Digital* considers the opportunities and limitations of digital CX management and how it interfaces (or does not!) with non-digital channels.

In **Chapter 18:** *Disruption* we consider the topic generally and the impact of COVID-19, both in terms of creating a new paradigm for humanity and also how it has had a specific impact on CX.

Please consider what impact these topics will have on your organization in the five Elements of our suggested approach as you develop your plan. Finally, we close with **Chapter 19:** *Summary* to help you recap your thinking within a high-level and practical overview.

CHAPTER 16
BEHAVIOUR

"No one is born with greed, prejudice, bigotry, patriotism and hatred; these are all learned behaviour patterns."

Jacque Fresco[1]

For all the advancements in technology to improve service delivery, the fact remains that we are human beings with human needs, desires, motivations and aspirations. Psychological research has classified six facial expressions that correspond to distinct universal emotions: disgust, sadness, happiness, fear, anger and surprise.[2] It is interesting to note that four of the six are negative emotions. Those emotions are essential when it comes to making quick decisions in day-to-day activities. The ability to recognize, understand and manage emotions in oneself and others is known as emotional intelligence, a key component in delivery of the customer experience.

Emotions play a crucial role in shaping the customer experience, influencing perceptions, decisions and customer loyalty. Studies have consistently shown the impact of emotions on customer behaviour.[3] Research by Deloitte found that 60% of long-term customers use emotional language to describe their connection to their favourite brands, the same language they would use for friends and family.[4] Positive emotions such as happiness and delight can lead to increased customer satisfaction, while negative emotions such as frustration or disappointment can result in dissatisfaction and can even cause customers to leave, also known as customer churn. In fact, the same Deloitte study found that 39% of customers switched brands after a bad experience. Therefore, organizations must strive to understand

and address customers' emotions throughout their journey, aiming to create positive emotional experiences that foster loyalty, advocacy and long-term success.

Positive emotions, such as happiness and satisfaction, have a profound impact on customer experience, leading to a range of benefits for organizations, particularly in driving customer loyalty and advocacy. Customers who have positive emotional experiences are six times more likely to repurchase, 12 times more likely to recommend the company, and five times more likely to forgive a mistake.[5] Additionally, customers who have the best past experiences spend 140% more compared to those who had the poorest past experience.[6] By prioritizing positive emotional experiences, organizations can not only boost customer satisfaction and loyalty but also gain a competitive advantage in the market, leading to increased revenue and business growth.

On the other side of the coin, negative emotions in customer experience, such as frustration and disappointment, can have a detrimental effect on organizations, leading to various shortcomings and challenges. Research consistently emphasizes the negative impact of poor emotional experiences on customer behaviour. One study found that 86% of unhappy customers will not willingly do business with a company again after experiencing bad service[7] and another that 32% of customers would stop doing business with a brand they loved after just one bad experience.[8] Furthermore, negative word-of-mouth spreads rapidly, with dissatisfied customers sharing their experiences with 15 people about a poor service experience.[9] This amplifies the negative impact, potentially leading to lost revenue and damage to the organization's reputation. The consequences of negative emotions highlight the need for organizations to proactively address and resolve customer issues, aiming to turn negative experiences into positive ones. By doing so, organizations can mitigate the shortcomings of negative emotions and foster customer loyalty, advocacy and long-term success.

Several approaches can be employed to address and alleviate negative emotions effectively. For example, many customers get frustrated because they need to repeat their issues to multiple representatives.[10] To mitigate this, organizations can focus on streamlining communication channels and implementing robust customer service processes that enable seamless issue resolution. Additionally, actively listening to customers and empathizing with their concerns can make a significant impact. By training customer-facing employees to demonstrate empathy and genuine understanding, organizations can provide emotional support and ease customer frustrations (see the section on problem resolution in **Chapter 9:** *Customer Experience*). Another strategy is to proactively seek feedback and address customer issues promptly. You might be surprised to learn that only 21% of customers who don't feel valued during a complaints process stay as a customer.[11] Organizations can actively welcome all feedback, then leverage technology and establish systems to ensure timely responses and resolutions, reducing customer disappointment.

Often, our emotions can drive behaviours that either instantly become, or evolve into, habits. Before we look into this in more detail, we will explore some key behaviours.

BEHAVIOUR

Human behaviours are shaped by a combination of nature and nurture, as well as the individuals and social circles we surround ourselves with. Nature refers to our genetic makeup and innate characteristics, while nurture refers to the environmental influences and experiences we encounter throughout our lives. The people we surround ourselves with, including family, friends and social circles, greatly influence our behaviours, regularly shaping our goals, attitudes and values through social norms and peer pressure.[12]

The cultural and societal norms prevalent in our communities can also shape our behaviours. Different cultures have distinct values, beliefs and practices that influence individual behaviours within those cultures. These cultures exist within organizations all over the world and the good news is that customer experience can be embedded as a culture and way of working for an organization.

Customer experience is influenced by several key behaviours that organizations must prioritize to ensure customer satisfaction and loyalty. Effective communication plays a vital role in shaping the customer experience, with studies showing that 86% of consumers are willing to pay more for better customer service.[13] Timely and responsive interactions are also crucial, as 46% of customers expect companies to respond faster than four hours, while 12% expect a response within 15 minutes or less.[14] Demonstrating empathy toward customers' needs and concerns is another significant behaviour, as 70% of buying experiences are influenced by how customers feel they are being treated.[15] There are a number of key behaviours that contribute to a great customer experience, but this list is by no means exhaustive.

First, trust forms the foundation, as it encompasses integrity, confidence and the fulfilment of customer expectations. Customers depend on the reliability and commitment of a business, and trust is what ensures their loyalty. The human aspect is equally crucial, as customers seek respect and a personal, personable interaction. It's about recognizing the individuality of each customer and tailoring the experience accordingly. Then there is ease, characterized by simplicity and clarity of the experience, making the customer journey smooth and enjoyable across channels and through all transitions. After 'ease' comes 'deliver': when a business can consistently deliver, supply and collaborate effectively, it enhances the customer's perception of value and reliability. Additionally, the ability to fix issues promptly through problem-solving, resolution and providing answers is pivotal in retaining customer trust and satisfaction. Finally, empathy, shown through understanding, compassion, and the ability to relate to customers' needs and emotions, is what truly sets apart a world-class customer experience from an ordinary one. These behaviours collectively create an environment where customers feel valued, heard and cared for, resulting in lasting customer loyalty and advocacy.

These behaviours are not mere buzzwords but fundamental elements that can significantly impact an organization's chance of success … or failure. By truly understanding customers' needs and preferences, organizations can tailor their communication strategies accordingly, ensuring that messages are clear, concise and personalized. When organizations prioritize these behaviours, they create positive experiences that resonate with customers, leading to increased customer satisfaction, loyalty and, ultimately, business growth.

Over the years, the field of customer experience and behaviour research has evolved significantly, driven by a growing understanding of consumer preferences and advancements in data analysis. This multidisciplinary area of study has provided valuable insights into the complex relationship between businesses and their customers, leading to improved strategies for enhancing customer satisfaction and loyalty.[16]

Our understanding of customer behaviours has been shaped by key theories and frameworks that have provided valuable insights into the factors influencing consumer decision making: Maslow's Hierarchy of Needs,[17] suggests that individuals have a set of hierarchical needs that drive their behaviour; McKinsey's Consumer Decision Journey (CDJ) framework[18] has been instrumental in understanding how customers interact with brands throughout their decision-making process, outlining four key stages – initial consideration, active evaluation, moment of purchase and post-purchase experience.

Technological advancements have also had a profound impact on customer behaviours, transforming the way individuals interact with organizations and influencing their expectations, and we'll explore this in detail in the next chapter, **Chapter 17:** *Digital.*

EMPLOYEE BEHAVIOURS

The role of employee behaviours in customer experience reflects a dynamic and ever-evolving landscape, shaped by shifting consumer expectations and technological advancements. Seventy-three per cent of consumers consider the customer experience to be a crucial factor in their purchasing decisions, highlighting the growing emphasis on delivering exceptional experiences that are driven by employee behaviours.[19]

Emotional Intelligence (EI) or Emotional Quotient (EQ)[20] is the ability to identify, evaluate, control and express one's own emotions, as well as perceive and assess others' emotions to facilitate thinking and understand emotional meanings. The level of EQ of employees in service organizations plays a significant role in shaping the customer experience, because it enables them to effectively understand and manage their own emotions, as well as recognize and empathize with the emotions of customers. By being aware of their own emotions, employees can regulate their behaviour and respond to customer needs in a composed and empathetic manner. They are also better equipped to establish meaningful connections with customers, leading to more positive and memorable interactions. This ability to manage emotions (self and others) helps create a calm and supportive environment, even during challenging situations, which can enhance customer satisfaction and loyalty.

Employee behaviours, driven by emotional intelligence, play a crucial role in shaping the customer experience and cultivating a customer-centric culture. First, active listening is key. This is not just listening or gathering feedback, but truly, deeply listening to what customers are saying. By attentively listening to customers, employees can better understand their needs and expectations, as well as appreciate their concerns, questions and complaints. The next, and second, stage is empathy, which is essential for delivering exceptional customer experiences. Forbes found that customers who have an emotional connection with a company are more likely to be loyal and spend more.[21] Employees are the face of the organization on a day-to-day basis, and those who display empathy, demonstrating a genuine understanding of customer concerns, are better equipped to provide appropriate solutions. On top of this, employees need to be responsive. While immediate responses aren't always possible, timely and efficient responses show customers that their concerns are valued. This can be achieved by implementing streamlined communication channels and empowering employees to make quick decisions. Technology can be helpful in this area through collection and communication of relevant data.

"Customer experience isn't an add-on,
it should be the DNA of your company."
Jeanne Bliss[22]

While implementing effective behaviours in support of the customer experience is simple, it is not easy. There is no magic switch to flick to make instant changes to behaviours, and it can be a challenging task, with significant barriers that need to be navigated. Eighty per cent of companies believe they provide superior customer service, while only 8% of customers agree.[23] This disconnect highlights the challenge of aligning internal perceptions with customer expectations, and a lot of it stems from embedding solid customer experience-focused behaviours across the organization. One major barrier to implementing these behaviours is the lack of a customer-centric culture within an organization. Building a culture that prioritizes the customer requires a shift in mindset, values and employee engagement to drive and embed the behaviour.

"A company's culture is the foundation for future innovation.
An entrepreneur's job is to build the foundation."
Shep Hyken[24]

Another challenge is the increasing complexity of customer touch-points and channels. With the proliferation of digital technologies and omnichannel interactions, providing a seamless and consistent experience across platforms can be daunting. Customers now expect seamless experiences between digital and physical touchpoints and 52% of consumers expect all offers to be personalized,[25] highlighting the need for organizations to integrate their channels effectively.

Shortcomings in data management and analysis present challenges in delivering personalized experiences. While many organizations have access to vast amounts of customer data, leveraging this data effectively is often not so straightforward. According to a survey by Gartner,[26] 63% of digital marketers find it challenging to execute personalized experiences using customer data. The key to success in this area is robust data analytics capabilities and the ability to extract meaningful insights. Internal silos, a lack of cross-functional collaboration and the absence of an overarching data management strategy can hinder effective customer experience implementation too. Departments working in isolation without shared goals, strategies and operating platforms can create disjointed experiences for customers.

CUSTOMER BEHAVIOURS

Understanding the psychological factors that influence customer behaviours is crucial for organizations to create effective strategies and deliver exceptional customer experiences. A study by Deloitte[27] shows that emotions play a critical role in customer loyalty and satisfaction, with emotionally engaged customers three times more likely to recommend a brand. This highlights the impact of emotions on customer behaviours.

A key factor that drives customer behaviours is the concept of social proof and 46% of consumers trust online reviews as much as personal recommendations.[28] When customers see positive reviews or endorsements from others, they are more likely to trust the brand and make a purchase.

The principle of scarcity has a powerful impact on customer behaviours, with consumers more likely to make a purchase when presented with a limited-time offer or a coupon.[29] Scarcity creates a sense of urgency and triggers the fear of missing out (FOMO), compelling customers to take action. The psychological concept of cognitive biases also influences customer behaviours. For example, the anchoring bias, where people rely heavily on the first piece of information they receive, affects how customers perceive prices and make purchasing decisions. Research by behavioural economist Dan Ariely has shown that even irrelevant and arbitrary reference points can impact price perceptions.[30] Understanding these cognitive biases can help organizations frame their offers and pricing strategies more effectively.

Perception and cognition play a vital role in customer decision making, influencing how customers perceive brands, products and services. A study showed that 53% of online shoppers abandon a website if it takes longer than three seconds to load, highlighting the impact of perception on customer decision making, as a slow-loading website can create a negative impression and lead to customer dissatisfaction. Customers' cognitive processes also play a crucial role in decision making, and the majority of consumers prefer to buy new products from brands they are familiar with.[31] Customers rely on their cognitive assessment of past experiences and information to make decisions. There is an important connection with branding and marketing strategies, and visual elements such as logos and packaging design can create strong associations and influence how customers perceive a brand.

When organizations have an understanding of the above and the drivers for customers' behaviours, they can respond with appropriate communications, language and initiatives at a strategic and tactical level to influence customers' perceptions and behaviours. Having said this, these efforts must be genuine and with good intent because, in our increasingly transparent, super-connected world, the truth often gets out, sometimes very fast, and any disingenuous activity can be exposed with potentially disastrous effects.

EMOTION & BEHAVIOUR FLOW

The relationship between emotions and behaviours profoundly impacts the flow of interactions between an employee, an internal customer, an external customer, and the feedback received by employees from the customer. Research suggests that emotions greatly influence how employees engage with both internal and external customers. Employees who experience positive emotions, such as happiness and enthusiasm, are more likely to provide superior customer service, resulting in increased customer satisfaction. On the other hand, negative emotions, such as frustration or anger, can hinder the quality of interactions and lead to dissatisfied customers.[32]

> "I've learned that people will forget what you said,
> people will forget what you did, but people will
> never forget how you made them feel."
> **Maya Angelou[33]**

Do you ever have days when your mood is determined by an emotional reaction to an event? Have you ever seen someone's mood change after an event that has led to an emotional reaction? Do you know anyone whose behaviour is commonly seen as negative? The answer to all of these is more than likely yes. Our emotional reactions can influence our behaviour for a short or sustained period of time – in some cases it becomes a habit.

The emotions experienced by an employee can significantly influence their behaviours in the workplace. Positive emotions, such as happiness and enthusiasm, can lead to behaviours characterized by friendliness, attentiveness and proactive engagement. When employees interact with internal customers, such as colleagues or team members, positive emotions can foster a collaborative and supportive work environment. A Gallup study found that employees who feel positive emotions during their interactions with internal customers are more engaged and demonstrate higher levels of teamwork.[34] These positive emotions induce positive behaviours that are established over time, helping to build a collaborative culture which, in turn, enhances productivity and innovation across the end-to-end value stream[35] and ultimately improves the service provided to external customers. Alternatively, when negative emotions are present during internal interactions, it has the opposite effect. Negative emotions, like frustration or stress, can result in behaviours such as disengagement, rudeness or even avoidance of interaction. Teams start to operate in isolation and more silos appear with very little collaboration and disrupted flow of information. Over time, this behaviour becomes ingrained as the way of working, with new joiners being indoctrinated to these negative behaviours. There will be individuals or teams that try to break through the silos and negativity, but when behaviours become habits that are deemed "the way we do things," it can be challenging to influence a change – although certainly not impossible. The power of positive emotions that engender engrained behaviours makes for a better culture and place to work, with alignment and focus on what needs to be achieved.

The emotions and behaviours of an employee also influence their direct interactions with external customers. Positive emotions and behaviours, such as empathy, patience and genuine care, contribute to a positive customer experience. Employees who display positive emotions are more likely to engage in behaviours that satisfy customer needs, provide excellent service and build customer loyalty. Conversely, negative emotions and behaviours can lead to dissatisfied customers, negative word-of-mouth and potential loss of business.

Positive and negative feedback from customers can significantly influence the behaviours of employees within an organization.[36] Positive feedback serves as a powerful motivator, reinforcing behaviours that contribute to customer satisfaction and loyalty. When employees receive praise and recognition from customers for their exceptional service or problem-solving abilities, it boosts their morale and sense of achievement. This positive reinforcement encourages employees to continue delivering high-quality experiences and go above and beyond to meet customer expectations. As a result, employees are more likely to exhibit behaviours such as active listening, empathy and responsiveness, which contribute to a positive customer experience.[37] On the other hand, negative feedback can serve as a catalyst for change and improvement. When customers express dissatisfaction or provide constructive criticism, it presents an opportunity for employees to reflect on their actions and behaviours. Negative feedback highlights areas where improvements are needed, allowing employees to identify gaps in their skills or knowledge and take steps to rectify them. Effective organizations view negative feedback as a valuable source of information and use it to drive continuous improvement. By analysing patterns in negative feedback, organizations can identify common issues and implement targeted training programmes or process enhancements to address them. Employees, in turn, learn from these experiences and adjust their behaviours to prevent similar issues from arising in the future.

CHALLENGING CUSTOMER BEHAVIOURS

It is crucial for organizations to identify and analyse challenging customer behaviours such as complaints, negative reviews and disengagement to improve customer satisfaction, and enhance the organization's overall reputation. Analysing customer behaviours can provide valuable insights into underlying issues or areas for improvement. So how best to achieve this? Ideally, you need an organization full of people that are empathetic, actively listening and taking action for the benefit of the customer. Dissatisfied customers usually generalize the organization and employee with a term such as 'you,' but the customer is usually dissatisfied with the organization, rather than the employee personally. Effective management of challenging customer behaviours is vital and can lead to positive outcomes (see the section on problem resolution in **Chapter 9:** *Customer Experience*). Displaying empathy to customers is incredibly important, whether it is in response to a complaint or more general feedback. It is important to ensure that customers feel that they are being heard and you can recap or paraphrase their issue to prove you understand. This is where the power of emotional intelligence comes into play.

Emotional intelligence allows employees to accurately perceive and understand the emotions of customers. By actively listening and observing nonverbal cues, employees can gauge customers' moods, preferences and concerns. This insight enables them to tailor their interactions and responses to align with customers' emotional states. For example, when a customer expresses frustration, an emotionally intelligent employee can respond with empathy and patience, defusing tension and working toward a solution. This empathetic approach demonstrates genuine care and fosters trust between the employee and the customer, enhancing the overall customer experience.

The way employees emotionally respond to feedback, whether positive or negative, can have a profound impact on the employees' mood, their effort and behaviour during the next task, and even on the organization's reputation and customer relationships. It could also impact the next interaction with a different customer or an internal customer.

To summarize, the relationship between emotions and behaviours is crucial for the flow of interactions between all stakeholders (employees, internal customers, external customers) and the overall feedback loop. It is important for organizations to promote emotional intelligence, provide support mechanisms, and cultivate a positive work culture to facilitate positive emotions and behaviours in the workplace. Behaviours are often a direct manifestation of an emotional state for everyone – employees and customers.

TWO TOP TIPS

- Remember that, from a customer perspective, employee behaviour often trumps technical competence.
- If there are negative emotions and behaviours that have become a habit, disrupt that negativity and create positive emotions and behaviours.

WANT TO KNOW MORE?

To explore this area further, you might enjoy the following articles and books.

Daniel Goleman. *Emotional Intelligence: Why It Can Matter More Than IQ.* Bantam Books.

Daniel Goleman and Cary Cherniss. *Optimal: How to Sustain Excellence Every Day.* Penguin Business.

Jay D. Lindquist and Joseph P. Sirgy. *The Psychology of Customer Behaviour.*

Roman Krznaric. *Empathy: Why It Matters, and How To Get It. Rider.*

Scott Magids, Alan Zorfas and Daniel Leemon. "The new science of customer emotions." *Harvard Business Review.*

Nathan Christensen. "Is ROI in empathy?" *Forbes.*

"Using psychology to design meaningful customer experiences." *CX Conversation.*

CHAPTER 17
DIGITAL

"When digital transformation is done right,
it's like a caterpillar turning into a butterfly, but when
done wrong, all you have is a really fast caterpillar."
often attributed to George Westerman[1]

Many people reading this chapter will remember when, as a customer, you had to physically visit a store to make a purchase. Sometimes this might have been a pleasant experience. At other times, you had to brave the elements, fight through crowds, plan your journey from one shop to another and endure the agony of finding a parking spot before closing time. But now, online shopping allows you to buy whatever you want with just a few clicks of a button, from the comfort of your own home at any time of the day or night, skipping from retailer to retailer, instantly.

Similarly, if there was a problem with a product or service you had bought, this involved at least one journey back to the retailer and waiting for hours or even days to get a response from customer service. Now, support is available by phone, email, online or social chat, sometimes 24/7. Need to cancel a subscription? Just click a button. Want to track your order? Check the app. Have a question about a product? Hop on live chat. The digital age has made customer service faster and more efficient than ever before. It has demonstrated how a digital environment can significantly reduce, if not totally eliminate, our dependence on time and place.

We also have voice recognition technology that has revolutionized the customer experience in remarkable ways. Gone are the days of cumbersome automated phone menus and frustrating hold times. Today, advanced voice recognition systems can swiftly identify and authenticate customers, offering a seamless and personalized service. But it doesn't stop there; emerging technologies like holograms have taken customer interactions to an entirely new level. Instead of merely hearing a voice, customers can now engage with lifelike holographic representations of customer service agents, making interactions more engaging and immersive.

And then there's the power of online reviews. We no longer have to rely on word-of-mouth recommendations or the opinions of so-called experts. With just a few clicks, we can read thousands of reviews from real (and sometimes not!) customers and make informed decisions about our purchases.

Technology has helped bridge the gap between virtual and physical, delivering a highly personalized and human-like experience that contrasts starkly with the 'old-fashioned way' of speaking on the phone. This more personal service is valued by customers, as it provides a sense of connection and individualized attention, fostering trust and loyalty in an era where exceptional customer experiences are paramount in building lasting relationships.

THE BEGINNING

The evolution of the digitalization of customer experience has been a fascinating journey that has spanned over two decades, beginning in the early 1990s. In the early days of the internet, companies primarily used their websites to provide information about their products and services. Then, as the internet became more sophisticated and accessible, companies began to realize the potential of digital channels to enhance customer experience. This led to the emergence of customer relationship management (CRM) systems that allowed companies to track customer interactions across multiple channels. With the advent of social media, mobile devices and the rise of e-commerce, companies have continued to refine their digital strategies to provide personalized, seamless and convenient experiences to their customers. Today, customers can engage with companies through a wide range of channels such as chatbots, voice assistants, social media and mobile apps, and companies can leverage data analytics and artificial intelligence (AI) to deliver personalized experiences.

The digital customer experience has been shaped by a range of key technologies and innovations that have revolutionized the way organizations interact with their customers. One of the most significant technological advances has been the emergence of data analytics and AI, which have allowed companies to collect, analyse and leverage vast amounts of customer data to gain insights into their preferences and behaviours. Cloud computing, the Internet of Things (IoT), and blockchain have also played a crucial role in the same area. This has enabled companies to provide seamless, convenient, personalized and tailored experiences to their customers and to anticipate their needs and expectations. Another key innovation has been the rise of mobile technology, which has made it possible for customers to access digital services and engage with companies from anywhere and at any time. Social media has also played a significant role in shaping the digital customer experience, providing a platform for customers to share feedback, reviews and opinions about products and services. The growth of e-commerce has transformed the way customers shop, and companies have responded by investing in technologies such as virtual try-ons, augmented reality and chatbots to enhance the online shopping experience. Voice assistants and natural language processing technologies have enabled customers to interact with companies in a more conversational and intuitive manner, further enhancing the digital customer experience.

Many businesses have successfully leveraged the digitalization of customer experience to improve their bottom line and here are three well-known examples:

1. Amazon is a prime example of a business that has leveraged the digitalization of customer experience to become one of the most successful e-commerce companies in the world. By providing a seamless and personalized customer experience through their website and mobile app, Amazon has built a loyal customer base that keeps coming back for more.

2. Netflix has transformed the entertainment industry by leveraging the digitalization of customer experience to provide a personalized and convenient streaming service. Their data-driven recommendations engine analyses user behaviour to suggest relevant movies and TV shows, leading to increased customer engagement and retention.

3. Starbucks has embraced digitalization to improve the customer experience through their mobile app, which allows customers to order and pay for their drinks ahead of time, reducing wait times and increasing convenience. The app also offers personalized rewards and promotions to customers, which has helped increase customer loyalty.

Digital technology that can be used by customers to improve their own experience has risen dramatically, with one of the best examples being Google's Translate app. Imagine being in a new city, confronted with signs, menus or documents in a language you do not understand. With the Google Translate app, you can simply take a picture of the text in question, and the app will swiftly translate it into your preferred language. This immediate accessibility breaks down the daunting language barrier that many face when navigating unfamiliar territories, making the world feel a little smaller and more interconnected. Such advances in technology not only demonstrate the rapid progress of digital tools but also highlight their potential in enhancing the customer experience, turning challenges into seamless interactions and fostering greater understanding and connection across cultures.

BIG DATA

The digital revolution has, therefore, not only made shopping more convenient, it has also completely transformed the customer experience. One of the main reasons for this is the ease with which customer behaviour and preferences can be tracked in the digital world, every single click. This information is used to tailor offerings and develop marketing strategies. You might be familiar with this example: you put some items in your online basket but get distracted and forget that you were ever shopping. A reminder arrives (by email, text or on your app) letting you know that you did not check out: "Was there anything that was missing?" or the best one, "Check out now for a 10% discount."

The ability to work with big data means that the days of receiving generic, mass-marketed emails from companies is rapidly disappearing. Instead, companies are increasingly using sophisticated algorithms and data analysis software to create highly personalized and targeted campaigns. You will no doubt notice that you now receive emails that address you by name and offer products that are tailored to your personal interests. The same big data allows companies to use your past purchases and online activity to create a profile of your preferences and habits, and then market directly to you. Predictive analytics can be used to identify new customers to target and potential risks, and anticipate customers needs, e.g., low tire pressure warnings in modern cars alert the driver to the risk before it becomes a problem. From a customer experience perspective, these advancements sound like they have had an enormous positive impact. But there is another side ...

The digital age has also brought with it a new set of challenges. With so much information and choice at our fingertips, it can be overwhelming to make a decision. And, as mentioned above, all that you read is not what it might seem in a world of fake reviews, social media influencers, phishing emails from seemingly legitimate enterprises and even fake websites. It can be hard to know who to trust. For example, Le Nouveau Duluth in Montreal, the city's highest TripAdvisor-rated restaurant, didn't even exist.[2]

On a less serious level, but nonetheless important at an emotional level, you might receive emails that address you by name (or not in some cases) or read as though the sender has known you personally for many years. You might feel like just another sales statistic, or possibly worse, that the company is not being authentic. This is where some companies have done the basics by implementing the technology but haven't invested in or even considered the customer experience and the emotions involved.

What about the scenarios when you need support to cancel a subscription or return an item and are not sure about the procedure, or want to resolve a problem? You notice the 'Live Chat' in the corner of the screen, you click that link, and you know after a few seconds that it's not a human at the other end – it's a chatbot.

CHATBOTS

Chatbots seem to be everywhere and regularly pop up after browsing a website for a few moments. But they are only as good as the information that is behind them. Chatbots are generally run from a knowledge base that consists of articles that enable the bot to return a message to the customer – whether it is useful or not is a different matter.

Recent research found that 93% of companies are offering chat as a digital channel for customer service, but 54% report that it is not good enough yet, 67% of companies feel happy with their current level of customer service offered via messaging channels, 25% of companies believe that consumers want to see less bots and 19% believe customers want more personalization.[3]

However, it seems that companies and customers have different points of view on the matter. Businesses believe that only 11% of consumers prioritize making self-service smarter, yet 36% of consumers say it's important to them. From the consumer perspective, the number one request (34%) is to improve self-service capabilities and to make self-service smarter – having the ability to digitally address more complex tasks than are currently being handled. Interestingly, 16% of consumers stated that they wanted to see fewer bots – the second highest request in the research.

Of course, there are benefits and disadvantages with chatbots. Some benefits are faster customer service, faster resolution, increased customer satisfaction, lower labour costs and a variety of uses across multiple industries. But, a word of warning: this is when chatbots are done well, and not all chatbots are equal. Disadvantages of chatbots can be limited or canned responses for customers, customer frustration and dissatisfaction, high costs for complex chatbots and not all businesses can deploy or use chatbots.

The more articles that a chatbot has access to, and the more detailed they are, then the better the response will be to the customer. Often, the canned phrases that are created as the default responses do not cover the range of questions that the bot may be presented with – nor can it show or display emotion.

In our opinion, it seems that many organizations are using chatbots as a buffer from speaking to an actual human who can help. They are like a triage service, albeit with an element of Russian roulette.

But that could all change very soon. The recent launch of AI, such as ChatGPT, has the ability to create emotive responses and can be integrated with existing knowledge bases and even enhance them. Perhaps this provides the capability for chatbots to be designed for the customer experience benefit first.

CRM SYSTEM

The evolution of the customer relationship management (CRM) system has been a significant driving force behind the digitalization of the customer experience. In the early days of the internet, CRM systems were used primarily as a tool for managing customer contact information.

However, as the internet became more sophisticated, organizations began to realize the potential of these systems to provide a holistic view of their customers' interactions across multiple channels. This led to the development of more sophisticated systems that allowed companies to track and manage customer interactions across multiple touchpoints, such as social media, email and chat – utilizing the big data that is available all around us.

Many experts believe that CRM systems are seen as the digital brain behind customer experience. This is because they enable businesses to better understand their customers, track interactions and provide targeted communications that improve customer satisfaction. Modern CRM systems have become an essential tool for companies looking to improve their customer experience by providing real-time insights into customer behaviour, preferences and needs. They use data analytics, machine learning and AI to provide companies with personalized insights into their customers' behaviour, allowing them to tailor their interactions to meet their customers' needs. This has enabled companies to deliver more personalized, seamless and convenient experiences to their customers, ultimately leading to increased customer satisfaction and loyalty.

Organizations that maximize their CRM systems are the ones that utilize it across all of the different channels and touchpoints to capture as much information as possible to inform the design of the end-to-end customer journey. The data generated can identify patterns and automate responses. This enables organizations to provide faster, more personalized support that meets, and even exceeds, customer expectations.

> "CRM systems allow us to track customer inquiries and respond in a timely manner, which is critical for maintaining customer satisfaction."
> **Jeff Bezos[4]**

ARTIFICIAL INTELLIGENCE & AUGMENTED REALITY

AI has revolutionized the customer experience by providing businesses with a powerful tool to automate and personalize interactions with customers. The evolution of AI in customer experience started with chatbots and virtual assistants that could answer simple customer queries, such as providing product information or tracking order status. As AI technology advanced, so did its ability to handle more complex interactions and provide personalized recommendations based on customer data. Today, AI-powered solutions such as predictive analytics and natural language processing are being used to identify customer needs, preferences and intent, enabling businesses to offer more personalized and proactive customer experiences.

AI-powered voice assistants like Amazon's Alexa and Google Home have also emerged as popular tools for customers to make purchases and interact with organizations, further advancing the capabilities of AI in customer experience. As AI continues to evolve and become more sophisticated, businesses can leverage its power to provide a seamless, personalized and convenient customer experience that drives loyalty and ultimately improves their bottom line. Organizations can also benefit from using APIs to integrate AI, like ChatGPT, to their chatbots to create more emotive responses that don't just rely on canned phrases or stored knowledge articles. ChatGPT is a hot topic right now, and the statistics back that up. According to OpenAI cofounder Greg Brockman, ChatGPT acquired one million users just five days after launching in November 2022,[5] and 100 million users after just two months.[6] By comparison, it took TikTok about nine months after its global launch and Instagram approximately two-and-a-half years to reach 100 million users.

Augmented Reality (AR) has had a profound impact on the way organizations engage with their customers, creating new opportunities for immersive experiences that drive customer satisfaction and loyalty. The global AR market size was valued at $31.97 billion in 2022, and is projected to reach $88.4 billion by 2026,[7] with applications ranging from retail and marketing to gaming and education.

One of the key benefits of AR is the ability to offer customers a more personalized experience. By using AR technology, clothes retailers can create virtual try-ons, allowing customers to see what products would look like on them before making a purchase. Another way AR is improving the customer experience is by providing interactive and engaging product information. IKEA, for example, has developed an AR app that allows customers to visualize furniture in their homes before making a purchase. This can create a more seamless experience for customers, enabling them to make more informed purchase decisions.

AR is transforming the way organizations interact with their customers, creating new opportunities for personalization, engagement and brand loyalty. As the technology continues to evolve and become more accessible, we can expect to see even more innovative uses of AR in the customer experience space.

SOCIAL MEDIA

Social media has revolutionized the way organizations interact with customers, offering new opportunities for engagement and communication. There are now over 4.2 billion active social media users worldwide, with users spending an average of 2 hours and 25 minutes per day on social media platforms.[8] In the past, unhappy customers wrote a strongly worded letter of complaint and would hope that it would reach the right person. Now, with the power of social media, customers can vent their frustrations to the world in real-time.

Companies are acutely aware of the power of social media and are investing heavily in their online presence. They are using social media platforms to engage with customers, respond to complaints and build brand loyalty. One of the key benefits of social media for businesses is the potential to build stronger relationships with customers.

"Social media enables us to have a direct line of communication with our customers, allowing us to better understand their needs and preferences."
Richard Branson

By engaging with customers on social media, organizations can respond to feedback and complaints in real-time, and provide personalized support that builds trust and loyalty. This environment has led to the rise of influencer marketing. Companies are now partnering with social media influencers to promote their products to a wider audience. It's like product placement, but instead of Tom Cruise drinking a Pepsi, it's Kylie Jenner using a new makeup product.

While the digitalization of customer experience offers many benefits, it also comes with potential shortcomings. One of the main concerns is data privacy and security. Collecting and using customer data can be a double-edged sword, as it can improve the customer experience but also exposes customers to data breaches and misuse of their personal information. In addition, organizations must take care not to alienate customers who prefer traditional channels, such as phone or in-person interactions – not all customers are comfortable with the use of chatbots or voice assistants.

Organizations must be prepared to invest in ongoing technology upgrades and maintenance to keep up with the rapidly changing landscape of digital channels and customer preferences. Failing to do so can result in outdated technology that hinders the customer experience and puts businesses at a competitive disadvantage. Overall, businesses must balance the benefits of digitalization with the potential risks and challenges to provide a seamless, personalized and secure customer experience that meets the needs of all customers.

So, what does the future hold for the digital customer experience? We think there will be even greater personalization and customization, with organizations using advanced technologies like AI and AR to create truly immersive and tailored experiences. We can also expect a greater emphasis on sustainability and social responsibility, with customers demanding that companies take action on issues like climate change and inequality.

Staying up to date with the latest trends and technologies is crucial for businesses looking to provide the best possible customer experience. With rapid advancements in technology and changes in customer behaviour, businesses must continuously adapt and innovate to stay ahead of the curve. However, it's important to note that there is no one-size-fits-all solution when it comes to the digitalization of customer experience. Just as in other parts of this book, it is all about context. Organizations must consider their unique customer base, industry and resources to determine the most effective digital strategies for their specific needs. This might involve experimenting with new technologies and channels to find the best fit for their customers, rather than simply adopting the latest trends. Ultimately, the key to providing a successful customer experience lies in finding the right balance between innovation, added value and practicality. By leveraging the latest trends and technologies in a way that aligns with their business goals and customer needs, organizations can stay competitive and provide a seamless, personalized and convenient experience that keeps customers coming back.

One thing is for sure, the digital revolution has completely transformed the customer experience, and there's no going back.

TWO TOP TIPS

- Adopting the latest digital innovation might be tempting but do the research to make sure it adds long-term value for your organization.
- Put yourself in the slippers of your customer when they're sitting at home in their pyjamas, sipping on a beverage of choice – ensure your digital experience is designed for their benefit.

WANT TO KNOW MORE?

To explore this area further, you might enjoy the following articles and books.

Klaus Schwab. *The Fourth Industrial Revolution. Penguin.*

Olivier Blanchard. *Social Media ROI: Managing and Measuring Social Media Efforts in Your Organization. QUE.*

Kai-Fu Lee. *AI Superpowers: China, Silicon Valley, and the New World Order. Harper Business.*

Chiara Valentina Misischia, Flora Poecze and Christine Strauss. "Chatbots in customer service: Their relevance and impact on service quality." *Science Direct.*

Wayne D. Hoyer, Mirja Kroschke, Bernd Schmitt, Karsten Kraume and Venkatesh Shankar. "Transforming the customer experience through new technologies." *Science Direct.*

"Digital customer experience: Everything to in 2023." *Qualtrics.*

"Four Pillars For A Best-In-Class Digital Experience Program In 2023 (And Beyond)." Aberdeen Strategy Research.

"How to Use AI for Intelligent Customer Service." KUSTOMER E-BOOK.

CHAPTER 18
DISRUPTION

"The arrogance of success is to think that
what you did yesterday will be sufficient for tomorrow."
Widely attributed to William Pollard[1]

In **Chapter 1:** *Introduction*, we noted that "the pace of change will never be this slow again" to describe the rate of change that is happening in the world. To put this into practical perspective, Uber was tested in New York in early 2010 using only three cars, and the official launch took place in San Francisco in May that year. By 2022, there were 5.4 million Uber drivers offering ridesharing services in over 10,000 cities across 72 countries. Sixty-four billion trips were taken, generating $31.8 billion in revenue[2] and Uber's market cap is higher than Ford Motor Company and General Motors Company. And if this exponential acceleration is not already enough of a challenge, there is another influencing factor to contend with: disruption. This is why the quote above has never been more relevant.

DISRUPTIVE INNOVATION

The term 'disruptive innovation' was coined and defined by Clayton M. Christensen in his book *The Innovator's Dilemma*.[3] Today the concept is present in our everyday language about innovation and seems to be used freely to describe a wide range of situations where industries experience change.

> "If you defer investing your time and energy until you see that you need to, chances are it will already be too late."
> **Clayton Christensen[4]**

To explain his theory, Christensen uses a comparison of Netflix and Uber. According to his theory, a disruptive business gains its foothold in a low-end market that has been ignored by the established companies, which have been more focused on profitable customers. Conversely, the disruptor must establish a completely new market, turning noncustomers into customers. Uber's case is not applicable to either of those assumptions, as it targets people who already use taxi services and doesn't create an entirely new market. According to Christensen, a truly disruptive business starts with a low-quality product, then ultimately covers the mainstream market by improving quality. He points out that Uber does not fit into this box either.

> "You're not that disruptive. Stop lying to yourself!"
> **widely attributed to Rameet Chawla[5]**

Christensen then uses the example of Netflix as a classic disruptive business. The initial Netflix mail-in subscription service definitely wasn't attractive to Blockbuster's mainstream customers, who rented new releases on demand. Netflix attracted only those who didn't care about new releases, were early adopters of DVD players or did online shopping. The company targeted segments of the population that had been overlooked by its competitor, delivering an inferior (but more tailored) alternative at a lower price. Eventually, Netflix moved upmarket by adding the things mainstream customers wanted. Then one day, there was no reason to use Blockbuster anymore. We agree that this is a great example of true disruption.

We think Christensen's examples help explain what disruption is and is not and are highly relevant for our book because they are both in the customer experience space. However, we also believe that there could be a better example to use than Uber because it is a business that is platform-based (rather than linear) and, at one level, we believe that Uber has caused disruption. Once a platform has established a strong network around its original core transaction, it can easily tap into that network to unlock new customer groups and create new markets. Networks are extensible in a way that traditional supply chains are not. In fact, most platforms create new markets. They succeed not by building sustaining innovations but by introducing disruptive innovations that build new networks, communities and marketplaces.[6] This is what Uber has done.

We also challenge the (what seems like a) technology-obsessed view of disruption. It might be true that new technology uproots, and eventually replaces, an existing technology (e.g., video streaming eventually replacing video rentals). However, this description still misses the point because disruption is not driven by technology *per se*. Instead, it is driven by customers. They are the ones behind the decisions to adopt or reject new technologies or new products and services. Using Uber again, customers valued the convenience and value of the Uber service, and the driver community valued the flexibility of the hours and the service delivery model. For this reason, large companies should focus on changing customer needs and wants to respond more effectively to digital disruption.

"Those who disrupt their industries change consumer behavior, alter economics and transform lives."
Heather Simmons[7]

Finally, we fully appreciate that innovation is an important dimension of disruption, especially with technological advancement. However, we prefer to take a broader view of the topic.

THE BIGGER PICTURE

We face a future of colliding megatrends, from rapid urbanization to climate change and resource scarcity to technological breakthroughs to shifts in economic global power, all against a backdrop of demographic and social change. We know that these shifts are reshaping societies, economies and behavioural norms around the world and redefining whole industries at a breathtaking pace. We also know that technology is a game-changer (see **Chapter 17:** *Digital*). At the same time, business leaders cannot be sure how they should be planning for what's to come. The past is no longer a reasonable guide to the future and there is so much hype, so many unknowns and such a degree of volatility in every dimension. Research shows that the 'pace of change' and related threats from business model disruption have become the top emerging risk for CEOs, with healthcare, insurance and industrial sectors fearing its consequences the most.[8]

> "Most industries experience disruption not from the sudden impact of a single force, but rather from a collision of interacting forces, and often with multiple, related consequences."
> **Sean Murphy[9]**

The notion of an organization with a fixed structure and supply chain offering a well-defined range of products or services in a stable market with a set of known competitors is disappearing fast. First, now and in the future, organizations should 'create their next cutting-edge' by embracing new technologies to develop potentially disruptive ideas, in and outside their current industry. Second, they should 'fund their future bets' by progressively bolstering and allocating their innovation investments to test and turn new ideas into commercial realities faster. Third, if organizations cannot build or fund the necessary skills and resources internally, they should find partners (including third parties and suppliers) to scale new ideas and provide access to technologies and specialized talent. Fourth, organizations should 'disrupt from the inside' by fostering an internal culture that views innovation as a benefit and establishing an 'innovation lab' or 'digital factory' to test new ideas.

Successful companies such as Google and Microsoft still spend billions of dollars trying to find new ways to avoid disruption by leaning into disruptive technologies, testing new ideas and learning how to remain close to the innovation frontier. We also believe that we will increasingly see the development of collaborative ecosystems replacing the traditional organization concept. A great example is a new Japan Airlines initiative dubbed "Any Wear, Anywhere," which offers passengers aboard JAL-operated flights the option to rent sets of clothing for the duration of their stay in the country, eliminating the need to pack.[10]

POST-COVID-19

"When written in Chinese, the word 'crisis' is composed of two characters – one represents danger and one represents opportunity."
John F. Kennedy[11]

When we are considering this broader perspective, how can we fail to reference COVID-19, the most profound disruption to lifestyles since the Second World War? The shock to the global economy from the pandemic was faster and more severe than the 2008 global financial crisis and even the Great Depression. These previous episodes saw stock markets collapse by 50% or more, caused credit markets to freeze, led to massive bankruptcies and pushed unemployment rates above 10%. But all of this took around three years to happen whereas, with COVID-19, similarly dire macroeconomic and financial outcomes materialized in just a few weeks.

As the number of lives lost as a result of the pandemic exceeds seven million,[12] there are signs that the impact of COVID-19 might result in fundamental long-lasting change. 'Unscaling' is causing the rapid reinvention of industries such as healthcare, education and manufacturing, and a historical shift in the way we work. Think of learning happening anywhere at any time rather than in one place at set times or how 3D printing can overcome the challenge of mass production in a single location with an expensive and complicated logistics infrastructure.

In summary, the impact of COVID-19 demonstrated how we are less constrained by time, geography and built environments than we previously appreciated. A global values assessment indicates that, at a personal level, there was a strong shift toward making a difference, adaptability, wellbeing and caring.[13] In workplaces, the traditional 'process' focus of finance, control and effectiveness was replaced by a focus on people, agility and communication. Health and wellbeing are now generally viewed as more important than economic wealth.[14] There were also early signs that consumers intended to reward more responsible retailers, particularly those that looked after their employees, and shop more on their local high streets and with smaller or independent retailers.[15] We wonder whether this will be a sustained shift, or a passing fad overtaken by events.

A heightened awareness of what is important to us on an individual and collective level has had a knock-on impact on organizations and we will now explore some of the factors to consider under the three main headings of our suggested approach. Our observations cannot be conclusive in any way because although the pandemic has been officially declared as ended, the long-term impact is still unfolding. However, we agree with the sentiment of John F. Kennedy's quote at the beginning of this section, even if it is factually incorrect.

BRAND IDENTITY

Marketing teams in all geographies, sectors, settings and platforms were challenged with the core issue that the coronavirus pandemic has been one of the most globally disruptive phenomena of all time, and no one could ignore it. In these circumstances, continuing with usual marketing activities would not have been wise and, understandably, would have been likely to cause a backlash from various stakeholder groups. As a result, many brands took to communicating their stance during the pandemic with a swathe of well-intended values-led messaging. However, many of these messages did not land well with the audience they were trying to reassure for several reasons: they were inward focused (on the brand) rather than focused on the real needs and concerns of the stakeholder; they were absent of any offer or helpful content; and they did nothing to differentiate the brand from all the other brands that were saying the same thing. At best, these messages might have been viewed as lacking in empathy or as disconnected from the core business and, at worst, they might have been seen as opportunistic, disingenuous and desperate. It is worth noting that brands have been behaving like this for some time, whether it is a brand using the Pride flag on its products for a month while not actually taking any constructive action to support the LGBTQ community or the numerous examples of environmental 'greenwashing.' What is needed instead is demonstrable action showing that an organization puts into practice what it has always preached about its brand's purpose and values, even more so in challenging times.

> "Watch what we do, not what we say."
> **John Mitchell**[16]

With a return to 'normality,' we are curious to know whether those brands that set aside opportunistic business gains and PR point-scoring during the COVID-19 period, and instead focused their efforts on the common good, will be remembered (and rewarded) by the people who built their brand in the first place. Of course, time will be the judge in this matter and in no way do we think this is a foregone conclusion, because people's memories can be short-lived. Having said this, we have a feeling that the emotions surfaced at this time might be longer lasting. Greater awareness of what is really important to us has touched a raw nerve. In the Values Economy, rhetoric no longer washes with customers, employees, service partners and local communities, however good the intentions.

EMPLOYEE ENGAGEMENT

The impact of COVID-19 turned the world of office work on its head, with an estimated 50% of employees working from home.[17] In **Chapter 8:** *Employee Engagement*, we outline seemingly contradictory findings in this area and we believe that at least three drivers have contributed to these. First, while at the onset of COVID-19 employees generally were impressed by the care employers showed for their employees' wellbeing, this is now wearing off. Second, the employment base has recovered strongly, and there is some indication that these newly employed people are less engaged in their jobs.

Third, many employees have taken the opportunity to reassess what is important in their lives and are now making work-related decisions in line with this new perspective.

The negative impact on wellbeing has been driven by the blurred distinction between professional and personal life, longer hours, and people struggling to concentrate, feeling bored and feeling less productive. These results suggest that while people may be working more hours at home, they're not necessarily delivering better work and may feel less efficient. In one survey, a significant proportion of people admitted that working from home makes them feel more stressed.[18]

The 'work-from-home' phase was followed by a 'return-to-work' phase, which we are still experiencing and which continues to develop. The pandemic period clearly demonstrated that the office is no longer a de facto place to work for many. There are wide variations in the stance being taken on the future direction, with some large organizations urging an immediate return to offices for people to be with their 'communities,'[19] others targeting a more gradual, meaningful return and some committing to working from home as the 'new normal.'[20] And it is not just the more progressive, tech-based organizations that seem to be open to a new alternative.

> "We've proven we can operate
> with effectively no footprint."
> **James Gorman**[21]

There are also indications that employees prefer to work from home[22] and signs of resentment from some toward their colleagues who continue to work from home, avoiding the time and cost of commuting.[23] Some experts estimate that pandemic-related working practices will reduce potential office capacity by more than 50%.[24] A more distributed workforce has clear implications for several areas, such as the tools and policies that are needed, the level of employee engagement, the organizational culture, informal knowledge transfer and even the case for a new social contract at work.

We believe that the traditional workplace model was already outdated compared to our general dynamic business environment, and the COVID-19 period laid this bare. We see this time as an opportunity to redefine how work is best organized, not just in a space dimension (office, home or other space) but also in terms of geography (city or suburbs and towns) and time of the day (if offices are used Monday to Friday, from 9am to 5pm, this foregoes over 75% of the capacity available!). At another level, this is also an opportunity to redefine the fundamental basis of the employer–employee relationship to be more in keeping with the concept of organizational citizenship. We find the way the term 'employee engagement' is used in an organizational context often verges on patronizing and is very organization-centric. Recent events might have increased the appetite and possibility of such a development, but it could also be counterbalanced by the current and future increase in unemployment numbers and a resultant swing in power to employers.

CUSTOMER EXPERIENCE

The coronavirus situation forced everybody to change in some way or another, whether they liked it or not. So much of everyday routine was disrupted, from the way people interacted with others to community movement patterns to the way purchases were found and bought, to personal priorities. A key challenge organizations face is to understand what has changed for their customers, the behavioural impact this has had, and to what extent these changes will be short term or long lasting.

Since the pandemic, customers have been engaging with retailers differently and are favouring more responsible operators. There has been a customer backlash against some operators that tried to continue trading despite unaddressed safety concerns being raised by employees or in the media.[25] A PwC survey found that more people (especially under-25s) are buying more from small companies and from brands that look after their employees, and even more people say they will increasingly do this in the future.[26]

We were already seeing decisions being made less on a rational and financial basis and more on a deeper, emotional (values) level and we believe this has been accentuated by recent events. Customers are even more focused on what a brand represents, what it offers, how it communicates with its customers and what it really stands for. The organizations that are closest to their customers, not just in terms of data collection but more in terms of genuine connection and being more 'human,' are best placed for success. In this age of Zoom and Facetime, how crude and clumsy does a chatline with a chatbot of limited capability feel? When you see the first positive customer comment about the organization next to the 'Buy Now' button, does this feel like a contrived sales tool or a genuine part of the customer experience?

The shift from face-to-face interactions toward omnichannel digital communications has accelerated and it is no big surprise that Adobe, Microsoft and Netflix have reported massive increases in demand for their products over the past couple of years. Buying online rather than in shops might not signal the demise of the high street as we know it. However, physical shops can no longer be regarded as the primary channel, perhaps with an online service as a 'backup.' Instead, customers will expect a truly integrated cross-channel approach with Amazon-like digital tools and they are just one click away from an alternative provider. We envisage a strange role reversal in the future where physical stores might help to differentiate online brands from their competition (see **Chapter 14:** *Nordstrom* for how the retailer is leading the way in this area).

> "Practice the art of heartfelt hospitality."
> **Alan Williams**

At a very practical level, we believe that the COVID-19 period had a dramatic impact on person-to-person customer experience. Service-people and customers alike were more acutely aware of the need for professional, considerate practice of personal hygiene and protection. Some businesses might also have had one eye on potential litigation for negligence. We believe that this focus might dilute the concept of service to make it more functional. In addition, the smile is one of the most powerful techniques to foster emotional engagement and we wonder whether there has been a negative legacy effect from when masks were being worn. Stakeholders in the hospitality sector have a challenge to recapture some of the magic of the industry, which does not seem to be held up as the best-in-class example of customer service that it once was.

STRONG FOUNDATIONS

'Pivoting' quickly became one of 2020's most popular business buzzwords and with it came much hype and mystery. Simply, we think of this as a combination of offering new products or services, identifying new target markets and using different channels to market. It could be one or all of these. Examples are a restaurant delivering takeaways (channel), hotels providing accommodation for asylum seekers (target market), and a brewery repurposing production facilities to produce hand sanitizer (product and target market). Such actions could be a short-term strategy or more long lasting.

We suggest that leaders can put in place three key foundations to give themselves the best chance of success in an environment that is being disrupted constantly. The first is to adopt and develop a quite different mindset from the one that has served so well in the past. Future success will no longer be driven by knowledge about past performance that is then applied in a detailed and well-executed plan to deliver incremental improvement. Instead, a mindset of possibility and continual adaptation, innovation and transformation will be more appropriate, alongside a willingness to work with ambiguity and operate in a 'messy' business as usual.

The second foundation is about keeping the organization's purpose and values as a strong 'North Star' rather than becoming too attached to a current set of products or customers or a specific delivery model. The Nordstrom mini case study (see **Chapter 14:** *Nordstrom*) describes how this North American retailer has retained absolute focus on its purpose of improving customer service and its values while at the same time not being limited to the upscale Nordstrom store setting or its expansion plans in Canada.

The third foundation relates to the concept of organization. One dictionary definition of 'organized' is "arranged according to a particular system" and "able to plan things carefully, keep things tidy and work effectively,"[27] and yet the word 'organization' can be traced back to the mid-15th-century medieval Latin *organizationem*, meaning "act or process of organizing, the arranging of parts in an organic whole."[28] Development of organizations over time has tended to gravitate toward the dictionary definition with structures, functions, forecasting and plans (classical theory), but we believe that this approach is no longer fit for purpose in such a dynamic world. Instead, organizations will be better served by the arranging of parts in an organic whole with decisions made closer to the point of service delivery and agility providing the ability to respond and react to developing or new situations. We like the way this spectrum of management evolution is described in Frederic Laloux's article, "The Future of Management Is Teal."[29] There are some parallels with our approach because the organizational structure is part of the Systems & Processes Element, the whole organization is driven by the purpose and values (Brand Identity), there is a focus on delivering the Customer Experience by 'one team' of brand ambassadors, while Measurement & Insight provides the intelligence for future decisions.

The after-effects of the pandemic continue to unfold and we believe that this state of readjustment will take many years, so it will be fascinating to see how much of the above materializes, to what extent and for how long.

TWO TOP TIPS

- Remind yourself that what you are building today might be redundant tomorrow – fast and agile is the best way.
- Take ownership of disruption in your organization or industry ... otherwise somebody else will.

WANT TO KNOW MORE?

To explore this area further, you might enjoy the following articles and books.

Neil Hodge. "Dealing with disruption." *Risk Management.*

A. Bhardawaj. "Organizational theories." *Economics Discussion.*

Steven Sinofsky. "The four stages of disruption." *Vox.*

Linda Jingfang Cai and Chris Yates. *Share: How Organizations Can Thrive in an Age of Networked Knowledge, Power and Relationships. New York: Bloomsbury Business.*

Global Consumer Insights Pulse Survey. "Consumers seek frictionless experiences in a world of disruptions." *PwC.*

CHAPTER 19
SUMMARY

"Customer service shouldn't just be a department,
it should be the entire company."
Tony Hsieh[1]

As we come to the end of this book, we trust that you will find it helpful to recap the core messages in a concise summary and, at the same time, that you will continue to revisit various chapters from time to time and explore some of the signposted additional resources.

The key context for customer service-focused organizations is a landscape that is volatile, uncertain, complex and ambiguous, and the meanings of these terms are continually becoming more extreme. The situation is fuelled by our ability (especially customers) to communicate information at lightning speed to millions of people. The very existence of the traditional organization is being challenged with new forms of collaboration and virtual organizations.

But against this dynamic landscape blurred by speed and change, customers remain, at the core, human beings with some basic and simple characteristics. We are emotional beings in need of a sense of purpose and a sense of belonging. These base needs are immensely powerful.

We believe that just three factors are combining to create a fundamental shift:

1. **Choice:** People are making decisions at a more emotional level, based on what is important to them and to express their opinion and identity.[2]
2. **Communication:** In our super-connected world, authenticity has become the new holy grail because organizations are no longer what

they say they are but are, instead, what others say they are,[3] especially customers.

3. **Control:** Organizations no longer 'own' their brands – the role of customers (past, current and potential) and other stakeholders as ambassadors for their organization has, in some ways, replaced the traditional marketing function.

These three factors are combining forces (we refer to this as C^3) to create a turbocharged shift in balance from traditional, fixed, singular organizational ownership and push marketing, to a less rigid, more complex concept of brand co-ownership and pull marketing. A perfect storm of values-driven choices, communication driving the power of stakeholder (especially customer) opinion and the concept of shared brand ownership has created a new paradigm that we refer to as the Values Economy.[4]

The traditional role of the organization was to bring order, direction and control. But, as the world becomes more dynamic, this approach is less and less relevant. It is more appropriate to have flexibility of objectives, action and reaction: to be able to adapt, to be agile. It takes too long for the traditional command-and-control approach to respond. Decentralized decision making is needed but this freedom needs to be exercised within a framework of 'the whole.' Alignment is key, summed up by Tony Hsieh's quote on the previous page (and first referenced in **Chapter 2**: *CX Evolution*): customer experience needs to be a deeply embedded mindset throughout the organization rather than viewed as the role of one function.

Of course, organizational alignment to deliver an excellent customer experience is no mean feat to achieve: it involves connecting organizations from the boardroom to the front line; aligning the hearts, minds and bodies of perhaps thousands of individuals to come together to represent a common way; overcoming barriers of individual interests, functions, different companies, geography and cultural differences; and doing this consistently, where customers can communicate any failure or shortcoming to millions in a flash. No mean feat indeed – but if it was easy to do, everybody would be doing it already. And we all know from personal experience that, while there are some notable exceptions, excellent customer experience is not commonplace.

While organizational alignment might not be easy to achieve in practice, we believe that it is nonetheless very straightforward and can be achieved by using our approach and framework, with the following key steps and supporting principles. We've kept these to the point, and you will have learned about the all-important detail in reading the book:

1. Clearly define your ambition to supercharge the customer experience with a values-led organizational alignment approach.
2. Establish a clear brand identity including a compelling purpose and set of values that engage customers and other stakeholders.
3. Embed the brand identity in every aspect of employee engagement from the first interaction to post-employment relationships.
4. Recognize the critical role of senior leadership behaviour in setting the example and reinforcing a customer experience focus for the organization.
5. Involve employees across hierarchies and functions throughout the alignment process.
6. Celebrate and share behaviours that represent the organization's values to positively reinforce them and create the 'heritage.'
7. Consciously design the customer experience to reflect the brand identity consistently across time, geography and channel.
8. Ensure that the organization's 'infrastructure' (systems and processes) supports and reinforces the brand identity, employee engagement and customer experience.
9. Proactively design the communication framework to maintain authenticity and alignment.
10. Make customer experience an organization-wide agenda, not confined to a single function.
11. Assess the impact of alignment at both quantitative and qualitative levels, with senior-level governance in place to ensure accountability.
12. Learn from other organizations but tailor solutions to your own unique context.
13. Adopt a mindset of continual improvement, refining what works well and enhancing what doesn't.
14. Recognize that leaders and organizations exist in a broader system and context.

And, last but not least:

15. Approach alignment with genuine good intention to build trust and authenticity.

As we say, very straightforward! You might wonder which of the steps is the most important, but we believe that the chance of success is optimized only by doing all of the above. The challenge is in the relentless pursuit of and obsession with authentic delivery: every action, every decision, every person, every day. And, as we have said before, we believe that practice makes more perfect. The added bonus is that delivering a great customer experience might also mean that the organization is performing more effectively, more efficiently and more profitably. And that the various stakeholders are proud of their association with the organization, becoming active advocates.

When you are considering what to introduce in your organization, you will achieve the best results by taking an aligned, joined-up view, so it is worth involving appropriate people from different disciplines when you are able. Here are four simple questions that are helpful to bear in mind:

1. How can the organization's brand identity (all aspects as detailed in **Chapter 7:** *Brand Identity*) be reflected in our people processes for directly employed employees and service partner employees (as detailed in **Chapter 8:** *Employee Engagement*)?

2. How can the organization's brand identity be reflected in all aspects of the customer experience (as detailed in **Chapter 9:** *Customer Experience*)?

3. How can the organization's systems and processes (all aspects as detailed in **Chapter 10:** *Systems & Processes*) support the alignment and coordination of the Brand Identity, Employee Engagement and Customer Experience Elements?

4. What measurement and insight processes (as detailed in **Chapter 11:** *Measurement & Insight*) can help us understand and assess impact and performance in the framework Elements: Brand Identity, Employee Engagement, Customer Experience, and Systems & Processes?

Finally, remember to consider all activities from strategy, management and delivery perspectives (vertical alignment, covered in **Part One:** *Backstory*) for the best impact.

As we highlighted in **Chapter 1:** *Introduction*, it is important to realize that the approach we suggest in itself is not what will make the difference. 'Content' (i.e., what you have read in this book) is vastly overrated and what is far more important is 'context' (i.e., how you choose to apply what you have learned). Each individual, group and organization's evolution is a process of constant interaction with and adaptation to the environment and context they find themselves in. It is, therefore, the way in which the approach is implemented by the people in an organization for its own situation that will determine the level of value creation.

Having said this, our approach does provide a framework that helps leaders in organizations to align and coordinate a range of various activities in a sustained way to supercharge the customer experience. It offers freedom within the framework to allow each organization to design and implement its own unique, fit-for-purpose solution, which can evolve over time. It enables synergies to be realized and duplication and waste to be minimized. And we know that it works – in organizations of different sizes, in different sectors and in different geographies. Conscious alignment of all aspects of the organization focused on the customer experience, informed throughout by the organization's purpose and values, is the core strength of the approach. It develops a level of agility that more traditionally organized businesses have struggled to achieve. As the pace of change and disruption continues to accelerate in the world, perhaps this deep sense of coherence will prove to be a priceless point of differentiation for organizations. Of course, it is not a 'fix-all' solution – nothing is – and successful application depends on effort, discipline and resilience.

We trust you have enjoyed *SUPERCHARGING THE CUSTOMER EXPERIENCE* and found much within our approach that resonates with you. We hope it has given you cause to think about your organization and 'the way things work around here,' and that it has stimulated ideas about how to design and deliver values-driven customer experience for sustained performance. We encourage you to do something different in the area of customer experience, small or large, as a result of what you have read. This is in keeping with our focus on action over knowledge. It will make the time you have spent reading our book worthwhile and also give us a great return on investment in our time writing it. We look forward to hearing your stories of how your thinking and practice have enabled you to supercharge the customer experience in your organization. And finally, just as we started this book with a quote (from Prime Minister Justin Trudeau), we would like to leave you with another. It is our variation on a saying by the Asaro tribe of Indonesia and Papua New Guinea that beautifully captures our approach to customer experience shared in this book: "If it is not in your muscles, it's just a rumour."

TWO TOP TIPS

- Take a whole-organization and culture perspective of customer experience rather than think of it as a function, process or toolkit.
- Reflect the values of the organization in the design and delivery of the customer experience.

TOP TIPS

TWO TOP TIPS COMPILATION

Chapter 1: *Introduction*
- No matter how volatile or uncertain the world may be, there will always be customers ... so treat them well.
- From the beginning, avoid treating customer experience in isolation because it is inextricably connected to the rest of the organization.

Chapter 2: *CX Evolution*
- Analyse the different ways customers interact with your organization and don't assume that what is in place today is good enough.
- Compare the experience your organization provides with experiences from other organizations, in other sectors and geographies because that's what your customers do.

Chapter 3: *Alignment*
- Examine how the different functions in your organization work together with the same objective and where they are working on their own in silos.
- Identify ways in which policies and procedures in your organization 'get in the way' of delivering a great customer experience and deal with them.

Chapter 4: *Beginning*
- Resist the temptation to plan forever – start implementing and adjust as you go.
- Take that leap of faith to collaborate – it can keep you accountable, innovate new ideas and take you out of your comfort zone.

Chapter 5: *SERVICEBRAND*
- Make decisions in the organization that are aligned with your values and benefit your customers.
- Experiment with how a proven framework could provide you with the guidance to make decisions to improve your customer experience.

Chapter 6: *Landscape*
- Pay attention to every detail in the customer journey because your customers can communicate their thoughts and feelings to millions of people all around the world in a heartbeat.
- Identify and close the gaps between the officially stated values of your organization and the way things are done in practice.

Chapter 7: *Brand Identity*
- Consider how customer-facing employees' remuneration packages could reflect the importance of their role as custodians of your organization's brand.
- Strive for brand identity consistency – every touchpoint, every day, everywhere.

Chapter 8: *Employee Engagement*
- Ask employees how to improve the customer experience, listen to suggestions and implement them.
- Do recognition well because it might be the best return on investment you ever make.

Chapter 9: *Customer Experience*
- Constantly remind yourself and all colleagues that without customers, your organization does not exist.
- Design the customer experience that you want to create and explore all of the CX tools at your disposal.

Chapter 10: *Systems & Processes*
- Clarify to support functions their role in supporting the alignment of the Elements: Brand Identity, Employee Engagement and Customer Experience.
- Put in place systems and processes in your organization that benefit the customer.

Chapter 11: *Measurement & Insight*
- Make decisions based on the measurement and insight being captured or stop capturing it.
- Resist the temptation to focus on the scores, because it's the feedback that helps you improve.

Chapter 16: *Behaviour*
- Remember that, from a customer perspective, employee behaviour often trumps technical competence.
- If there are negative emotions and behaviours that have become a habit, disrupt that negativity and create positive emotions and behaviours.

Chapter 17: *Digital*
- Adopting the latest digital innovation might be tempting but do the research to make sure it adds long-term value for your organization.
- Put yourself in the slippers of your customer when they're sitting at home in their pyjamas, sipping on a beverage of choice – ensure your digital experience is designed for their benefit.

Chapter 18: *Disruption*
- Remind yourself that what you are building today might be redundant tomorrow – fast and agile is the best way.
- Take ownership of disruption in your organization or industry … otherwise somebody else will.

Chapter 19: *Summary*
- Take a whole-organization and culture perspective of customer experience rather than think of it as a function, process or toolkit.
- Reflect the values of the organization in the design and delivery of the customer experience.

NOTES

Chapter 1: *Introduction*

1. Justin Trudeau, PC MP (born 1971) is a Canadian politician who became prime minister of Canada in 2015 and has led the Liberal Party since 2013. See Justin Trudeau, "Justin Trudeau's Davos address in full," *World Economic Forum*, last modified 23 January 2018. https://www.weforum.org/agenda/2018/01/pm-keynote-remarks-for-world-economic-forum-2018.

2. Waltraud Glaeser. *VUCA-WORLD*. https://www.vuca-world.org/vuca-bani-rupt-tuna/. Accessed 22nd June 2023.

3. Fairtrade International. 2020-2021 Annual Report. https://www.fairtrade.net/library/2020-2021-annual-report. Accessed 22 June 2023.

4. ET2C. "The rise of green consumerism," 28 September 2020. *ET2C International*. Accessed 15 May 2023.

5. Wentzel, D. "The effect of employee behavior on brand personality impressions and brand attitudes." *J. of the Acad. Mark*. Sci. 37, 359–374 (2009). https://doi.org/10.1007/s11747-009-0140-6. Accessed 10 October 2023.

6. State of Global Customer Service Report, Microsoft (2017). http://info.microsoft.com/rs/157-GQE-382/images/EN-CNTNT-Report-DynService-2017-global-state-customer-service-en-au.pdf. Accessed 10 October 2023.

7. McKinsey & Company. "The state of customer care in 2022," 8 July 2022. https://www.mckinsey.com/.../the-state-of-customer-care-in-2022. Accessed 22 May 2023.

8. Forrester (2022). "Forrester's US 2022 customer experience index: nearly 20% of brands see drop in customer experience quality." Accessed 10 October 2023.

9. Blake Morgan (2021). "10 stats showing the growth of CX." *Forbes*. https://www.forbes.com/sites/blakemorgan/2021/08/09/10-stats-showing-the-growth-of-cx/?sh=38062ac05f23. Accessed 10 October 2023.

10. B. Joseph Pine II and James H. Gilmore. "Welcome to the experience economy." *Harvard Business Review*, last modified July–August 1998. https://hbr.org/1998/07/welcome-to-the-experience-economy.

11. Maya Vautier, (2021). "EY Future Consumer Index: 68% of global consumers expect companies to solve sustainability issues," *EY Press Release*. https://www.ey.com/en_us/news/2021/06/ey-future-consumer-index-68-of-global-consumers-expect-companies-to-solve-sustainability-issues. Accessed 22 May 2023.

12. Andrew Morgan (2015). "The True Cost." Untold Creative in association with Life is My Movie Entertainment. https://truecostmovie.com/about/.

13. "Global consumer trust is on the offensive, survey finds." *SAI Global*, last modified 20 May 2019. https://www.saiglobal.com/hub/sai-global-newsroom/global-consumer-trust-is-on-the-offensive-survey-finds-2.

14. Maya Angelou (1928–2014) was an American poet, singer, memoirist and civil rights activist.

15. Howard Schultz and Dori Jones Yang (1997), *Pour Your Heart into It: How Starbucks Built a Company One Cup at a Time*. New York: Hyperion

Chapter 2: *CX Evolution*

1. Lewis P Carbone and Stephan H Haeckel (1994). "Engineering customer experiences." *Marketing Management*, https://www.researchgate.net/publication/265031917_Engineering_Customer_Experience. Accessed 30 August 2023.

2. Henry Ford (1863–1947) was an American industrialist and business magnate. He was the founder of Ford Motor Company, and chief developer of the assembly line technique of mass production.

3. Bruce Temkin is often referred to as the 'Godfather of Customer Experience' and is cofounder of the Customer Experience Professionals Association (CXPA).

4. Samuel Moore Walton (1918–1992) was an American business magnate best known for founding the retailer Walmart in 1962.

5. Harry Gordon Selfridge (1858–1947) was an American retail magnate who founded the London-based department store Selfridges.

6. Marshall Field (1834–1906) was an American entrepreneur and the founder of Marshall Field and Company, the Chicago-based department store.

7. https://www.cxpa.org/home. (Accessed 9 August 2023).

8. Peter Drucker (1909–2005) was an Austrian-American management consultant, educator and author, whose writings contributed to the philosophical and practical foundations of modern management theory.

9. PwC (2018). "Experience is everything: Here's how to get it right." https://www.pwc.com/us/en/advisory-services/publications/consumer-intelligence-series/pwc-consumer-intelligence-series-customer-experience.pdf. Accessed 4 September 2023.

10. Jeff Bezos (1964–) is the founder, executive chairman, former president and CEO of Amazon, the world's largest e-commerce and cloud computing company.

11. Gartner (2023). "Gartner's top customer service trends and priorities for 2023." https://www.gartner.com/en/customer-service-support/insights/service-leaders-priorities. Accessed 10 October 2023.

12. Tony Hsieh (1973–2020) was an American internet entrepreneur and venture capitalist. He retired as the CEO of the online shoe and clothing company Zappos in August 2020 after 21 years.

13. Rachel Diebner, Mike Thompson, David Malfara, Kevin Neher and Maxence Vancauwenberghe (2021). "Prediction: The future of CX." https://www.mckinsey.com/capabilities/growth-marketing-and-sales/our-insights/prediction-the-future-of-cx. Accessed 5 September 2023.

14. International Trade Statistics (1962). "International Trade Statistics 1900–1960." https://unstats.un.org/unsd/trade/imts/Historical%20data%201900-1960.pdf. Accessed 5th September 2023

15. Henry Ford (1863–1947) was an American industrialist and business magnate. He was the founder of Ford Motor Company, and chief developer of the assembly line technique of mass production.

16. United Nations Conference on Trade and Development (2018). "50 years of review of maritime transport, 1968-2018." https://unctad.org/system/files/official-document/dtl2018d1_en.pdf . Accessed 5 September 2023.

17. Fred Smith (1944–) is the founder and chairman of FedEx Corporation, the world's largest transportation company.

18. Kevin Bartley. "Big data statistics: How much data is there in the world?" https://rivery.io/blog/big-data-statistics-how-much-data-is-there-in-the-world/. Accessed 5 September 2023.

19. Bill Gates (1955–) is an American business magnate, investor and philanthropist best known for cofounding the software giant Microsoft.

20. Salesforce (2023). "State of the connected customer 3rd edition." https://www.salesforce.com/eu/form/pdf/state-of-the-connected-customer-3rd-edition/. Accessed 5 September 2023.

21. McKinsey (2021). "The value of getting personalization right—or wrong—is multiplying." https://www.mckinsey.com/capabilities/growth-marketing-and-sales/our-insights/the-value-of-getting-personalization-right-or-wrong-is-multiplying. Accessed 5 September 2023.

22. Colin Jeffrey, Oliver Vernon-Harcourt and Harvey Lewis (2019). "The Deloitte consumer review. Made-to-order: The rise of mass personalization." https://www2.deloitte.com/content/dam/Deloitte/ch/Documents/consumer-business/ch-en-consumer-business-made-to-order-consumer-review.pdf. Accessed 5 September 2023.

23. Blake Morgan (2020). "50 stats showing the power of personalization." https://www.forbes.com/sites/blakemorgan/2020/02/18/50-stats-showing-the-power-of-personalization/. Accessed 5 September 2023.

24. Paige Bennett (2022). "How customer experience has evolved over the last decade." https://blog.hubspot.com/service/how-customer-experience-has-evolved#:~:text=,move%20on%20with%20their%20life. Accessed 10 October 2023.

25. Kelsey Jones (2018). "Personalized marketing is more than just a name." https://www.salesforce.com/ca/blog/2017/12/personalized-marketing.html#:~:text=According%20to%20Salesforce%27s%20Fourth%20Annual,vendor%20doesn%27t%20personalize%20communications. Accessed 5 September 2023.

26. Alec Bokman, Lars Fiedler, Jesko Perrey and Andrew Pickersgill (2014). "Five facts: How customer analytics boosts corporate performance." https://www.mckinsey.com/capabilities/growth-marketing-and-sales/our-insights/five-facts-how-customer-analytics-boosts-corporate-performance. Accessed 5 September 2023.

27. Howard Schultz (1953–) is an American businessman and author who served as the chairman and CEO of Starbucks from 1986 to 2000, from 2008 to 2017, and as interim CEO from 2022 to 2023.

28. Daniel Lemin (2023). "Customer experience evolution: From 2015 insights to 2023 realities." *Convince & Convert*, https://www.convinceandconvert.com/customer-experience/customer-experience-evolution-from-2015-insights-to-2023-realities/#:~:text=,told%20consumers%20about%20their%20products. Accessed 10 October 2023.

29. Salesforce. "What are customer expectations, and how have they changed?" https://www.salesforce.com/resources/articles/customer-expectations/?bc=DB&sfdc-redirect=369. Accessed 5 September 2023.

30. Zendesk (2020). "Customer service gets conversational." https://www.zendesk.com/publications/customer-service-gets-conversational/. Accessed 10 October 2023.

31. Emma Sopadjieva, Utpal M. Dholakia and Beth Benjamin (2017). "A study of 46,000 shoppers shows that omnichannel retailing works." https://hbr.org/2017/01/a-study-of-46000-shoppers-shows-that-omnichannel-retailing-works?utm_source=Triggermail&utm_medium=email&utm_campaign=P. Accessed 5 September 2023.

32. Pradeep Vasudev (2023). "Omnichannel customer engagement: How to manage effectively." https://www.sprinklr.com/blog/omnichannel-customer-engagement/. Accessed 5 September 2023.

33. Deloitte & Informatica (2023). "5 ways to enhance the customer experience with cloud data management." https://www2.deloitte.com/content/dam/Deloitte/us/Documents/about-deloitte/us-five-ways-to-enhance-the-customer-experience-with-cloud-data-management.pdf. Accessed 5 September 2023.

Chapter 3: *Alignment*

1. Halford Edward Luccock (1885–1960) was a prominent American Methodist minister, professor of Homiletics at Yale's Divinity School (1928–1953) and author.

2. Sir John Reginald Hartnell Bond (1941–) is a businessman who has served as chairman of HSBC, Vodafone and Xstrata. Quoted in Jeffrey W. Bennett, Thomas E. Pernsteiner, Paul Kocourek and Steven B. Hedlund, "The organization vs. the strategy: Solving the alignment paradox." *Strategy+Business*. https://www.strategy-business.com/article/14114?gko=183ff. Last modified 1 October 2020.

3. Alan Williams and Sam Williams (2021). *The Values Economy: How to Deliver Purpose-Driven Service for Sustained Performance*. LID Publishing, London.

4. Arvind Hickman, "Oxfam sex scandal wiped 400m from brand valuation, report reveals." *PRWeek*. https://www.prweek.com/article/1522440/oxfam-sex-scandal-wiped-400m-brand-valuation-report-reveals. Last modified 9 January 2019.

5. John Francis Welch Jr. (1935–2020) was chairman and CEO of General Electric between 1981 and 2001. Quoted in Noel Tichy and Ram Charan, "Speed, simplicity, self-confidence: An interview with Jack Welch." *Harvard Business Review*. https://hbr.org/1989/09/speed-simplicity-self-confidence-an-interview-with-jack-welch. Last modified 2 March 2020.

6. Robert S. Kaplan and David P. Norton. "The office of strategy management." *Harvard Business Review*. https://hbr.org/2005/10/the-office-of-strategy-management. Last modified October 2005.

7. Peter M. Senge, Bryan Smith, Art Kleiner, Richard Ross and Charlotte Roberts (1994). *The Fifth Discipline Fieldbook: Strategies and Tools for Building a Learning Organization* (New York: Currency Doubleday).

8. Ken Perlman is one of today's best-known clawhammer banjo players and an executive consultant. Quoted in John Kotter, "When CEOs talk strategy, 70% of the company doesn't get it." *Forbes*. https://www.forbes.com/sites/johnkotter/2013/07/09/heres-why-ceo-strategies-fall-on-deaf-ears. Last modified 9 July 2013.

9. Stephen R. Covey (1932–2012) was an American educator and businessman. See Stephen R. Covey, A. Roger Merrill and Rebecca R. Merrill (1995), *First Things First.* New York: Simon & Schuster.

10. Jonathan Trevor and Barry Varcoe. "How aligned is your organization?" *Harvard Business Review*. https://hbr.org/2017/02/how-aligned-is-your-organization. Last modified 7 February 2017.

11. Christopher M. Branson. "Achieving organizational change through values alignment," *Journal of Educational Administration* 46 (2008): 376–395.

12. Le Fevre et al (2023). "Does a conscious connection to personal values have value? A mixed methods exploration of individuals' lived experience." *Occupational Psychology Outlook* 2(1):14-23. BPS - The British Psychological Society. Accessed 29 August 2023.

13. Natalia Karelaia (2020). "INSEAD knowledge, the advantages of being (seen as) authentic." https://knowledge.insead.edu/leadership-organisations/advantages-being-seen-authentic#:~:text=Essentially%2C%20as%20social%20creatures%2C%20we,to%20individuals%20we%20can%20trust. Accessed 29 August 2023.

14. Maria Guadalupe, Zoe Kinias and Florian Schloderer (2020). "Individual identity and organizational identification: Evidence from a field experiment." *American Economic Association*, AEA Papers and Proceedings, VOL. 110, May 2020 (pp. 193-98. https://www.aeaweb.org/articles?id=10.1257/pandp.20201092#:~:text=Abstract,on%20average%20reduces%20organizational%20attachment. Accessed 29 August 2023.

15. George Labovitz is a businessman, author and award-winning professor at the Boston University School of Management. Quoted in Derrick Vikiru. "Strategic alignment drives greater results." *Envision*. https://www.envsionmag.com/2020/09/09/strategic-alignment-drives-greater-results. Last modified 9 September 2020.

16. "The high cost of low performance: The essential role of communications." *Project Management Institute*. 2013. https://www.pmi.org/-/media/pmi/documents/public/pdf/learning/thought-leadership/pulse/the-essential-role-of-communications.pdf?v=e1f0e914-4b3a-456f-b75e-40101632258b&sc_lang_temp=en. Accessed 10 November 2020.

17. Erik Berggren and Jac Fitz-enz. "How smart HCM drives financial performance." *Docplayer.net*. https://docplayer.net/14010836-Financial-performance-by.html. Accessed 7 March 2020.

18. Chris Houpis. "Sales and marketing alignment: Collaboration + cooperation = peak performance." Aberdeen Research, 2010. https://www.dnb.com/content/dam/english/dnb-solutions/sales-and-marketing/aberdeen_report_sales_and_marketing_alignment_2010_09.pdf. Accessed 10 November 2020.

19. Henry Ford (1863–1947) was an American industrialist and business magnate. He was the founder of Ford Motor Company and chief developer of the assembly line technique of mass production.

20. Dan Witters and John H. Fleming. "Do consumers 'get' your brand?" *Gallup*. https://news.gallup.com/businessjournal/153005/Consumers-Brand.aspx?utm_source=google&utm_medium=rss&utm_campaign=syndication#3. Last modified 29 February 2012.

21. Robert S. Kaplan (1940–) is a Harvard Business School emeritus professor famous for creating the Balanced Scorecard with David P. Norton. See Robert S. Kaplan, "Mapping your board's effectiveness." *Harvard Business School*. https://hbswk.hbs.edu/item/mapping-your-boards-effectiveness. Last modified 30 August 2004.

Chapter 4: *Beginning*

1. Arthur Robert Ashe Jr. (1943–1993) was an American professional tennis player who was the only Black man ever to win the singles titles at Wimbledon, the US Open and the Australian Open.

2. *BQF website*. https://www.bqf.org.uk/about-us/. Accessed 29 August 2023.

3. "EFQM model." *EFQM*. https://www.efqm.org/index.php/efqm-model. Last modified 9 July 2013.

4. "How we assess." *Hospitality Assured*. http://www.hospitalityassured.com/quality-is-everything. Accessed 4 September 2020.

5. See https://www.investorsinpeople.com.

6. James L. Heskett, Thomas O. Jones, Gary W. Loveman, W. Earl Sasser, Jr. and Leonard A. Schlesinger. "Putting the service-profit chain to work." *Harvard Business Review*. https://hbr.org/2008/07/putting-the-service-profit-chain-to-work. Last modified July-August 2008.

7. Steve Jobs (1955–2011) was an American business magnate famous worldwide as a cofounder of Apple. Interview in *Business Week*, 25 May 1998.

Chapter 6: *Landscape*

1. The original version is a calypso song written by jazz musicians Melvin 'Sy' Oliver and James 'Trummy' Young.

2. "Paris Fashion Week: Innovation and Progressive Values Take Centre Stage." *The Global Herald*. Last modified 28 February 2020. https://theglobalherald.com/news/paris-fashion-week-innovation-and-progressive-values-take-centre-stage.

3. See www.worldvaluesday.com.

4. Kate Taylor. "McDonald's is flipping its iconic golden arches upside down in 'Celebration of Women' — and people are freaking out." *Business Insider*. http://businessinsider.com/mcdonalds-flips-arches-international-womens-day-2019-3?r=US&IR=T. Last modified 8 March 2018.

5. McDonald's 2021–2022 Global Diversity, Equity and Inclusion Report. McDonald's 2021–2022 Global Diversity, Equity and Inclusion Report (*mcdonalds.com*).

6. Simon Sinek. "Start with why." TEDx Puget Sound. https://www.youtube.com/watch?v=u4ZoJKF_VuA&t=8s. Last modified 28 September 2009.

7. Anjali Lai. "The values-based consumer." *Forbes*. https://www.forbes.com/sites/forrester/2017/03/22/the-values-based-consumer/?sh=665cb9ef23af. Last modified 22 March 2017.

8. *Forrester Data Consumer Technographics North American Omnibus Survey* (2017). Cambridge, Mass.: Forrester.

9. Ibid.

10. With the advent of AI, it's no longer 'human' to do or to think; now, human beings' expressions of compassion set them apart. See Thomas L. Friedman, "From hands to heads to hearts." *The New York Times*. https://www.nytimes.com/2017/01/04/opinion/from-hands-to-heads-to-hearts.html. Last modified 4 January 2017.

11. Oxford Dictionaries' 2016 word of the year was 'post-truth,' meaning "circumstances in which objective facts are less influential in shaping public opinion than appeals to emotion and personal belief." See "Word of the Year 2016." *Oxford Languages*. https://languages.oup.com/word-of-the-year/2016. Last modified 16 November 2016.

12. A sense of purpose or meaning is a deep-seated drive that is critical to our psychological health, adaptation and survival. In fact, a study by researchers from Stanford University even proves that a sense of meaning leads to long-lasting wellbeing, while positive emotional experiences yield temporary effects. See Emily Esfahani Smith and Jennifer Aaker, "In 2017, pursue meaning instead of happiness." *The Cut*. https://www.thecut.com/2016/12/in-2017-pursue-meaning-instead-of-happiness.html. Last modified 30 December 2016.

13. 2020-2021 Annual Report – *fairtrade.net*. https://www.fairtrade.net/library/2020-2021-annual-report

14. Julia Naftulin, Tyler Sonnemaker, Juliana Kaplan and Tanya Dua. "The biggest companies no longer advertising on Facebook due to the platform's lack of hate-speech moderation." *Business Insider*. https://www.businessinsider.com/companies-no-longer-advertising-on-facebook-after-poor-speech-moderation-2020-6?r=US&IR=T. Last modified 1 July 2020.

15. Ashley Armstrong and Katherine Griffiths. "Aberdeen Standard Investments dumps Boohoo shares over pay scandal." *The Times*. https://www.thetimes.co.uk/article/aberdeen-standard-investments-sells-stake-in-boohoo-amid-factory-pay-row-xzjrksskc. Last modified 10 July 2020.

16. "Consumer-goods' brands that demonstrate commitment to sustainability outperform those that don't." *Nielsen*. https://www.nielsen.com/us/en/press-releases/2015/consumer-goods-brands-that-demonstrate-commitment-to-sustainability-outperform. Last modified 12 October 2015.

17. Bill Pelster, Josh Bersin and Jeff Schwartz. "Culture and engagement: The naked organization." *Quartz*. https://qz.com/374973/culture-and-engagement-the-naked-organization. Last modified 1 April 2015.

18. Thomas Stewart. "Who owns your brand?" *CBS News*. https://www.cbsnews.com/news/who-owns-your-brand. Last modified 26 April 2011.

19. Alan Williams, "Shhh ... the Values Economy has arrived." *World Values Day*. https://www.worldvaluesday.com/values-economy-arrived. Accessed 29 April 2018.

20. Sir John Whitmore (2009.) *Coaching for Performance: GROWing Human Potential and Purpose*, 4th ed. London: Nicholas Brealey Press.

21. James C. Collins and Jerry I. Porras (1994.) *Built to Last: Successful Habits of Visionary Companies*. New York: Harper Collins.

22. Eric Flamholtz. "Corporate culture and the bottom line." *European Management Journal* 19 (2001): 268-275.

23. See John P. Kotter and James L. Heskett (1992). *Corporate Culture and Performance*. New York: Free Press; James C. Collins and Jerry I. Porras (1994), *Built to Last: Successful Habits of Visionary Companies*. New York: HarperCollins. And Rajendra S. Sisodia, David B. Wolfe and Jagdish N. Sheth (2007) *Firms of Endearment: The Pursuit of Purpose and Profit*. Upper Saddle River, NJ: Wharton School Press.

24. Quoted in Laura Chamberlain, "Four key enablers to employee engagement." *Personnel Today*. https://www.personneltoday.com/hr/four-key-enablers-to-employee-engagement. Last modified 27 January 2012.

25. Howard D. Schultz (1953–) is an American businessman. He served as the chairman and chief executive officer (CEO) of the Starbucks Coffee Company from 1986 to 2000 and from 2008 to 2017.

26. Rafe Offer has been a leader in the areas of teams and innovation at some of the world's most widely known brands. For example, he has been global marketing director of Coca-Cola, director of global marketing at The Walt Disney Company and a director of innovation for the global drinks giant Diageo.

27. Ivan Misner. "In business, culture eats strategy for breakfast." *FOX Business*. http://smallbusiness.foxbusiness.com/legal-hr/2012/09/27/in-business-culture-eats-strategy-for-breakfast/#ixzz2CkyBVqMi. Last modified 27 September 2012.

28. *Leading Through Connections: Highlights of the Global CEO Study* (IBM, 2012). https://www.ibm.com/downloads/cas/3O8OG8RL. Accessed 10 November 2020.

29. Thomas Peters and Waterman (1982). *In Search of Excellence: Lessons from America's Best-Run Companies*. New York: Harper & Row.

30. See https://jobs.netflix.com/culture

31. Djuna Thurley, Federico Mor, Lorna Booth and Lorraine Conway. "The collapse of Carillion." *UK Parliament*. https://researchbriefings.parliament.uk/ResearchBriefing/Summary/CBP-8206. Last modified 14 March 2018.

32. PwC. "Australian government refers PwC tax leaks scandal to police." *Financial Times* https://www.ft.com/content/ca2dd8fc-b3a4-43fd-a474-d600f4498687. Accessed 20 July 2023.

33. Donald Sull, Stefano Turconi and Charles Sull. "When it comes to culture, does your company walk the talk?" *MIT Sloan Management Review*. https://sloanreview.mit.edu/article/when-it-comes-to-culture-does-your-company-walk-the-talk. Last modified 21 July 2020.

34. Ken Blanchard and Phil Hodges (2003). *The Servant Leader* (Nashville: Thomas Nelson).

35. *Employee Outlook*. CIPD, 2012. https://www.bl.uk/collection-items/employee-outlook-autumn-2012. Accessed 24 November 2020.

36. Ken Blanchard, Michael O'Connor and Jim Ballard (1997). *Managing by Values*. San Francisco: Berrett-Koehler.

37. *Employee Outlook* (CIPD, 2012).

38. Ibid

39. Peter Cheese, CEO of the Chartered Institute for Personnel and Development (CIPD) in the UK. See *Employee Outlook* (CIPD, 2012).

40. Margaret Heffernan (2011). *Wilful Blindness: Why We Ignore the Obvious at Our Peril.* London: Simon & Schuster.

41. Lawrence Peter 'Yogi' Berra (1925–2015) was an American professional baseball catcher, manager and coach.

Chapter 7: *Brand Identity*

1. Jeff Bezos (1964–) is the founder, CEO and president of the technology company Amazon.

2. Seth W. Godin (1960–) is an American author and entrepreneur. See Seth Godin, "Define: Brand." *Seth's Blog*, https://seths.blog/2009/12/define-brand. Last modified 13 December 2009.

3. Kathryn Wheeler. "Brand identity: How to develop a unique & memorable brand in 2023." *Hubspot*. https://blog.hubspot.com/agency/develop-brand-identity. Accessed 12 October 2023.

4. Ross Kimbarovsky. "Brand identity: The definitive guide to building a strong, consistent, and memorable brand image in 2023." *Crowdspring*. https://www.crowdspring.com/blog/brand-identity/. Accessed 10 October 2023.

5. "Sharing an employer's core values is leading driver to boost employee engagement." *CISION PRWeb*. https://www.prweb.com/releases/2009/10/prweb3134014.htm. Last modified 30 October 2009.

6. Charles A. O'Reilly, III, Jennifer Chatman and David F. Caldwell (2017). "People and organizational culture: a profile comparison approach to assessing person-organization fit." *Academy of Management Journal* Vol. 34, No. 3. https://journals.aom.org/doi/abs/10.5465/256404. Accessed 29 August 2023.

7. Philip Kotler. "Branding: from purpose to beneficence." *The Marketing Journal*. https://www.marketingjournal.org/brand-purpose-to-beneficence-philip-kotler. Last modified 22 March 2016.

8. Scott David Cook (1952–) is an American businessman and a cofounder of Intuit.

9. Sam Nathan and Karl Schmidt. "From promotion to emotion: Connecting B2B customers to brands." *Think with Google*. https://www.thinkwithgoogle.com/marketing-resources/promotion-emotion-b2b. Last modified October 2013.

10. Marc Schenker. "Icon, mark, brand, emblem: The missing guide to logo design terms." *Creative Market*. https://creativemarket.com/blog/logo-design-terms. Last modified 6 March 2017.

11. Ina Verstl (2023). "Reaching maturity: US craft beer in 2022." *Brauwelt International*. https://brauwelt.com/en/international-report/the-americas/645628-reaching-maturity-us-craft-beer-in-2022#:~:text=The%20number%20of%20operating%20craft%20breweries%20continued%20to,3%2C838%20taproom%20breweries%2C%20and%20261%20regional%20craft%20breweries. Accessed 26 June 2023.

12. "The top 50 biggest craft breweries in America in 2021 by sales volume." *Craft Brewing Business* (2021). https://www.craftbrewingbusiness.com/featured/the-top-50-biggest-craft-breweries-in-america-in-2021-by-sales-volume/. Accessed 26 June 2023.

13. "How we're structured." Ben & Jerry's. https://www.benjerry.co.uk/about-us/how-were-structured. Accessed 4 August 2020.

14. Howard D. Schultz (1953–) is an American businessman. He served as the chairman and chief executive officer (CEO) of the Starbucks Coffee Company from 1986 to 2000 and from 2008 to 2017. See Howard Schultz and Dori Jones Yang (1997). *Pour Your Heart into It: How Starbucks Built a Company One Cup at a Time.* New York: Hyperion.

15. Ann Hodge. "5 examples of brand authenticity to help you make a profit." *Instapage.* https://instapage.com/blog/building-brand-authenticity. Last modified 24 June 2020.

Chapter 8: *Employee Engagement*

1. Stephen R. Covey (1932–2012) was an American educator and businessman. See Stephen R. Covey. *The 7 Habits of Highly Effective People.* New York: Free Press, 1989.

2. Timothy R. Clark (1964–) is an author and management consultant who specializes in organizational change, leadership development and strategy. See Timothy R. Clark. "The 5 ways that highly engaged employees are different." *TLNT.* https://www.tlnt.com/the-5-ways-that-highly-engaged-employees-are-different. Last modified 19 June 2012.

3. "Business Process Outsourcing." *Statista.* https://www.statista.com/outlook/15200/100/business-process-outsourcing/worldwide. Accessed 10 October 2023.

4. "Employee engagement benchmark study, 2017." *Qualtrics.* https://www.qualtrics.com/xm-institute/employee-engagement-benchmark-study-2017. Accessed 18 March 2020

5. Denise Lee Yohn (2023). "Engaged employees create better customer experiences." *Harvard Business Review,* https://hbr.org/2023/04/engaged-employees-create-better-customer-experiences#:~:text=,driver%20of%20the%20customer%20experience. Accessed 10 October 2023.

6. "Q12 employee engagement center." *Gallup.* https://www.gallup.com/products/170969/q12-employee-engagement-center.aspx. Accessed 10 November 2020.

7. "US brand marketing in a crisis: Why now is not the time for silence." *Opinium,* 2020. https://www.opinium.com/wp-content/uploads/2020/03/Opinium-US_Brand-marketing-in-a-crisis_4.5.2020.pdf. Accessed 4 August 2020.

8. Shane Green (1970–2020) was a technology entrepreneur, self-made millionaire and advocate of internet privacy. See "Company culture: A Q&A with Shane Green, president of SGEi." *Benbria.* https://www.benbria.com/company-culture-qa-shane-green. Last modified 27 October 2016.

9. "Gallup's state of the global workforce 2023 report: The voice of the world's employees." https://www.gallup.com/workplace/349484/state-of-the-global-workplace.aspx. Accessed 11 October 2023.

10. A phenomenon that describes record numbers of people leaving their jobs after the COVID-19 pandemic ends. https://www.weforum.org/agenda/2021/11/what-is-the-great-resignation-and-what-can-we-learn-from-it/. Accessed 10 October 2023.

11. Jeanne Meister. "Employee activism is on the rise: Workers protest return to office." *Forbes.* https://www.forbes.com/sites/jeannemeister/2023/06/05/employee-activism-workers-protest-return-to-office/?sh=40a48cbf29af. Last updated 5 June 2023.

12. David MacLeod, OBE, is a cofounder of the Employee Engagement Task Force, launched by the UK prime minister in 2011. See "What is employee engagement?" Engage for Success. https://engageforsuccess.org/what-is-employee-engagement. Accessed 18 March 2020.

13. Ibid.

14. John Gibbons. "Employee engagement: A review of current research and its implications." Conference Board, 2006. https://www.conference-board.org/publications/publicationdetail.cfm?publicationid=1238&centerid=4. Accessed 19 March 2020.

15. David MacLeod and Nita Clarke. "Engaging for success." *Department for Business, Innovation and Skills,* 2009. https://engageforsuccess.org/wp-content/uploads/2015/08/file52215.pdf. Accessed 10 November 2020.

16. Zameena Mejia. "Nearly 9 out of 10 millennials would consider taking a pay cut to get this." *CNBC News*. https://www.cnbc.com/2018/06/27/nearly-9-out-of-10-millennials-would-consider-a-pay-cut-to-get-this.html. Accessed 14 November 2019.

17. Jeanne Meister (2023). "Employee activism is on the rise: Workers protest return to office." *Forbes*. https://www.forbes.com/sites/jeannemeister/2023/06/05/employee-activism-workers-protest-return-to-office/?sh=269d051529af. Last modified 5 June 2023.

18. "Sharing an employer's core values is leading driver to boost employee engagement." *CISION PRWeb*. https://www.prweb.com/releases/2009/10/prweb3134014.htm. Last modified 30 October 2009.

19. Annamarie Mann and Nate Dvorak. "Employee recognition: Low cost, high impact." *Gallup*. https://www.gallup.com/workplace/236441/employee-recognition-low-cost-high-impact.aspx. Last modified 28 June 2016.

20. Claire Hastwell. "Creating a culture of recognition." *Great Place to Work*. https://www.greatplacetowork.com/resources/blog/creating-a-culture-of-recognition. Last modified 27 January 2020.

21. "The human capital platform." *Deloitte*. https://www2.deloitte.com/us/en/pages/human-capital/topics/bersin-insights-and-services-for-hr.html. Accessed 20 March 2020.

22. "The global state of employee engagement." *Office Vibe*. https://officevibe.com/state-employee-engagement. Accessed 18 March 2020.

23. Mary Kay Ash (1918–2001) was an American businesswoman who founded Mary Kay Cosmetics.

24. "Is Your Organization Simply Irresistible?" *Deloitte*, 2019. https://www2.deloitte.com/content/dam/Deloitte/at/Documents/human-capital/at-is-your-organization-simply-irresistible.pdf. Accessed 20 March 2020.

25. "Employee recognition survey." *Globoforce*, 2012. http://go.globoforce.com/rs/globoforce/images/SHRMFALL2012Survey_web.pdf. Accessed 20 March 2020.

26. Sir Richard Branson (1950–) is the founder of the Virgin Group and an author and philanthropist.

27. Marcus Buckingham and Curt Coffman (2005). *First, Break All the Rules*. London: Simon & Schuster.

28. John Gibbons. "Employee engagement: A review of current research and its implications." *The Conference Board*, 2006. https://www.conference-board.org/publications/publicationdetail.cfm?publicationid=1238&centerid=4.), Accessed 19 March 2020.

29. Vijaya Mani. "Analysis of employee engagement and its predictors." *International Journal of Human Resource Studies* 1 (2011). https://pdfs.semanticscholar.org/5266/d4025e1169f39a8e8f2f4459db9b0e28d783.pdf?_ga=2.3355065.80399140.1550527229-1396868609.1548349636. Accessed 18 March 2020.

30. Santiago Jaramillo. "Four lessons from companies that get employee engagement right." *Forbes*. https://www.forbes.com/sites/forbeshumanresourcescouncil/2018/06/22/four-lessons-from-companies-that-get-employee-engagement-right/#958aa2e21bd2. Last modified 22 June 2018.

31. Schrita Osborne and Mohamad S. Hammoud. "Effective employee engagement in the workplace." *International Journal of Applied Management and Technology* 16 (2017): 50–67. https://scholarworks.waldenu.edu/ijamt/vol16/iss1/4/. Accessed 10 October 2023.

32. Joe Dettmann and Jeff Stier. "Five leadership behaviors for all of us during COVID-19." *EY Workforce*. https://www.ey.com/en_gl/workforce/five-leadership-behaviors-for-all-of-us-during-covid-19. last Modified 18 August 2020.

33. Vijaya Mani. "Analysis of employee engagement and its predictors." *International Journal of Human Resource Studies* 1 (2011). https://pdfs.semanticscholar.org/5266/d4025e1169f39a8e8f2f4459db9b0e28d783.pdf?_ga=2.3355065.80399140.1550527229-1396868609.1548349636. Accessed 18 March 2020.

34. "Engagement and the global workplace." *SteelCase*. https://info.steelcase.com/global-employee-engagement-workplace-report?utm_campaign=2016-WPR-Campaign-En&utm_medium=HomeInsights&utm_source=Steelcase.com#engagement. Accessed 10 November 2020.

Chapter 9: *Customer Experience*

1. Samuel Moore Walton (1918–1992) was an American businessman and entrepreneur best known for founding the retail chain Walmart, which grew to be the world's largest corporation. See *Sam Walton: Made in America, My Story* (1993). New York: Bantam.

2. Henry Ford (1863–1947) was an American industrialist and business magnate. He was the founder of Ford Motor Company, and chief developer of the assembly line technique of mass production.

3. Rebecca Hinds and Sarang Gupta (2023). "Customer experience is everyone's responsibility." *Harvard Business Review*. https://hbr.org/2023/04/customer-experience-is-everyones-responsibility. Accessed 27 June 2023.

4. "Customer Experience Management (CEM)." *Gartner Glossary*. https://www.gartner.com/it-glossary/customer-experience-management-cem. Accessed 9 August 2019.

5. Steve Cannon is an American businessman who is president and CEO of the AMB Group. Quoted in Jim Tierney. "Mercedes Benz CEO: Customer experience is the new marketing." *Loyalty 360*. https://loyalty360.org/content-gallery/daily-news/mercedes-benz-ceo-customer-experience-is-the-new-marketing. Last modified 8 October 2014.

6. Matthew Dixon, Karen Freeman and Nicholas Toman. "Stop trying to delight your customers." *Harvard Business Review*. https://hbr.org/2010/07/stop-trying-to-delight-your-customers. Last modified July–August 2020.

7. Matthew Dixon, Nick Toman and Rick DeLisi (2013). *The Effortless Experience: Conquering the New Battleground for Customer Loyalty*. London: Portfolio.

8. David Clarke and Ron Kinghorn. "Experience is everything: Here's how to get it right." *pwc.com/future-of-cx*. https://www.pwc.com/us/en/services/consulting/library/consumer-intelligence-series/future-of-customer-experience.html. Accessed 10 October 2023.

9. Douglas 'Sandy' Warner (1946–) began his career as an officer's assistant in 1968 and later became chairman of the board of J. P. Morgan.

10. Steve Jobs (1955–2011) was an American business magnate famous worldwide as a cofounder of Apple. See "Steve Jobs – Business Strategy: Start with your customer and work backwards to a product or service." YouTube. https://www.youtube.com/watch?v=48j493tfO-o. Last modified 6 August 2017.

11. Leonardo da Vinci (1452–1519) was an Italian polymath of the Renaissance whose areas of interest included invention, drawing, painting, sculpture, architecture, science, music, mathematics, engineering, literature, anatomy, geology, astronomy, botany, palaeontology and cartography.

12. Simon Sinek (2011). *Start with Why: How Great Leaders Inspire Everyone to Take Action*. London: Penguin.

13. Alfonso Pulido, Dorian Stone and John Strevel. "The three Cs of customer satisfaction: Consistency, consistency, consistency." *McKinsey*. https://www.mckinsey.com/industries/retail/our-insights/the-three-cs-of-customer-satisfaction-consistency-consistency-consistency. Last modified 1 March 2014.

14. "A consistent customer experience builds a trusted brand." *Forrester*. https://go.forrester.com/blogs/14-05-07-a_consistent_customer_experience_builds_a_trusted_brand. Last modified 7 May 2014.

15. Lucy Hunt. "How consistent branding is being challenged in the digital age." *Techipedia*. http://www.techipedia.com/2011/consistent-branding. Last modified 9 November 2011.

16. Jake Sorofman. "In customer experience, consistency is the new delight." *BW CIO World*. http://bwcio.businessworld.in/article/In-Customer-Experience-Consistency-is-the-New-Delight/23-09-2015-109488. Last modified 23 September 2015.

17. James Allen, Frederick F. Reichheld, Barney Hamilton and Rob Markey. "Closing the delivery gap." *Bain & Company*, 2005. https://www.bain.com/contentassets/41326e0918834cd1a0102fdd0810535d/bb_closing_delivery_gap.pdf. Accessed 12 November 2020.

18. Christopher McCormick is an American businessman and the former CEO of L. L. Bean, a mail-order, online and retail company. Quoted in Blake Morgan. "101 of the best customer experience quotes." *Forbes*. https://www.forbes.com/sites/blakemorgan/2019/04/03/101-of-the-best-customer-experience-quotes/?sh=60a81b4b45fd. Last modified 3 April 2019.

19. Alfonso Pulido, Dorian Stone and John Strevel. "The three Cs of customer satisfaction: Consistency, consistency, consistency." McKinsey. https://www.mckinsey.com/industries/retail/our-insights/the-three-cs-of-customer-satisfaction-consistency-consistency-consistency. Last modified 1 March 2014.

20. Oprah Winfrey (1954–) is an American media executive, actress, talk show host, television producer and philanthropist.

21. Bill Gates (1955–) is an American business magnate, software developer, investor and philanthropist who is best known as the cofounder of Microsoft. See Bill Gates (2009) *Business @ the Speed of Thought: Succeeding in the Digital Economy.* London: Hachette.

22. Wayne Huang, John Mitchell, Carmel Dibner, Andrea Ruttenberg and Audrey Tripp. "How customer service can turn angry customers into loyal ones." *Harvard Business Review.* https://hbr.org/2018/01/how-customer-service-can-turn-angry-customers-into-loyal-ones. Last modified 16 January 2018.

Chapter 10: *Systems & Processes*

1. Simon Sinek (1973–) is a British-born American author and motivational speaker most famous for his book *Start with Why* (2011). See Simon Sinek via Facebook. https://www.facebook.com/simonsinek/posts/10154654688426499.

2. Ralph Stacey. "Comment on debate article: Coaching Psychology coming of age: The challenges we face in the messy world of complexity." *International Coaching Psychology Review* 7 (2012): 91–95. https://psycnet.apa.org/record/2012-11404-006. Accessed 10 October 2023.

3. Bob Hodge. "Coaching for a complex world." *International Coaching Psychology Review* 7 (2012): 109–113. https://researchdirect.westernsydney.edu.au/islandora/object/uws:13177. Accessed 10 October 2023.

4. Carrie Wilkerson (1972–) is an American speaker, award-winning author and business consultant.

5. Mary E Shacklett (2023). "Let customer experience guide processes, systems." *Information Week.* https://www.informationweek.com/it-leadership/let-customer-experience-guide-processes-systems#:~:text=,service%20options%20to%20customers. Accessed 10 October 2023.

6. Stephen R. Covey (1932–2012) was an American educator and businessman. See Stephen R. Covey (1989), *The 7 Habits of Highly Effective People.* New York: Free Press.

7. William Edwards Deming (1900–1993) was an American engineer, statistician and management consultant noted for originating what became the Plan, Do, Check, Act cycle. See "Don't gamble with your company's culture." *The Deming Institute.* https://deming.org/2589-2. Last modified 8 June 2017.

8. This widely quoted saying is a paraphrase of an assertion in Deming's *Out of the Crisis* (1982). See "Appreciation for a system." *The Deming Institute.* https://deming.org/appreciation-for-a-system. Last modified 26 October 2012.

9. Peter Drucker (1909–2005) was an Austrian-born American management consultant, educator and author, whose writings contributed to the philosophical and practical foundations of the modern business corporation.

10. Allaya Cooks-Campbell (2022). "Communication is key in the workplace. Here's how to improve." *Better Up Blog.* https://www.betterup.com/blog/why-communication-is-key-to-workplace-and-how-to-improve-skills. Accessed 29 August 2023.

11. William H. Whyte. "Is anybody listening?" *Fortune*, September 1950. https://quoteinvestigator.com/2014/08/31/illusion/#f+9667+1+1. Accessed 2 February 2024.

12. Therese J. Borchard. "Words can change your brain." *PsychCentral.* https://psychcentral.com/blog/words-can-change-your-brain-2. Last modified 27 May 2019.

13. J. P. Pathak (2015). *Fundamentals of Management.* New Delhi: Vikas Publishing House.

14. Gill Corkindale. "The importance of organizational design and structure." *Harvard Business Review.* https://hbr.org/2011/02/the-importance-of-organization. Last modified 11 February 2011.

15. Information Technology Infrastructure Library's (ITIL) Foundation Course Glossary. https://itil.it.utah.edu/downloads/ITILV3_Glossary.pdf. Accessed 24 November 2020.

16. Richard Harshaw is an American CEO and inventor of the Monopolize Your Marketplace system. See Richard Harshaw (2005). *Monopolize Your Marketplace: Separate Your Business from the Competition then Eliminate.* (Provo, Utah: Executive Excellence).

Chapter 11: *Measurement & Insight*

1. John H. Holcomb (1991). *The Militant Moderate* (n.p.: Rafter).

2. "Are Profit-Based Incentives Compatible with a Risk Culture?" *FINSA*, 2017. https://www.mq.edu.au/__data/assets/pdf_file/0008/759617/Experimental-Research-Report_FINAL.pdf. Accessed 20 April 2020.

3. Simon Caulkin. "The rule is simple: Be careful what you measure." *The Guardian* https://www.theguardian.com/business/2008/feb/10/businesscomment1. Last modified 10 February 2008.

4. Barack Obama (1961–) was the 44th President of the US. See Barack Obama, "Remarks by the President in State of Union Address." *The White House.* https://obamawhitehouse.archives.gov/the-press-office/2011/01/25/remarks-president-state-union-address. Last modified 25 January 2011.

5. Joseph Stiglitz. "Towards a better measure of well-being." *Financial Times.* https://www.ft.com/content/95b492a8-a095-11de-b9ef-00144feabdc0. Last modified 13 September 2009.

6. Robert S. Kaplan and David P. Norton. "The Balanced Scorecard: Measures that drive performance." *Harvard Business Review.* https://hbr.org/1992/01/the-balanced-scorecard-measures-that-drive-performance-2. Last modified January–February 1992.

7. Quoted in Simon Caulkin, "The rule is simple: Be careful what you measure." *The Guardian.* https://www.theguardian.com/business/2008/feb/10/businesscomment1. Last modified 10 February 2008.

8. Stemming from ideas about experiential learning. For more background and research into learning, see David A. Kolb, Richard E. Boyatzis and Charalampos Mainemelis, "Experiential learning theory: Previous research and new directions." in *Perspectives on Thinking, Learning, and Cognitive Styles,* eds. R. J. Sternberg and L. F. Zhang (Mahwah: Lawrence Erlbaum, 2001); David A. Kolb (1984). *Experiential Learning: Experience as the Source of Learning and Development.* Upper Saddle River: Prentice-Hall.

9. Greg Kihlstrom (2021). "Real-time insights are the future of customer experience measurement." *Forbes.* https://www.forbes.com/sites/forbesagencycouncil/2021/07/22/real-time-insights-are-the-future-of-customer-experience-measurement/?sh=4a4e75321d36. Accessed 10 October 2023.

10. Ivan Pavlov (1849–1936) was a Russian physiologist. He won the Nobel Peace Prize for physiology in 1904.

11. B. F. Skinner (1904–1990) was an American psychologist best-known for his influence on behaviorism. He was the Edgar Pierce Professor of Psychology at Harvard University from 1958 until his retirement in 1974.

12. Charles Duhigg (2012). *The Power of Habit: Why We do What We do in Life and Business.* London: William Heinemann.

13. Edward L. Deci and Richard M. Ryan (1985). *Intrinsic Motivation and Self-Determination in Human Behaviour.* New York: Plenum.

14. Quoted in Carinne Piekema, "Does money really motivate people?" *BBC Future.* https://www.bbc.com/future/article/20120509-is-it-all-about-the-money. Last modified 18 November 2014.

15. "What is Net Promoter?" *NICE Satmetrix.* https://www.netpromoter.com/know. Accessed 20 April 2020.

Chapter 12: *Hanbury Manor*

1. Alan Williams and Alison Whybrow (2008). *The 31 Practices: Release the Power of Your Organization's Values Every Day.* London: LID Publishing.

Chapter 14: *Nordstrom*

1. "About Us" (Nordstrom), accessed 10 November 2020, https://press.nordstrom.com/about.

2. "Nordstrom: Mission | Vision | Core Values (2024 Analysis)." *Business Strategy Hub*, last modified 19 May 2020, https://bstrategyhub.com/nordstrom-mission-vision-core-values.

3. Robert Spector and breAnne O. Reeves (2017). *The Nordstrom Way to Customer Experience Excellence: Creating a Values-Driven Service Culture*. Hoboken: John Wiley & Sons.

4. Ibid.

5. Ibid.

6. "Millennials at work reshaping the workplace." https://www.pwc.com/co/es/publicaciones/assets/millennials-at-work.pdf. Accessed 24 November 2020.

7. Ashley Lutz. "Nordstrom's employee handbook has only one rule," *Business Insider*. https://www.businessinsider.in/Nordstroms-Employee-Handbook-Has-Only-One-Rule/articleshow/44804035.cms. Last modified 13 October 2014.

8. Abha Bhattarai. "Nordstrom is getting into the used-clothes business; here's how it will work." *The Washington Post*. https://www.seattletimes.com/business/nordstrom-enters-burgeoning-used-clothes-business/. Last modified 31 January 2020.

9. *Careerbliss.com*. https://www.careerbliss.com/nordstrom/. Accessed 10 October 2023.

10. "Department stores global 2019 digital IQ index." *Gartner*. https://www.gartner.com/en/marketing/research/department-stores-global-2019. Last modified 11 June 2019.

Chapter 15: *BT Group*

1. *This is Money*. https://www.thisismoney.co.uk/money/news/article-4153860/And-winner-annual-Wooden-Spoon-Award-BT.html#:~:text=Once%20again%2C%20BT%20has%20been,last%20four%20Wooden%20Spoon%20awards. Accessed? 25 January 2017.

2. "Definition of value stream." *Gartner*. https://www.gartner.com/en/information-technology/glossary/value-stream#:~:text=A%20value%20stream%20is%20the,from%20customer%20request%20to%20delivery. Last accessed 4 December 2023.

3. "What is agile?" *McKinsey*. https://www.mckinsey.com/featured-insights/mckinsey-explainers/what-is-agile. Accessed 27 March 2023.

4. "What is DevOps?" *Microsoft*. https://learn.microsoft.com/en-us/devops/what-is-devops, Accessed? January 2023.

Part Six: *Future*

1. Pamela Hinds. "Research: Why best practices don't translate across cultures." *Harvard Business Review*. https://hbr.org/2016/06/research-why-best-practices-dont-translate-across-cultures. Last modified 27 June 2016.

Chapter 16: *Behaviour*

1. Jacque Fresco (1916–2017) was an American futurist and self-described social engineer. Self-taught, he worked in a variety of positions related to industrial design.

2. Y. Yacoob and L. S. Davis. "Recognizing human facial expressions from long image sequences using optical flow." *IEEE Transactions on Pattern Analysis and Machine Intelligence* 18 (1996): 636–642. https://ieeexplore.ieee.org/document/506414. Accessed 10 October 2023.

3. Scott Magids, Alan Zorfas and Daniel Leemon (2015). "The new science of customer emotions." *Harvard Business Review*. https://hbr.org/2015/11/the-new-science-of-customer-emotions. Accessed 31st August 2023.

4. "Exploring the value of emotion-driven engagement." Deloitte (2019). https://www.deloittedigital.com/content/dam/deloittedigital/us/documents/offerings/offerings-20190521-exploring-the-value-of-emotion-driven-engagement-2.pdf. Accessed 31 August 2023.

5. Tempkin Group Research. *Customer Experience Matters*. https://experiencematters.wordpress.com/temkin-group-research/. Accessed 31 August 2023.

6. Peter Kriss (2014). "The value of customer experience, quantified." *Harvard Business Review*. https://hbr.org/2014/08/the-value-of-customer-experience-quantified. Accessed 31 August 2023.

7. "Customer service and experience infographics." *Shep Hyken* (2023). https://hyken.com/customer-service-and-experience-infographics/. Accessed 31 August 2023.

8. "Experience is everything: Here's how to get it right." *PwC* (2018). https://www.pwc.com/us/en/advisory-services/publications/consumer-intelligence-series/pwc-consumer-intelligence-series-customer-experience.pdf. Accessed 4 September 2023.

9. Esteban Kolsky (2015). "CX for executives." *Slideshare*. https://www.slideshare.net/ekolsky/cx-for-executives#2. Accessed 4 September 2023.

10. John Dick (2021). "Live chat exposes a fatal flaw in your go-to-market." *blog.hubpost*. https://blog.hubspot.com/sales/live-chat-go-to-market-flaw?hubs_content=blog.hubspot.com%2Fservice%2Fcustomer-service-stats&hubs_content-cta=HubSpot%20Research. Accessed 4 September 2023.

11. "Complaints outlook 2022." *Huntswood*. https://www.huntswood.com/uploads/documents/CO2022.pdf. Accessed 4 September 2023.

12. David McClleland (1988). *Human Motivation*. Cambridge University Press.

13. Daniel Newman (2020). "4 actionable customer experience statistics for 2020." *Forbes*. https://www.forbes.com/sites/danielnewman/2020/06/23/4-actionable-customer-experience-statistics-for-2020/. Accessed 4 September 2023.

14. Jeff Toister. "How quickly should you respond to email?" *toistersolutions.com*. https://www.toistersolutions.com/blog/how-quickly-should-you-respond-to-email. Accessed 4 September 2023.

15. Marc Beaujean, Jonathan Davidson and Stacey Madge (2006). "The 'moment of truth' in customer service." *McKinsey*. https://www.mckinsey.com/capabilities/people-and-organizational-performance/our-insights/the-moment-of-truth-in-customer-service. Accessed 4 September 2023.

16. Sagi Eliyahu (2020). "The impact of employee experience on customer experience." *Forbes*. https://www.forbes.com/sites/forbestechcouncil/2020/03/30/the-impact-of-employee-experience-on-customer-experience/?sh=534cc90061fc. Accessed 10 October 2023.

17. A. H. Maslow (1943). "A theory of human motivation." *Psych Classics*. http://psychclassics.yorku.ca/Maslow/motivation.htm. Accessed 4 September 2023.

18. David Edelman and Marc Singer (2015). "The new consumer decision journey." *McKinsey*. https://www.mckinsey.com/capabilities/growth-marketing-and-sales/our-insights/the-new-consumer-decision-journey. Accessed 10 October 2023.

19. "Experience is everything: Here's how to get it right." PwC. https://www.pwc.com/us/en/advisory-services/publications/consumer-intelligence-series/pwc-consumer-intelligence-series-customer-experience.pdf. Accessed 4 September 2023.

20. Daniel Goleman (1995). *Emotional Intelligence – Why it Can Matter More Than IQ. Bloomsbury*.

21. Shep Hyken (2022). "Customer loyalty comes from an emotional connection." *Forbes*. https://www.forbes.com/sites/shephyken/2022/10/23/customer-loyalty-comes-from-an-emotional-connection/. Accessed 4 September 2023.

22. Jeanne Bliss is a leadership and customer experience advisor and keynote speaker.

23. James Allen, Frederick F. Reichheld, Barney Hamilton and Rob Markey (2005). "Closing the delivery gap." *Bain & Co.* https://media.bain.com/bainweb/PDFs/cms/hotTopics/closingdeliverygap.pdf. Accessed 4 September 2023.

24. Shep Hyken is a customer service and experience expert, an award-winning keynote speaker, and a *New York Times* and *Wall Street Journal* bestselling author

25. Ted Levine (2022). "What does today's consumer want? Personalized, seamless, omnichannel experiences." *Forbes.* https://www.forbes.com/sites/forbesbusinesscouncil/2022/03/11/what-does-todays-consumer-want-personalized-seamless-omnichannel-experiences/. Accessed 28 September 2023.

26. Kelly Blum and Gloria Omale (2021). "Gartner says 63% of digital marketing leaders still struggle with personalization." *Gartner.* https://www.gartner.com/en/newsroom/press-releases/-gartner-says-63--of-digital-marketing-leaders-still-struggle-wi. Accessed 28 September 2023.

27. "Exploring the value of emotion-driven engagement." *Deloitte.* https://www.deloittedigital.com/content/dam/deloittedigital/us/documents/offerings/offerings-20190521-exploring-the-value-of-emotion-driven-engagement-2.pdf. Accessed 28 September 2023.

28. Sammy Paget (2023). "Local consumer review survey 2023." *Bright Local.* https://www.brightlocal.com/research/local-consumer-review-survey/. Accessed 4 September 2023.

29. J. Jeffrey Inman and Leigh McAlister (1994). "Do coupon expiration dates affect consumer behaviour?" *JSTOR.* https://www.jstor.org/stable/3152229?seq=1#page_scan_tab_contents. Accessed 4 September 2023.

30. "The importance of irrelevant alternatives." *The Economist.* https://www.economist.com/democracy-in-america/2009/05/22/the-importance-of-irrelevant-alternatives. Accessed 4 September 2023.

31. "1 in 2 visitors abandon a website that takes more than 6 seconds to load." *Digital.* https://digital.com/1-in-2-visitors-abandon-a-website-that-takes-more-than-6-seconds-to-load/. Accessed 4 September 2023.

32. Ashira Prossack (2019). "How employee satisfaction affects customer satisfaction." *Forbes.* https://www.forbes.com/sites/ashiraprossack1/2019/05/31/employee-satisfaction-customer-satisfaction/. Accessed 4 September 2023.

33. Maya Angelou, born Marguerite Annie Johnson (1928–2014) was an American memoirist, poet and civil rights activist.

34. "What is employee engagement and how do you improve it?" *Gallup.* https://www.gallup.com/workplace/285674/improve-employee-engagement-workplace.aspx. Accessed 4 September 2023.

35. "Value stream is the sequence of activities necessary to deliver a product, service or experience to a customer, internal or external." Gartner. https://www.gartner.com/en/information-technology/glossary/value-stream#:~:text=A%20value%20stream%20is%20the,from%20customer%20request%20to%20delivery. Accessed 4 September 2023.

36. Guofo Chen and Shuhao Li (2021). "Effect of employee–customer interaction quality on customers' prohibitive voice behaviors: Mediating roles of customer trust and identification." *Frontiers.* https://www.frontiersin.org/articles/10.3389/fpsyg.2021.773354/full. Accessed 4 September 2023.

37. Misun (Sunny) Kim & Jichul Jang (2021). "The impact of employees' perceived customer citizenship behaviors on organizational citizenship behaviors: The mediating roles of employee customer-orientation attitude." *International Journal of Hospitality & Tourism Administration*, Volume 24, 2023 – Issue 4. https://www.tandfonline.com/doi/abs/10.1080/15256480.2021.2025191#:~:text=This%20study%20serves%20as%20one,customer%20citizenship%20behavior%20Employee%20perception. Accessed 10 October 2023.

Chapter 17: *Digital*

1. George Westerman is a Senior Lecturer at the MIT Sloan School of Management and founder of the Global Opportunity Initiative.

2. Leyland Cecco. "Best restaurant in Montreal according to Tripadvisor does not exist." *The Guardian.* https://www.theguardian.com/world/2023/feb/03/montreal-restaurant-that-never-was-online-reviews-canada. Accessed 4 September 2023.

3. "Digital-first customer experience report." *Nice.* https://get.nice.com/rs/069-KVM-666/images/0003959_en_digital-first-cx-report.pdf. Accessed 31 August 2023.

4. Jeff Bezos (1964–) is the founder, executive chairman and former president and CEO of Amazon, the world's largest e-commerce and cloud computing company.

5. Greg Brockman (2022). "ChatGPT just crossed 1 million users; it's been 5 days since launch." *Twitter.* https://twitter.com/gdb/status/1599683104142430208. Accessed 5 September 2023.

6. Krystal Hu (2023). "ChatGPT sets record for fastest-growing user base." *Reuters.* https://www.reuters.com/technology/chatgpt-sets-record-fastest-growing-user-base-analyst-note-2023-02-01/. Accessed 31 August 2023.

7. "Augmented reality market by device type." *Markets and Markets.* https://www.marketsandmarkets.com/Market-Reports/augmented-reality-market-82758548.html. Accessed 5 September 2023.

8. "Social media trends 2024." *Hootsuite.* https://www.hootsuite.com/research/social-trends. Accessed 31 August 2023.

Chapter 18: *Disruption*

1. William Pollard (1828–1893) was an English Quaker writer and recorded minister.

2. Harry Campbell (2023). "Uber statistics 2024: Drivers, riders, revenue & more." *RideShareGuy.* https://therideshareguy.com/uber-statistics/. Last updated 22 March 2023.

3. Clayton Christensen (1997). *The Innovator's Dilemma: When New Technologies Cause Great Firms to Fail.* Boston: Harvard Business Review Press.

4. Ibid.

5. Rameet Chawla is an expert in mobile design, start-ups, product strategy, ecommerce and user experience.

6. Alex Moazed and Nicholas Johnson. "Why Clayton Christensen is wrong about uber and disruptive innovation." *TechCrunch.* https://techcrunch.com/2016/02/27/why-christensen-is-wrong-about-uber-and-disruptive-innovation. Last modified 27 February 2016.

7. Heather Simmons (2015). *Reinventing Dell: The Innovation Imperative* (Toronto: Murmurous Publishing).

8. "Gartner survey shows pace of change as top emerging risk concerning organizations in 2Q19." *Gartner.* https://www.gartner.com/en/newsroom/press-releases/2019-07-24-gartner-survey-shows-pace-of-change-as-top-emerging-r. Last modified 24 July 2019.

9. Sean Murphy is managing director of BDO's Crisis Management and Business Continuity practice. Quoted in Neil Hodge, "Dealing with disruption." *Risk Management.* http://www.rmmagazine.com/2019/10/01/dealing-with-disruption. Last modified 1 October 2019.

10. Charlie Hobbs (2023). "Conde Nast Traveler, Japan Airlines will now rent you clothes so you don't have to pack." https://www.cntraveler.com/story/japan-airlines-renting-clothes-to-passengers. Accessed 20 July 2023.

11. John F. Kennedy (1917–1963) was the 35th president of the US. See John F. Kennedy, "Remarks at the Convocation of the United Negro College Fund, Indianapolis, Indiana, April 12, 1959." *John F. Kennedy Presidential Library and Museum.* https://www.jfklibrary.org/archives/other-resources/john-f-kennedy-speeches/indianapolis-in-19590412. Accessed 14 November 2020.

12. "COVID-19 coronavirus pandemic." *Worldometer.* https://www.worldometers.info/coronavirus/. Last updated August 31, 2023.

13. Crystal Wiedemann. "The great transformation? The cultural implications of COVID-19." *Barrett Values Centre.* https://www.valuescentre.com/articles/the-great-transformation-the-cultural-implications-of-covid-19. Accessed 20 August 2020.

14. Fiona Harvey. "Britons want quality of life indicators to take priority over economy." *The Guardian.* https://www.theguardian.com/society/2020/may/10/britons-want-quality-of-life-indicators-priority-over-economy-coronavirus. Last modified 10 May 2020.

15. "ONS retail sales: PwC's Lisa Hooker comments." PwC. https://www.pwc.co.uk/press-room/press-releases/ons-lisa-hooker.html. Last modified 24 April 2020.

16. John Mitchell (1913–1988) was the 67th Attorney General of the US. Quoted in Eric Salzman, "Watch what we do, not what we say." *SWBC Blog.* https://blog.swbc.com/lenderhub/watch-what-we-do-not-what-we-say. Last modified 10 April 2017.

17. "50% of UK workforce to work remotely by 2020." hSo. https://www.hso.co.uk/leased-lines/technology-news/homeworking-news/50-of-uk-workforce-to-work-remotely-by-2020. Accessed 19 March 2020.

18. Harriet McCulley, "Lockdown: Homeworkers putting in extra hours – instant messaging up 1900%." *The HR Director.* https://www.thehrdirector.com/business-news/the-workplace/new-data-over-a-third-38-admit-to-working-longer-hours-when-working-from-home. Last modified 27 April 2020.

19. Angharad Carrick, "Barclays urges staff back to the office as HSBC eyes September return." *CityAM.* https://www.cityam.com/barclays-boss-calls-on-staff-to-return-to-the-office. Last modified 29 July 2020.

20. Rob McLean, "These companies plan to make working from home the new normal – as in forever." *CNN Business.* https://edition.cnn.com/2020/05/22/tech/work-from-home-companies/index.html. Last modified 25 June 2020.

21. James Gorman (1958–) is the chairman and CEO of Morgan Stanley. Quoted in Erik Schatzker, "Gorman sees Morgan Stanley future with 'much less real estate.'" *Bloomberg.* https://www.bloomberg.com/news/articles/2020-04-16/gorman-sees-morgan-stanley-future-with-much-less-real-estate. Last modified 16 April 2020.

22. "National survey: A Majority of US employees want remote work arrangement to stay." *GetAbstract.* https://journal.getabstract.com/wp-content/uploads/2020/04/ga_remote_survey_2020_compressed.pdf. Accessed 4 August 2020.

23. Sophie Tanno and Rory Tingle. "Workers who have battled into the office during the pandemic are resentful of those still working from home – and are being offered pay rises and perks to keep them happy, HR staff reveal." *Mail Online.* https://www.dailymail.co.uk/news/article-8590111/Workers-resentful-colleagues-working-home-HR-staff-say.html. Last modified 4 August 2020.

24. Matt Hall. "Research finds 7.8 million office workers will be unable to return to work when lockdown ends." *Punchline Gloucester.* https://www.punchline-gloucester.com/articles/aanews/research-finds-almost-eight-million-office-workers-will-be-unable-to-return-to-work-when-lockdown-is. Last modified 28 April 2020.

25. Josie Wexler. "Ten companies to avoid over their response to COVID-19." *Ethical Consumer.* https://www.ethicalconsumer.org/ethical-shopping/ten-companies-avoid-over-their-response-covid-19. Last modified 12 May 2020.

26. "Consumer sentiment survey – Autumn 2020." *PwC.* https://www.pwc.co.uk/industries/retail-consumer/insights/consumer-sentiment-survey.html. Accessed 4 August 2020.

27. "Organized." *Cambridge Dictionary.* https://dictionary.cambridge.org/dictionary/english/organized. Accessed 31 July 2020.

28. "Organization." *Online Etymological Dictionary.* https://www.etymonline.com/word/organization. Accessed 13 November 2020.

29. "The future of management is teal." *Strategy+Business.* https://www.strategy-business.com/article/00344?gko=30876. Last modified 6 July 2015.

Chapter 19: *Summary*

1. Tony Hsieh (1973–2020) was an American internet entrepreneur and venture capitalist, best known as CEO of Zappos.

2. "Consumer-goods' brands that demonstrate commitment to sustainability outperform those that don't." *Nielsen*. https://www.nielsen.com/us/en/press-releases/2015/consumer-goods-brands-that-demonstrate-commitment-to-sustainability-outperform. Last modified 12 October 2015.

3. Thomas Stewart. "Who owns your brand?" *CBS News*. https://www.cbsnews.com/news/who-owns-your-brand. Last modified 26 April 2011.

4. Alan Williams., "Shhh... the Values Economy has arrived." *World Values Day*. https://www.worldvaluesday.com/values-economy-arrived. Accessed 29 April 2018.

ABOUT THE CX SUPERHERO, AUTHORS AND ILLUSTRATOR

CAI, ILLUSTRATION
CX SuperHero

Cai is a gender-neutral name of Latin and Welsh origin. Meaning 'rejoice' or 'happy', Cai is a diminutive of Caius, a Roman male name. It's particularly popular in Wales, where it's the Welsh variant of Sir Kay, an important character in Arthurian mythology. Sir Cai is prominent in medieval Welsh texts about the fabled King of Camelot and is said to have many super-human qualities.

Cai sees the ultimate objective of CX to create delight and happiness that both customers and service providers can enjoy, celebrate and rejoice in. The neutrality of their name reflects Cai's inclusive philosophy to customer service, which welcomes anybody and everybody (irrespective of background, race, sexual orientation, gender, faith, neuro, physical and mental characteristics, and capability). The next step is to seek to understand their needs and wants, and then deliver a customer experience accordingly. The heroic, chivalrous and fabled super-human roots of the name represent Cai's laser focus on and commitment to the customer. They have a magical, intuitive quality to sense what the customer needs and deliver this in a way that they will appreciate and enjoy. Finally, Cai's distinctive name is indicative of how they are always striving to be better and different, summed up beautifully by a workshop attendee Anton who said, "Customer service is something that is delivered, whereas a customer experience is taken away."

ALAN WILLIAMS, COAUTHOR
Founder & MD, SERVICEBRAND GLOBAL

Alan coaches progressive leaders of service sector organizations, internationally and in the UK, to deliver values-driven service for sustained performance. He is a published author and speaker whose projects have delivered measurable business results across a balanced scorecard and been recognized with industry awards.

With more than 20 years' senior management experience in demanding customer service environments, Alan's rare mix of extensive operations and coaching experience enables him to create and implement holistic SERVICEBRAND® strategies for sustainable impact. Alan has applied this approach as a consultant and in senior leadership roles for global blue-chip organizations as well as smaller entrepreneurial companies.

Alan is passionate about the importance of employees at the point-of-service delivery and their role in delivering remarkable customer experience. He thrives on leading the values-driven transformation of service, culture and behaviour and is an expert facilitator of experiential learning workshops. His previous coauthored books, *The 31 Practices: Release the Power of Your Organization's Values Every Day*, *My 31 Practices: Release the Power of Your Values for Authentic Happiness* and *The Values Economy, How to Deliver Purpose-Driven Service for Sustained Performance* all received international critical acclaim.

Alan graduated in Hotel and Catering Administration at Surrey University, where he has been a visiting lecturer, and was a global train-the-trainer for the Marriott International Spirit to Serve programme. He is a past president of the Meetings Industry Association, a fellow of the Institute of Hospitality, a nonexecutive director of BQF, a director of the UK Values Alliance and founder of the Global Values Alliance.

DAVE STUBBERFIELD, COAUTHOR
Director & Principal Consultant, Carter Consultancy

With over a decade's worth of experience in business transformation, Dave has been involved with and managed complex and comprehensive projects to improve a variety of businesses with a customer-centric focus. By empowering people from the ground up and gaining total sponsorship from senior leaders, Dave ensures complete coverage of the transformation across the organization. He applies his expertise in continuous improvement, customer experience and change management to create bespoke implementation solutions for businesses of all sizes and reach their goals, embedding and sustaining these methodologies.

Dave has enabled the transformation of a cloud contact centre organization from an NPS score of -11 to +76 over a five-year period through detailed and meticulous project management, ensuring that tasks and assignments are scoped appropriately with the correct level of resource and training across all levels of the business. He has a natural ability to lead by example, showcasing behaviours through role-modelling and a hands-on approach to gain buy-in and traction with all stakeholders creating natural momentum, engagement and enthusiasm.

JOHN MONTGOMERY, ILLUSTRATOR
Founder & managing director, Fastcom IT Ltd

John is a collaborative communicator who cocreates with interesting people to get ideas out of their heads and onto (digital) paper.

He works with large organizations and subject matter experts all over the world on subjects as diverse as climate change, values, customer service, anti-smoking, leadership, agile and private equity investment.

In the business communication world, John is best known for making whiteboard animations or doodle videos ... 'a sort of doodling on steroids.' Images, metaphors, concepts and visual models are all powerful ways to think, create and help ideas emerge and form. John believes that visuals and visual literacy are a powerful and efficient but largely untapped vehicle for creativity and communication that is open to everyone with a little bit of practice.

Once described as 'project therapy,' it's fair to say he is more than just a 'pencil for hire.'

"Of course work is about the end result, but it is great working with people who really know their stuff or are just enthusiastic about it – for me it's like learning by osmosis."